UNIX
Administration
Quick
Guide

Saket Jain

UNIX
Administration
Quick
Guide

Saket Jain

First Step
Publishing
Paving Ways For New Writers

First Published in India in 2015 by First Step Publishing

Editorial / Sales / Marketing Office at
303-304 Garnet Nirmal Lifestyles Ph 2
Behind Nirmal Lifestyles Mall
LBS Marg Mulund West
Mumbai 400080
E-Mail:- info@firststepcorp.com
www.firststepcorp.com

ISBN: - 978-93-83306-25-1
Publisher and Managing Editor: Rohit Shetty
Branding, Marketing and Promotions by: Design Fishing
Digital Management by: First Step Corp
Typeset in Book Antique
India PaperBack: ₹ 550
Rest Paperback: $ 15

About the Author

 Saket Jain is an Indian computer science engineer with over 4.5 Years of experience in Linux/UNIX System Administration in Ericsson Global India Pvt. Ltd, Ericsson Egypt and HCL Technologies Ltd. His current affiliations include being "Tier –II Engineer" in BSS (Business support system) in Ericsson, Gurgaon. His name had been included in Limca Book of Records in the year 2012 for creating the "World's First One Page Blog on Internet".

He has obtained his B.E. from Jagannath Gupta Institute of Engineering and Technology (JNIT), Jaipur and PGDM (Systems) from IMT Gaziabad. He is fond of creating new innovative things and had also created various tools which include NIS User Password Management through Web Portal, Notes management software, Links Management Portal, an Online Word Dictionary, etc.

He is associated with Art of Living which helps him to stay focused, motivated and encouraged. He is also a moderate Yoga Practitioner cum Trainer associated with Bhartiya Yog Sansthan(Regd.), New Delhi and used to practice Yog Sadhna or Yoga regularly.

Certification Details

1. RHCSA (Redhat Certified System Administrator) and RHCE(Redhat Certified Engineer) on RHEL6(Red Hat Enterprise Linux 6) ☐ Certificate No. 110-380-425.
2. RHCE(Red Hat Certified Engineer) on RHEL5 ☐ Certificate No. 805008382433073.
3. Limca Book of National Records 2012 Certified.

Author Blog

http://saketjain.com ~ World's First One Page Blog

http://blog.saketjain.com ~ One page blog replicated in wordpress. The beauty of this page is that it automatically posts new articles or comments which were posted on main page saketjain.com The reason why I have created is that, AJAX pages are not crawled by google search, so to make the posts appear in google search I need to create this blog page.

Preface

The primary goal of this work is to make people aware of what is unix, or linux and how we can work on these operating systems especially Oracle's Unix flavour known as Solaris Operating system. Another objective is to make the guys aware about ins and outs of Unix administration by providing them practical examples in the form short tips that will help them to learn these tasks quickly.

This book is helpful for all persons who work on Unix or Linux, and provides in depth administration tips for Unix operating systems. This book is also helpful for all Unix beginners, for all those guys, who want some perfection in Unix administration with deep understanding and want to know how we as Linux or Unix Administrator manages the servers in an organization.

The book is must for all Linux/unix administrators working in different organizations around the world since it contains most of the things a technical unix guy should be aware about.

This book is targeted for all technical guys who work on Unix platform and will be very fruitful to the Linux/unix profile persons. A beginner, student, teacher, or professional anyone can take benefit from it by quickly learning from the quick tips and concepts shared.

Dedication

I want to dedicate this book to my parents and my sisters; they are the one without whom this would have never taken the shape of a book. Along with this, I also want to thank my seniors and colleagues who are always there to support me and encouraged me to complete this work. I can't name all persons; however there are few persons who hold a unique place in my life and with this book, i want to pay my gratitude towards them.

- Prabal Tripathi, Ramachandra Rao Poluri, Pavneet Singh, Himanshu Pathak, and Sanghamitra Khuntia from Extreme Networks, HCL Technologies.
- Ravi Gudivaka, and Rahul Kumar Singh, Xerox Midrange, HCL Technologies.
- Manoj Kumar, Pankaj Singla, and Sanyukt Sharma, EGIL(Ericsson Global India Limited)
- Mahmoud Omar and Mohamed Mahfouz, Ericsson, Egypt
- Frank and Van Loock Patrick, HP, Belgium
- Yogesh Chandra Bhatt, Tan Singh Chauhan, Rohit Jain, Girishma Singh, Manish Rawat and Mohammad Sarfaraz, JNIT, Jaipur, India.
- Mitra Bandyopadhyay(Banerjee Mam) and Saji Manuel, St. Anselms School, Alwar, India
- Dilip Kumar Saini , Yog Sadhna Teacher, Bhartiya Yog Sansthan, Delhi, India
- Puneet Agarwal, Art of Living Teacher, Gurgaon, India

Last but not the least I want to thank my idols God Shiva and *Gau Mata*, my foremost beliefs for providing me enough strength to complete this work.

Index

Chapter-1
Theory - Introduction

Chapter -2
Working with Solaris FS and Device Administration
Day - 1

Chapter -3
Networking, Zpool/ZFS/Snapshots, Package/Patch Administration
Day – 2

Chapter -4
SMF, NFS and AutoFS
Day 3

Chapter -5
User and Core file Administration
Day 4

Chapter -6
Solaris Zones and Volume Manager
Day 5

Chapter -7
Solaris Installation/Upgrade and Troubleshooting
Day 6

APPENDIX

LAB

FEW ISSUES

Chapter-1
Theory – Introduction

1.   History of UNIX/Solaris

UNIX is one of the first operating systems written in high level language C. The first version of UNIX Operating System (OS) was developed in 1969 by Kenneth Thompson and Dennis Ritchie, engineers at AT&T Bell Laboratories in assembly language which was installed on Programmed Data Processor -7(PDP-7) hardware. PDP-7 is a small computer produced by Digital Equipment Corporation, an American company, as a part of their PDP series computer hardware(s). This OS has no official name, however the developer team used to call it as UNICS which is a rhyming word matches with MULTICS (Multiplexed Information and Computing Service) which later on became UNIX. UNICS is based on time sharing operating system and also named as Time Sharing System.

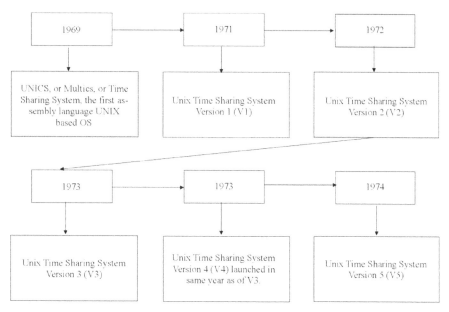

Fig. 1.1 : Evolution of UNIX from 1969 to 1974

In 1975, UNIX Time Sharing System Version 6 was released which was the turning point in the development of this operating system. It enabled different organizations to derive their own versions of UNIX to launch for sale, in the market. Fig. 1.1 summarizes the evolution of Unix from 1969 to 1974.

Fig. 1.2 below shows the evolution of UNIX OS in the subsequent years after 1975.

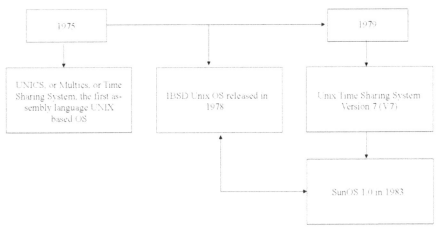

Fig. 1.2 Development of UNIX from 1975 to 1979

Note : In past, there were many other UNIX derivatives which were launched by different organizations but diminished with time. However we will only look those UNIX versions which mainly contributed to the development of Sun OS. Solaris OS is most widely used UNIX OS today after Apple OS UNIX which is also known as Mac OS.

There were many derivatives of UNIX OS(Operating System) developed in which the most famous was BSD or Barkeley Software Distribution which was evolved in 1977 by Computer Systems Research Group (CSRG).

CSRG initially shared its codebase with AT&T and later on came with its own UNIX version called Barkeley UNIX which was also known as BSD1.0 which was launched on march 9, 1978. In 1980s, BSD UNIX was widely adopted by different vendors in the form of proprietary UNIX variant. BSD 4.1 was released in June, 1981 which was referenced by Sun Microsystems to make their own UNIX OS known as SunOS, introducing a new most popular UNIX workstation of the future.

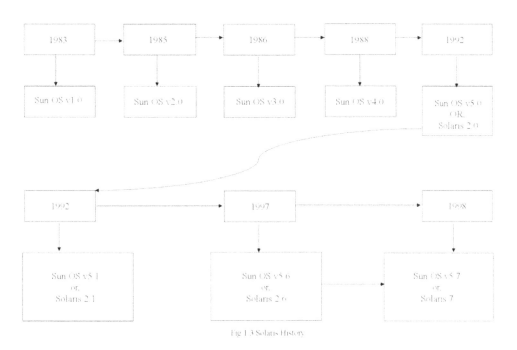

Fig 1.3 Solaris History

SunOS v1.0 was released in year 1983 by Sun Microsystems. With ongoing development, several other versions released which were known as SunOS 2.0(May 1985), SunOS 3.0(Feb 1986), SunOS 4.0(Dec 1988), SunOS 5.0(June 1992). SunOS 5.0 was alternatively come to known as Solaris 2.0 by Sun Micro system marketing team.

This is called as second version Solaris because there were major advancement to Sun OS 4.0 or first version of solaris, which includes

Open Windows GUI and Open Network Computing (ONC) functionality. Thereafter Sun Microsystems released different SunOS or Solaris Versions which were Solaris 2.1(or Sun OS 5.1), Solaris 2.2(or Sun OS 5.2), Solaris 2.3(or Sun OS 5.3), Solaris 2.4(or Sun OS 5.4), Solaris 2.5(or Sun OS 5.5), solaris 2.6(or Sun OS 5.6).

In November 1998, with the release of SunOS 2.7, Sun Microsystem decided to drop "2." from its marketing name "Solaris 2.6", and the new version came to be known as Solaris 7 . Similarly Solaris 8 was released in February 2000, and Solaris 9 was released in May2002.

Solaris 10, the most stable and reliable UNIX OS, finally released on January 31, 2005,. On 27 January 2010, SUN was acquired by Oracle Corporation, and this is the reason why Solaris is now known as Oracle Solaris.

2.   Introduction to Solaris

Oracle Solaris is known for its reliability and scalability, especially on SPARC hardware systems with Oracle Database providing high speed and performance compared to other operating systems. Solaris is famous for innovation of many features such as ZFS(Zetta Byte File System), DTrace, etc. Solaris supports both SPARC-based and x86-based servers from Oracle Sun and other vendors like HP, IBM. Earlier Solaris was supported only for sun sparc workstations but with time, it is now supported on major x86 platforms, with continuing development to include support for almost all x86/x64 platforms.

Solaris was historically developed as proprietary registered software of SUN. However in June 2005, Sun Microsystems released OpenSolaris, an open source project revealing most of its codebase including solaris kernel. With OpenSolaris, the company aimed to build a developer and user base around the internet. After the acquisition of Sun, Oracle decided to discontinue the OpenSolaris development as they reported that this could provide a thriving alternative to Oracle Solaris and can affect their solaris license and support contract numbers.

Now Oracle no more provides public updates to the source code of their Solaris Kernel. Also from Solaris 11 onwards, the company preferred to make this a completely closed source proprietary operating system except for those linux parts/programs which are already in GPL(open source) license whose source code can still be downloaded from oracle website.

2.1.   Linux/UNIX Architecture concept (shells and kernel).

The first thing we should understand before programming or running command on UNIX is its architecture. UNIX is an Operating system and hence we should know how it takes commands from users and how it translates and executes it. For every OS , there are few standards that were defined and are followed even with new generation operating systems. Any UNIX/UNIX-Like(Linux) OS may adhere to standards like Single UNIX Specification (SUS) or POSIX(Portable Operating System Interface) IEEE(Institute of Electrical and Electronics Engineers) standard(usually followed by linux). SUS or POSIX standards include the basic guidelines like what commands, definitions, system interfaces, various services/daemons that should be common and should comply with the mentioned guidelines.

If we talk about Solaris, then we found that it is registered as compliant with the Single UNIX Specification i.e. SUS. And linux is a POSIX complaint UNIX-Like OS. Don't get confuse that they are different, SUS involves the POSIX complaint from 1988 onwards. So likely or unlikely, both UNIX and Linux are almost same. However there are few differences exist when we talk about their kernel and hence few functionalities/commands differ in them.

Now lets have a look at a diagram to understand how our UNIX like Operating systems work, and how it executes the command(s) fired on it by the users. We know an OS can take user commands, and shows us the result. In the background how our bare hardware processes these commands which can only understand a language of bits i.e. 0 and1. So this is all a game of the OS architecture which has made it so intelligent.

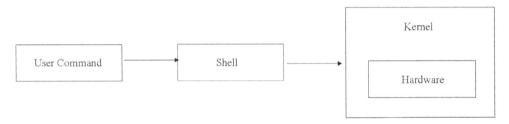

Fig 1.4 Unix OS Architecture

Here we can see that the user commands are first processed by UNIX shell, lets say bash shell and when the shell prepares an object code, it sends the code to kernel which converts it to the byte codes and process it on the system hardware. Now what we have understood by this, a kernel is the core of the Operating system which is responsible of converting the executable programs to bit code and everything depends on a system kernel. Its efficiency, speed and multitasking. Obviously hardware stays at the core, but utilizing hardware efficiently all depends upon the kernel efficiency.

Due to this kernel software, UNIX was prominently dominating the market earlier before the launch of Linux kernel by Linus torwalds in the year 1991 and after that the complete market has experienced a powerful change when we talk about OS development. However I will not cover linux history in brief over here. The main motive of this section is to understand how user applications executed on a linux/UNIX system and why UNIX was dominating the market with its expensive licence which was deeply affected with the launch of Linux kernel.

2.2. Common in Linux and Solaris

Obviously as we have seen UNIX and linux are based on two different standards. Solaris is based on SUS and linux is based on POSIX IEEE with much ongoing advancement by different groups worldwide since its an open source software. However since solaris also include libraries to support POSIX(Portable Operating System Independent UNIX), hence there are major possibilities that an application designed for linux can be deployed on Solaris, or vice versa without much changes. Only few modification or checks can make a program capable to run on both operating systems. Now lets look at few major similarities between linux and Solaris(or UNIX-like) operating systems.

1.   Base command Set
The base commands for both UNIX and linux are almost same like ls(to list files), date(to see system date), cp (to copy), etc.

2.   File system structure
The file system structure defines how the directories are made inside the OS and how the files/programs are placed including binaries, etc. For example:- In windows, the file system structure is first at top we see an icon "My Computer", and inside that we can see our drives like "C:", "D:", "G:" , etc.

Similarly in linux or UNIX like operating systems we have hierarchical architecture as shown in Fig 2 with / as topmost file system location.

The figure shows the simple file system hierarchy in UNIX systems. / is the root directory under which all directories of the system resides like root, usr, home,etc. Futher this fig. shows bin and sbin are some sub-directories created under usr directory.

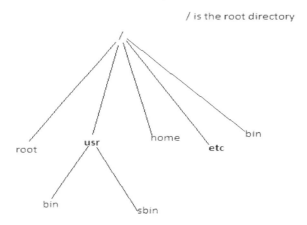

Fig.1.5 File system Hierarchy

➢ / --> Root Directory (top most location) of the entire linux file system

➢ /bin/ --> Contains all binary commands/executables that are required by users for their day to day operation on the system. For example ls(list command), cat(display file command), cp(copy command), etc are stored in /bin directory.

➢ /boot/ --> Contains the essential files to boot the operating system like kernel, initrd image(initial ramdisk used to load temporary files onto the system) and their associated linkage files.

➢ /dev/ --> It contains the list of connected devices to the system. In linux every hardware device is saved in software files and their configuration can be easily changed by modifying these files located in /dev directory.

➢ /etc/ --> This directory contains all the configuration files of the system and system applications. To change the user preferences we can modify these configuration files.

➤ /home/ --> This directory contains the user personal files or personal settings. It can be considered as a home for a user to reside everything personal. It contains separate directories for each user created so that each user can have a part of /home storage. In solaris, /export/home is the actual directory used in place of /home(which is mounted using autofs, you will undertsand it later in autofs chapter.)

➤ /root/ --> It is the home directory for root in linux, root is the super user that has all the powers and permissions. In Solaris, / the topmost directory is served as root home directory by default.

➤ /tmp/ --> Contains the temporary files which are removed on each system boot.(Temporary files are also stored at /var/tmp)

➤ /usr/ --> It contains all the user data i.e. the applications installed on the system and the different utilities required by all users.

○ Remember that /usr contains the application data common to every user whereas /home contains the personal data unique for each user on the system.

➤ /var/ --> Contains the variable data.(the data that has the possibility to change frequently).

3.   Runlevel Concept and admin commands like shutdown, init

Another thing which is common to both Linux and Solaris Operating system is their basic administration commands like init, shutdown. All such commands are avail ble on both UNIX and linux. Also the runlevel concept on UNIX and linux are same. It means init 1 will execute all scripts placed in /etc/rc1.d/ directory same as in Linux.

4.   Shells

A shell, as we had seen earlier, provides an interface which accepts the user input and passes to kernel. Hence this interface is also common for linux and Solaris. It means the same bourne shell, bash shell, c shell, korn shell can be installed on both UNIX and Linux. It makes the working environment look and behavior similar in both UNIX and linux.

5.   Kernel tuning

The kernel can be tuned on both operating systems namely Linux and UNIX. However the syntax and paramters supported are different. For example:- lets set the socket buffer size to some large value to avoid dropping large buffer packets.

On Linux:

sysctl -w net.core.rmem_max=2092304

sysctl -w net.core.wmem_max=2092304

On Solaris:

ndd -set /dev/udp udp_max_buf 2092304

6.   Applications and GUI manager

Mostly all third party applications provide support for UNIX and UNIX-like operating systems. For example:- Editors like vi/vim, window managers like kde, gnome are available on both UNIX and UNIX like operating systems(linux), and utilities like adobe reader, vlc player, etc.

2.3.   **Difference between Solaris and Linux**

After the above similarities, you might be thinking that both OS seems same so is there any difference between them. Yes there are many differences between them. The similarities itself indicates the differences. Let's have a look at the following points.

1.   Kernel – Hardware Specific

The major difference between UNIX and linux is their kernel and hence we can't deny the fact that there may be few tasks that can be achieved on Linux kernel and can't be achieved on UNIX/Solaris Kernel and vice versa. For example:- Solaris kernel earlier doesn't support x86 hardware, even today on few hardwares, it causes issue(s). On the other hand, linux kernel, open source software, provides support for almost every x86 hardware.

Other examples of UNIX as hardware specific OS:
.   Solaris   -->   Sparc (in 2005, added support for x86)
Hp-UX   -->   Supported on itanium, PA-iris series servers.
AIX   -->   IBM Powerseries Server.

On left, you can see the OS name, and on right the hardware on which it is supported.

2.   Init, mount, grep, etc Commands.
The same init command is used in Linux as well as in Solaris. But don't confuse with same command name. Since the command versions are different and hence the options used with same command on UNIX and linux may vary in their meaning. For example:- init 5 is used to enter graphical mode in Linux, whereas in Solaris it is used to completely power off the system So be ware before using the command options. And similarly there are few options in grep and mount which you find only supported on linux or solaris. You need to check manual page to get help of any such command is this case. (# man <commandname>)

3.   Added System Specific commands
In each distribution whether we talk about UNIX or UNIX-like(linux) operating systems, we found many system specific commands which can only be executed on that OS. For example:- prtdiag(in Solaris), ioscan (in HP), system-config-*(in linux). These commands are an example that even many commands are same between different flavors of UNIX and UNIX like OS, but there are tons of commands and functionalities exists which are still different and make each OS appropriate for their unique processing features.

4. Volume Managers

Every UNIX or linux system has its own volume management software. Volume manager is a software which is helpful in managing disks efficiently. For example:- if we want to increase/decrease disk space on a partition in real time, then these volume managers are very helpful and provide a greater flexibility to achieve this task on the fly in running system. Also in case we want to setup redundancy like raid, then also these provides various ways to achive it.

When we talk about linux, it provides LVM(Logical volume manager) to manage disks. The commands and usage of lvm is completely different from those found in UNIX operating system. However the concept behind it remains the same.

In Solaris, we have SVM(Solaris Volume Manager) which provides nice way to achieve RAID implementation, however it appears a little complex to beginners due to metadb(or volume database) creation. Solaris now provides a new file system ZFS(Z file system) which can also be used as a volume manager providing better flexibility than SVM. With Solaris 11, we find even the root file system is on ZFS which simplifies the task of disk management activities.

Symantac also provides a platform independent Volume manager called VxVM, which is very useful when we consider a distributed environment where we may need to sync data between different OS platforms. Since we need to purchase licence to use this volume manager, hence it is a little less preferred as compared to other volume managers.

5. Hardware Troubleshooting Commands

Since UNIX OS is hardware specific, so the commands required to troubleshoot issues with this OS are different from those commands that are required to troubleshoot issues with Linux, or any other UNIX or UNIX-like operating system. For example:- in linux we refer dmesg, however in solaris we have utilities like cfgadm to find the device connection status.

6.   <u>UNIX requires License, Linux is free/open-source</u>

The major difference that we already know is that UNIX requires a valid license, whereas Linux is available free of cost without any licensing software.

3.   What is file system

A file system is a way in which files are stored on disk, and provides a mechanism to access different media files comfortably. In windows, we see "My Computer" as top most location of file system under which we see c drive, d drive, etc where we can store our data. So our windows file system hierarchy is as follows:

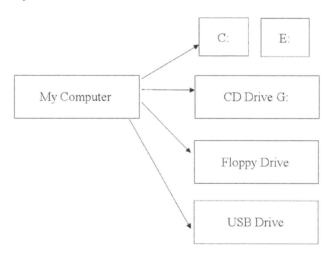

Fig 1.6 Windows File System

Now think "My Computer" as a file system. Windows will be installed in C drive. You will store your movies on D: drive. CD can be accessed in G drive, etc. So a file system provides an efficient way how we can access and retrieve data. Suppose there is no file system, then the information will become a large body of data with no way to determine where one piece of information ends and the next begins.

Similarly, in linux we have "/" as root, compare it with "my computer" in windows. Under /, you find some directories like:

1.   /var/log ---> Where all logs are stored.
2.   /export/home or /home --> Where user home directories are stored.
3.   /boot --> Where Grub/kernel image is kept.
4.   /dev, /devices --> To access connected devices with the system.
5.   /bin, /sbin, /usr/bin, /usr/sbin --> To access executable binaries/programs/commands like init, etc.
Similarly you can mount cd drive on /mnt, or any other drive and can access it. You can create your own partition under /, say /mydata and can access /check it by going under root(/) directory with ease.

So in solaris/linux, the top most location in a file system hierarchy is / followed by different locations/directories to access all system data/devices.

Lets look at the file system hierarchy again:

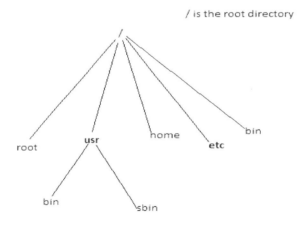

Fig.1.7 Unix File system

The UNIX or UNIX like systems follow the same hierarchy in file system. The name "file system" itself signifies a system responsible for managing files. And in UNIX or UNIX-like operating systems, everything is treated as a file whether it's a device connected with operating system, or its a software. We can access any device files directly by mentioning its complete absolute path under /devices.

3.1. What are disks and slices

A computer system usually consists of a hard disk on which we install the operating system and do our work. Suppose you have 5 hard disks of 100gb each, in this case you can format each disk seperatly and can use each disk for different purpose.

Now in case you have a single hard disk of 500gb, then you will prefer to create few partitions like c: drive with 100gb, d: and e: drive of 200gb each. This partition is known as slice in UNIX or UNIX-like operating system.

A disk is the complete hard disk or lun(a storage part coming from emc/netapp, it appears as a separate disk to the system), and a slice is a part of hard disk which can also be treated as a separate hard disk and used similarly.

As we know a disk is made of sectors or blocks. So a slice can be referred to as a single set of contiguous blocks which can be assigned a seperate name, and hence this complete name can be used as if we have a separate device.

So concluding the above description, we can say a slice is a subset of disk which can be utilized in the same manner as if a separate disk (only with an exception that further sub parts or slices can not be made from a slice).

3.2. UFS file system

A disk/slice is composed of the blocks, and the concern is, how user can store data on blocks directly. There should be some software/mechanism which can manage how data will be stored, which blocks will be used, and how they will be referred when accessed in future.

UFS or UNIX file system provides a mechanism to manage the hard disk/slice. When we format a disk/slice in UFS, then few starting blocks are reserved for boot blocks, one superblock is used to hold tuning paramters of hard disk including a magic number which is used to identify this as a UFS file system, thereafter few blocks are used to hold number of cylinder groups. Each cylinder group contains all inode numbers, file attributes, and backup copy of superblock, and in the end our original data is saved.

Just like UFS, we have many other formats available in UNIX or UNIX-like operating system, which includes BSD/OS, FreeBSD, Xenix, AIX, ZFS, etc. In linux, we usually find ufs, or ufs2(new version of ufs) as file system type. Till solaris 10, ufs is used for root / partition, and zfs is preferred for other mount points. But from Solaris 11, zfs is used even for root / partition as it provides greater flexibility to manage system administration activities and it can also serve as a volume manager. We will read about volume manager in the next section.

3.3. Introduction to RAID.

RAID stands for redundant array of inexpensive disks. So to understand what RAID is, let's look at its full form again "Redundant array of inexpensive disks" which simply means multiple or number of repetitive low cost disks: which are helpful in providing data redundancy in case of any drive failure.

RAID can also provide performance tuning by spreading large data onto multiple disks and hence the big data will be accessed from multiple disks simultaneously which decreases IO overhead per disk and hence increasing the overall time to get the data.

RAID provides different levels of redundancy and performance improvement based on which there are many standard RAID levels like RAID-0,1,2,3,4,5 and many hybrid RAID levels like RAID 10,01, etc. It all depends how data is duplicated between different disks to provide data redundancy, and hence providing an assurance of almost no data loss, and in case of one drive failure the same can be recovered from another disk.

Let's have a look at different standard and hybrid raid levels in short to understand how they configure the disks.

1.   RAID 0 (Striping/concat) :- RAID 0 simply combines several disks in either stripe or concat type. It does not provide any data redundancy or fault tolerance, but can improve performance through parallelism of read and write operations across multiple drives(striping), or flexibility of adding/extending space in existing volume(concat).

2.   RAID 1(mirroring):- RAID -1 is also called mirroring where the data is written identically on two (or more) drives which helps in creating a "mirrored set of data". So the read request can be serviced by any of the mirrored drive containing the requested data which can improve performance as the data is read from alternate disks.

3.   RAID 2,3,4 (striping with dedicated parity):- RAID 2, 3 and 4 provides data striping i.e writing data to alternate disks. RAID 2 provides bit-level, RAID-3 provides byte-level and RAID-4 provides block level data striping with dedicated parity. These raid levels are not used nowadays.

4.   RAID 5:- RAID 5 uses block-level striping with distributed parity on all disks. Unlike RAID 2,3,or 4, the parity information is distributed between all the drives. It requires not all drives but at least one to be present for operation. If there is a failure of any single drive, subsequent reads can be calculated from the distributed parity on other disks, such that no data loss. RAID 5 requires at least three disks to be present.

5.   RAID6:- RAID 6 is just an extension to RAID5 with an additional parity block. Hence it takes into account two parity blocks alongwith block level string among the disks.

6.   RAID 1+0 and 0+1 :- RAID 10 and RAID 01 are different from each other. RAID 10 creates mirror of striped disk groups (data striped on two or more disks), whereas RAID 01 stripes mirrored data(data of each disk is mirrored separately.

4.   What is Volume Manager?

A volume manager provides a flexible and an efficient way to manage the disks/slices. Now you might be thinking that we already have ufs available then what is the use of Volume managers. Suppose you have formatted disk in ufs, and later there is a requirement to increase / (root) partition size because there is some patch needs to be installed and it requires extra disk space. Then it becomes very difficult and challenging to achive this task, to copy data to some tape drive, make new partition, format it and then transfer the data. If the root disk was made on some volume manager then this task can be achieved very easily with just five minutes of downtime.

4.1.   Logical Volume Manager(specific to Linux OS)

A linux/logical volume manager takes physical disks/space inside it, and creates a logical group of one single big space. On this single large space, we can create logical volumes or partitions which will act as disks for the operating system and when we want to increase disk space, we can easily extend the partition on the fly without any downtime. The best configuration is when we setup LVM over hardware raid.

Let's have a look at the following diagram to understand LVM

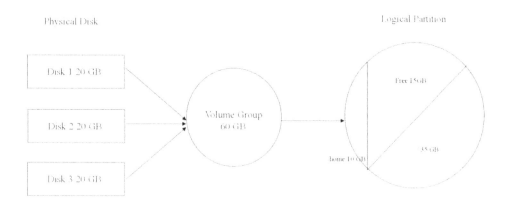

Fig 1.8 Concept of Volume Group

As we see in figure 1.8, there are different physical disks available, and we combine them to create a logical group of space known as volume group or VG. And thereafter we can divide the VG into different logical volumes of any sizes, for example:- . /home of 10GB, / of 35gb , and keep some space free which can be used to increase the space on any of the logical volume in future. So this provides a greater flexibility.

Below is a figure that shows the process, how we can create a logical volume from physical raw disks. First we create physical volume of each raw disk, so we have one physical volume against each physical disk. Thereafter we can combine any number of physical volumes to create a big logical space which is known as Volume Group. And in the last, we can divide this big volume group into any number of logical volumes.

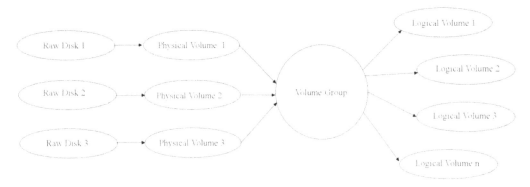

Fig 1.9 Process to create a Logical Volume

4.2.   SVM (Solaris Volume Manager)

The Solaris volume manager introduced with the Solaris Version 9. This is also known as Solstice DiskSuite in earlier versions of Solaris. Several new features were included like soft partitions, access via SMC , and monitoring active disks. We can create a RAID 0 concatenation or stripe, or a RAID 1 configuration mirroring the root, var and swap slices and we can also create RAID 5.

For increasing the size of the partition, we need to add a new slice/disk and similarly to reduce the space we can remove any spare slice/disk. Like LVM, we can increase/decrease disk space because in SVM we use complete space allocated. However the similar functionality can be achieved by createing extra slices as per our requirements.

SVM creates logical volume on each disk/slice and then we can setup any RAID configuration , and is efficient for creating, modifying and controlling RAID-0 (concatenation/stripe) , RAID-1 (mirror) , RAID 0+1 , RAID 1+0 , RAID-5 volumes, and soft partitions. SVM provides a easy way to setup and manage the software raid on Solaris OS.

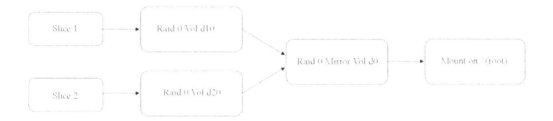

Fig 1.10: Use of SVM to create RAID1 mirror d0 volume

The above figure explains a practical use of SVM which is mostly used on Solaris servers where RAID1 is configured. Here we can see there are 2 slices created, and then on each slice we configured RAID 0 volumes namely d10 and d20, now finally we created another volume d0 with two volumes d10 and d20 in mirror.

We could have used the slices directly instead of d10 and d20 RAID0 volumes, but suppose you want to increase size of these individual volumes then that could not be possible easily if the disks/slices are used directly.

Now we can easily increase space by adding another slice along with existing d10 volume in concat, which cannot be implemented in case of using slices directly instead of raid 0 volume.

4.3.   Z file system

The Z file system (ZFS) was first introduced by Sun which is designed for maximum data integrity, supporting data snapshots, checksums and multiple copies of data. It uses data replication model which is also known as RAID-Z. RAID-Z ensures redundancy equivalent to hardware RAID, however it also overcomes some of the limitations of hardware RAID.

According to oracle, the ZFS file system is a revolutionary new type of file system which has changed the way file systems, disks and storage can be administered, with some unique features that are not found in any other file system available today.The definition is absolutely correct when we consider other file systems, but in other file systems also using few tweaks and explicit configuration changes we can achieve similar functionality. However why anyone will waste extra man hours on tweaking a ufs or any other file system when all the features are already provided with zfs file system.

ZFS combines the features of a file system as well as a volume manager. It means all features of a volume manager are available in ZFS. So we only need to configure our file system as zfs and there is no need to chase up for any other volume manager.

The concept of ZFS is similar to LVM. First we need to create a logical volume group called as pool and then we create logical file systems called as zfs file system. Lets have a look at the following diagrams.

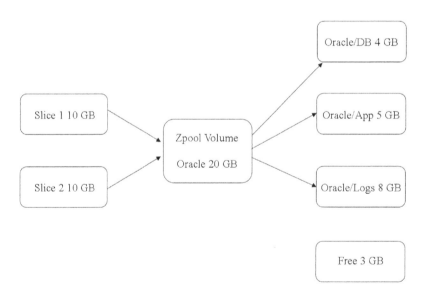

Fig.1.11. ZFS as a Volume Manager and File system

In the above figure, we can see two slices combined into one big volume oracle which is called as zpool in solaris. And thereafter we have created sub file systems oracle/db, oracle/app and oracle/logs of different sizes as per requirements. This size limit is just like quota in ZFS, so we can increase/decrease the limit in runtime. Also since the file systems are created on logical space, so we can also add new slice/disk in the zpool at runtime only. As we can see, we can do almost all tasks without any downtime, and hence zfs plays an important role in Solaris.

With Solaris 11, we have an option to select ZFS file system for root / during OS install also. With ZFS, oracle aims to attract new customers to go for OracleUnix OS instead of Linux or any other version of UNIX or UNIX like OS. Not only volume manager, zfs provides many new features as we can see below:

a.   ZFS Snapshots:- Oracle ZFS provides a unique feature of snapshots, with the help of which we can create a read-only backup copy of the original data which occupies zero size(concept of hard links in linux with LOFS file system)

b.   Copy on write Technology:- In ufs file system scheme, there are chances of data corruption in case there is power failure between data copy. But ZFS provides a new technology called copy on write technology, here the data is never overwritten, and any operation is either entirely committed or ignored. Because of this, the file system can never be corrupted through accidental loss of power or a system crash, however there are little chances of data loss but the file system will always be consistent.

c.   Self Healing Data:- ZFS also provides a new feature of data self healing. ZFS checks the data corruption in background and if it founds any data corruption, it used to recover the original copy from the backup copy.

d.   High Scalability:- ZFS is 128 bit file system and hence allows upto 256 quadrillon zettabytes of storage. The metadata is allocated dynamically, and hence there is no need to tune inode numbers and other paramters.

4.4.   ZFS Vs LVM

We had seen LVM, and then ZFS. We know that the same functionality can be achieved in Linux by using RAID + LVM, and in Solaris by using SVM, or ZFS. Now the most common question usually asked by few people is what will be the best. So the answer is simple when you check out below points.

a.   ZFS is faster, provides more data integrity but it requires extra memory or high RAM availablility compared to LVM.
b.   High amount of data can be stored on small disk using compression and deduplication.
c.   ZFS came out to be safer than traditional ext2/ext3 partitions when we talk about data corruption rates.

So the first priority goes to ZFS when we talk about storage, or high amount of data. However for small data you can even go with LVM+RAID, or simply LVM and tape backup or it depends upon the requirement.

5.   What is package and patch in UNIX.
A package is just like an archive which contains some set of binary complied files which are copied on the target system in order to install/update a new program alongwith few scripts to update system files. We can install a new program via package file. A patch file is just a script file/binary program that updates the text or package files to

correct/remove any vulnerability in the existing program or package files.

UNIX provides a command called "patch" which can be used to apply a patch. The patch command first changes/updates the required files as listed under the patchfile and thereafter runs diff or similar UNIX utility to list the changes between old and new changed files.

A package is a compiled code which alongwith program files, provides information about its dependencies and description. To install any new package, first we need to install all dependencies and this task is really cumbersome to first check all dependencies and install them. So to simplify this task, we have many package management utilities introduced in UNIX or UNIX like operating systems.

5.1 Package Format and Package managers

The problem when we install any software with source code is that sometimes the installation fails due to slight change in source code and we should have enough knowledge to troubleshoot such issues which could be time consuming and cumbersome task. To make it simplier UNIX or UNIX like operating systems provides a package management facility or different package managers.

RPM or Redhat package manager is a package format available for redhat-derived linux operating systems. RPM provides an easy way to install the packages on redhat linux, the package files are identified using .rpm extension. Similarly Ubuntu provides .deb format package files and solaris provides .pkg format files.

Now we have package format available to avoid any compile time error in case of source code, but still people used to face dependency issues. For example:- when we try to install a package using pkgadd/rpm command in our system, the system will throw an error if any dependency is not met, suppose you are trying to install GUI server like GNOME, then you need to install about hundreds of dependencies first to successfully install the gnome x server or desktop.

To resolve this dependency issue, a new concept of package management system is introduced. When we fire a command to install any specific program or software, we need not to worry of any dependencies. Package manager will automatically search the dependencies on its one central location(also called repository) and install all required dependencies followed by the required software.

To easily understand the difference among package, package format, and different package management utilities, we can have a look at the following table.

UNIX/UNIX Like OS	Package Format	Package Management System
Redhat Linux/ RHEL	RPM (Redhat Package Manager)	YUM
Solaris	PKG	Pkgadd, Image Packaging System, and OpenCSW(online open community that maintains a collection of packages)
Ubuntu/Debian Linux	DEB	Dpkg, APT, Ubuntu Software Center

OS X	Pkg/pkgsrc	Mac App Store, Steam

Table 1.1 Different Package formats

Similarly we have different package manager for every other UNIX or UNIX like operating system. However we can install a package by downloading the source code and compiling it on any target system regardless of the package manager software.

UNIX also provides a wonderful tool "Alien" which can convert different Linux package formats. Conversion between Linux Standard Base/compliant .rpm packages, .deb, Solaris (.pkg) and Slackware (.tgz, .txz, .tbz, .tz) packages are supported by this utility.

6.   **What is meant by Snapshot?**

A snapshot is the system state at a particular point in time. Snapshot is derived from photography, like a photograph it captures the particular system state and saves it for future reference in case we want to recover data by looking at the snapshot. Different linux and UNIX systems provides different features when we talk about snapshots in linux, and snapshots in oracle solaris zfs file system. For example:- In linux lvm, the snapshots' data can be changed, however in zfs snapshots, they are a read-only copy of data. On the other hand, zfs provides easy way to manage snapshots as compared to linux LVM.

Unlike backup, snapshot takes a very small time to finish and can be taken in running live production systems without any chances of data corruption. In backup strategies, the major challenge faced was how to take backup of live system when there are multiple write operations going on and there are great chances of data corruption. And taking downtime in a production live system is not possible, so the snapshot came into picture.

A snapshot takes only fraction of time as compared to complete backup copy and the data remains intact with no effect when original data is modified. The initial size of snapshot can be very small in MBs for GBs of file system, but with increasing changes on original file system/partition, we may need to increase the size of the snapshot.

6.1. LVM Snapshot

In linux LVM, we can create snapshots to store a particular state of the file system and this just requires only few MBs to copy the inode values and when we make changes to the original file system, a new inode number is created and hence the space occupied in snapshot increases gradually.

Lets take an example how to create LVM snapshot.

a.   In My system, I have two LVs created in one volume group and has 224 MB free. First lets check LVs and VGs on a system.

```
[root@avivr2 ~]# lvs
LV      VG      Attr   LSize Origin Snap%  Move Log Copy%  Convert
LogVol00 VolGroup00 -wi-ao 4.69G
LogVol01 VolGroup00 -wi-ao 1.44G

[root@avivr2 ~]# vgs
VG      #PV #LV #SN Attr   VSize VFree
VolGroup00  1  2  0 wz--n- 6.34G 224.00M
```

b.   A snapshot only takes few MBs, hence we can create a snapshot in a very less space (in 100MB only) and here we have enough space available. So lets create a new snapshot LV.

[root@avivr2 ~]# lvcreate --size 100M --snapshot --name snap1 /dev/VolGroup00/LogVol00
  Rounding up size to full physical extent 128.00 MB
  Logical volume "snap1" created

[root@avivr2 ~]# lvs
  LV   VG   Attr LSize   Origin   Snap% Move Log Copy% Convert
  LogVol00 VolGroup00 owi-ao 4.69G
  LogVol01 VolGroup00 -wi-ao 1.44G
  snap1   VolGroup00 swi-a- 128.00M LogVol00 0.31

c.   Now lets mount it and check.
[root@avivr2 ~]# mount /dev/mapper/VolGroup00-snap1 /mnt
[root@avivr2 ~]# df -h
File system   Size Used Avail Use% Mounted on
/dev/mapper/VolGroup00-LogVol00   4.6G 2.2G 2.2G 50%
/
/dev/mapper/VolGroup00-LogVol01   1.4G 35M 1.3G 3%
/tmp
/dev/mapper/VolGroup00-LogVol00   4.6G 2.2G 2.2G 50%
/mnt
/dev/mapper/VolGroup00-snap1   4.6G 2.2G 2.2G
50% /mnt

d.   If you try to write data into this file system, then you can observe that this snapshot is read-write and you can make changes into it.

[root@avivr2 mnt]# touch hello.txt

```
[root@avivr2 mnt]# ls -il hello.txt
97076 -rw-r--r-- 1 root root 0 Feb 18 19:23 hello.txt
[root@avivr2 mnt]# pwd
/mnt
[root@avivr2 mnt]#
[root@avivr2 mnt]# ls -il /hello.txt
ls: /hello.txt: No such file or directory
```

Now when we look at ZFS snapshots later we will identify they are just read only copies, but they offer better flexibility when we talk about snapshot management. Here the snapshot size need to be increased when they cross the defined size and this sometimes creates problems when there are major changes on some file system and the snapshot size is very small.

Few Questions

Q.1. What is Solaris ?

Q.2 How Solaris/UNIX is different from Linux ?

Q.3 What is UFS and ZFS file system ?

Q.4 What is Volume Manager ? Which Volume manager is used in Linux and Solaris ?

Q.5 Difference between patch and package in UNIX ?

Q.6 What do you mean by a Snapshot ?

Chapter -2
Working with Solaris FS and Device Administration

Now with this chapter, we will more emphasize on practical commands and very less on theoretical part to make ourselves comfortable in solaris operation. In this chapter, we will see the Solaris File system and device administration basics and the common issues, basics of device management that as a Solaris User or administrator you must be aware.

Instead of going on with theory, I have made different topics and when you practice each topic on your solaris 10 Test machine, in the end you will observe that we had covered all the topics and you are now comfortable with these operations on your Solaris Machine.

I assume you have installed Solaris 10 on a VM or you already have a test machine configured. If not, please install Solaris 10 OS as a VM machine on your PC and login to the machine as root user. Once you are logged in, you are ready to execute below excercises and you are now ready to learn Solaris operating system.

1.   Check file systems mounted on OS.

First step to deal with file systems and devices, we need to check what type of file systems are mounted on the system and their format. To check which all file systems are mounted, we can use any of the below commands.

a.   The most common command used is ""df" with "-h" option that means human readable i.e. shows space in GB/MB.
bash-3.2# **df -h**
File system   size used avail capacity Mounted on
/dev/dsk/c0d0s0   14G 8.4G 5.0G 63%   /

b.   Another good command to check all mounted partitions and their types is mount command.

bash-3.2# **mount -v | grep /**

/dev/dsk/c0d0s0 on / **type ufs**

read/write/setuid/devices/rstchown/intr/largefiles/logging/xattr/on

error=panic/dev=1980000 on Thu Mar 27 10:02:51 2014

c.   Another way to identify type of file system is to use "-n" to know type of file system. In linux, we can use "-t" to have a nice output with type of file system.

bash-3.2# **df -n | more**

/   : ufs

/devices   : devfs

/system/contract   : ctfs

/proc   : proc

/etc/mnttab   : mntfs

Note: Can we convert UFS root to ZFS in Solaris 10 ?

Yes we can convert UFS root file system to ZFS, however to convert UFS into ZFS, system requires reboot, it can't be done online. In Solaris 10, there is no option to setup rpool(root pool) i.e. ZFS formatted / partition, but in Solaris 11, it will ask if we want ufs or zfs file system for root partition during install.

2.   **UNIX Directory Structure**

Let's have a quick review of UNIX directory structure file system. We have several directories created when we install solaris 10.

/ --> Topmost file system Location under which everything is installed.

/root --> Root user home directory in few flavors, doesn't exist on Solaris.

/dev --> Contains logical device names through which we access the file system data.

/boot --> Contains kernel and initrd(Initial RAM disk) image files necessary to boot OS.

/home --> An autofs mount point directs to /export/home.

/export --> Commonly shared file system.

/lib --> SMF executables, and shared executables.

/mnt --> Temporary mount point, usually used by administrator or few root programs.

/opt --> Default dir for addon application packages(3rd party).

/sbin --> Contains System binary for superuser commands

/bin --> Keeps binary executable programs usually linked to /usr/bin.

bash-3.2# ls -l /bin
lrwxrwxrwx 1 root   root   9 Jan 10 12:12 **/bin -> ./usr/bin**

Few other common directories in UNIX.
/proc, /etc/mnttab --> In memory directories, contains information provided by kernel at runtime.

/tmp --> Mounted on swap, contents refreshed/removed on reboot.
bash-3.2# df -h /tmp/

File system	size	used	avail	capacity	Mounted on
swap	2.0G	44K	2.0G	1%	/tmp

2.1.   Quick Tip 1: User Home Directory in Linux and Solaris

Linux --> /home
Solaris --> /export/home --> Autofs to /home/

bash-3.2# ls -ld /export/home/
drwxr-xr-x **3** root   root   512 Mar 12 15:50 /export/home/

bash-3.2# ls -ld /home/
dr-xr-xr-x **1** root   root   1 Mar 27 10:03 /home/
Link count is 1, so its a autofs directory not a normal directory.
Link count for a directory is always 2 and for a file it is 1.

bash-3.2# cd /home/
bash-3.2# df -h .
File system   size used avail capacity Mounted on
auto_home   0K   0K   0K   0%   /home

2.2.   **Quick Tip 2**: **Why /home is autofs by default in Solaris?**

Sun Microsystem developed servers like NIS(Network Information System), and NFS (Network File System)
Due to this, Sun has reserved /home for LDAP (Light Directory Access Protocol) or NIS user administration and hence this directory is controlled via autofs by default.
However in linux, we need to configure /home under autofs manually.

2.3.   **Quick Tip 3**: **Difference between /usr/bin and /usr/sbin executable?**

/usr/bin contains basic UNIX commands which are usually required by all users, however /usr/sbin contains commands that make changes to the system, and their access is limited to users having sudo, root group access. For example:- "ls(to list files) command is available under /usr/bin", and useradd is available under /usr/sbin.

bash-3.2# type ls
ls is hashed (/usr/bin/ls)
bash-3.2# **which ls**

/usr/bin/ls

bash-3.2# **which useradd**
/usr/sbin/useradd

2.4.   <u>Quick Tip 4</u>: **Difference between /sbin and /usr/sbin directories**
We have seen difference between /bin and /usr/sbin, but do you know
what is there is /sbin directory.
In single user mode during troubleshooting, only /sbin loaded but
/usr/sbin is not loaded. /usr/sbin is loaded only in multiuser mode. So
/sbin only contains few major system troubleshooting commands that
are necessary for an administrator to troubleshoot the issues with the
system in single user mode.

For example:- Init is available in both. However when running system in
multiuser mode, the path is loaded from /usr/sbin.
bash-3.2# ls -l /sbin/init
-r-xr-xr-x 1 root   sys   43432 Sep 29 2012 **/sbin/init**
bash-3.2# which init
/usr8/sbin/init.

3.   **System architecture**
Solaris is supported on SPARC, as well as x86/x64 systems of few
common manufacturers, however now the support is extended to
maximum possible vendors. Since sparc is Oracle's own hardware so it
provides additional features like OK prompt over other hardware and
hence it is easier to manage sparc servers over x86 running solaris OS.

3.1.   **Sparc and x86 difference**
Sparc and x86 are two different hardware architectures available on
which we can install the Solaris OS. Since the OS is same, there is no
difference between them w.r.t the software i.e. operating system. Hence

after OS comes up, there is no difference whether its sparc or x86. Now the point is where the difference lies then.

a.   Sparc and x86 are two different hardwares, so the major difference lies between then is of hardware efficiency to boost OS performance.

b.   Another major difference lies is that system boot up procedure is different in both. Means in X86, we have BIOS whereas in Sparc we have OK prompt.

3.2.   Quick Tip 5: Check OS whether its x86 or Sparc.

We can identify whether our Solaris OS is installed on a x86 machine or sparc machine by running the most basic command i.e. "uname -a" which shows "sparc" in case of SPARC system and in case of x86/x64 of another vendor, it will show i86pc or x64.

On x86 machine:

bash-3.2# uname -a

SunOS Solaris10 5.10 Generic_147441-25 i86pc i386 i86pc

On sparc these would have shown sparc instaed of 86.

On Sparc Machine:

root@bhminsat1 # uname -a

SunOS bhminsat1 5.10 Generic_147440-26 sun4u sparc SUNW,Netra-T12

3.3.   Quick Tip 6: Change first boot device from OS in Solaris on SPARC architecture.

On sparc, we can change first boot device from OS, but this can not be done in case of X86 systems. This can be done using eeprom command. There are several boot time parameters available for an administrator to change from Solaris OS. Lets have a look at this command and usage how we can change the boot device.

```
# eeprom
output-device=virtual-console
input-device=virtual-console
auto-boot-on-error?=false
load-base=16384
```
auto-boot?=true
```
network-boot-arguments: data not available.
boot-command=boot
boot-file: data not available.
```
boot-device=/pci@780/pci@0/pci@9/scsi@0/disk@0,0:a disk net
```
multipath-boot?=false
boot-device-index=0
use-nvramrc?=false
nvramrc: data not available.
error-reset-recovery=boot
```

Above we can see the parameter boot-device which displays the value of the device which is used for Solaris system booting at present. So now you can edit this parameter value to any other device to boot from that device.

The value can be changed by using below command:
 # eeprom boot-device=new-value

3.4.   Quick Tip 7: Checking OS bit level (64 bit or 32 bit) in Solaris

In Solaris, we can check the system bit level by using a command "isainfo". If isainfo shows both 64-bit and 32-bit in its output then its 64 bit OS, and if only one 32-bit output is shown then it's a 32-bit OS.

For example:- Below we can see isainfo output on a 64-bit OS.

bash-3.2# isainfo -v

64-bit amd64 applications

avx xsave pclmulqdq aes sse4.2 sse4.1 ssse3 popcnt tscp cx16 sse3 sse2

sse fxsr mmx cmov amd_sysc cx8 tsc fpu

32-bit i386 applications

avx xsave pclmulqdq aes sse4.2 sse4.1 ssse3 popcnt tscp cx16 sse3 sse2

sse fxsr mmx cmov sep cx8 tsc fpu

However for Solaris 11, no 32 bit version is available, so any Solaris 11 system will be 100% 64 bit OS. We can also check the bit level in BIOS.

4. Kernel

A kernel is a program that acts as an interface between OS and the system hardware i.e CPU. The OS instructions are translated to a language (assembly or bit level) by a kernel program which is then executed on system hardware. A kernel can be classified as monolithic or microkernel based on where kernel stores its code. A monolithic kernel stores all the kernel code and kernel related threads in kernel space which is safe from any user modification and hence more reliable but less flexible. Usually in Linux/Solaris and most of UNIX flavors we have monolithic kernel. Microkernel is another type of kernel in which few kernel threads are stored in user space which provides more flexibility when we talk about online system changes; however the performance becomes poor as it takes time to load such threads back to memory.

The Solaris kernel was first introduced by Sun Microsystems, and is monolithic in nature and the unique feature supported by solaris kernel is of zones. The kernel settings gets loaded when system boots up and we can't make changes directly in the kernel at real time except for few parameters that can be tuned at run time.

4.1. Understanding Solaris Kernel Directory Structure

In Solaris the kernel files and settings are stored in two directories namely /kernel and /platform. /kernel contains the kernel components common to all hardware platforms within a particular instruction set that are required for booting the system. /platform contains the platform definition files that are required by different platforms to bring the system up. The changes made in /platform directory will be reflected only after the system reboot i.e., it serves in the role of static kernel in solaris.

bash-3.2# pwd
/platform/i86pc/kernel/cpu

bash-3.2# ls
amd64   cpu_ms.GenuineIntel.6.45
cpu_ms.AuthenticAMD   cpu_ms.GenuineIntel.6.46
cpu_ms.AuthenticAMD.15   cpu_ms.GenuineIntel.6.47
cpu_ms.GenuineIntel   cpu.generic

4.2. Solaris Kernel Insiders

Solaris kernel has two parts, one is static kernel which can't be changed at runtime, and another part is dynamically loaded kernel in which we can change the parameters at runtime. In case any changes need to be done in static kernel, then our solaris system needs a reboot. Let's have a small look at the following directories in solaris file system.

➢ /kernel --> It is referred as Dynamic kernel (since the changes can be made on fly, means in running kernel, and in reboot it will be added into static kernel.

➢ /platform --> Static kernel (it requires a reboot)

➢ Genunix --> Name of the kernel file in solaris, vmlinux in linux(vmlinux in linux(vm stands for virtual machine depicting support of virtual machines in linux)

➢ /etc/system file --> for kernel tuning configuration in Solaris 10 OS. ---> comment starts from *, instead of #. --> changes will require a reboot to implement.

➢ Any wrong changes in /etc/system--> OS will go in cyclic reboot.

Kernel has two parts/settings which are, modules and parameters that we can modify to add/remove system features and tune its performance. Lets have a look of these features of Solaris Kernel.

1. Modules: A kernel module is a set of code usually written in C or assembly language which is loaded into the kernel and extends/adds some functionality to it. For example: - When we attach some new hardware to our system, the kernel loads few modules to read and interact with that hardware. In windows, we usually call them as device drivers, and in UNIX we call them up kernel modules. Even in case of few OS utilities to function we need to load kernel modules. Hence we can classify the kernel modules into two types.

a. Drivers
b. OS utility (NFS, LVM, etc.)

Module Check
To check all available kernel modules which are already loaded into the system kernel, we can use command modinfo. In Solaris, all functions like TCP IP, SCSI, FS Operations, etc are carried out by different kernel modules.

bash-3.2# modinfo | more
 Id   Loadaddr   Size Info Rev Module Name
  0 fffffffffb800000 18ec50 - 0 UNIX ()
  1 fffffffffb906bf0 3ef32 - 0 krtld ()
  2 fffffffffb93b8e0 27f720 - 0 genunix ()
--------------output truncated--------------------

Here in modinfo output, we can see Id which is the module ID, loadaddr is the starting text address in hexadecimal format, size is the size of text, data, and bss in hexadecimal bytes, Info is module specific information, Rev is the revision number of the loaded modules, and Module Name is the description of the module.

To check all scsi modules loaded, we can grep scsi from modinfo command output.

bash-3.2# modinfo | grep scsi
 27 ffffffff7851000 17ba8 174 1 scsi_vhci (SCSI VHCI Driver 1.77)
 28 ffffffff7868000 24f58 - 1 scsi (SCSI Bus Utility Routines)
106 ffffffff7c9a000 37428 73 1 iscsi (Sun iSCSI Initiator v20110524-0)

Load/Unload Module

To load or unload kernel modules, we can use the two commands /usr/sbin/modload and /usr/sbin/modunload. Modload and modunload command uses an argument "-i ID" to load/unload the module corresponding to the Id mentioned.

Let's have a look how to unload a module.

bash-3.2# **modinfo | grep -i scsi**
 27 ffffffff7851000 17ba8 174 1 **scsi_vhci (SCSI VHCI Driver 1.77)**
 28 ffffffff7868000 24f58 - 1 scsi (SCSI Bus Utility Routines)
106 ffffffff7c9a000 37428 73 1 iscsi (Sun iSCSI Initiator v20110524-0)
108 ffffffff7c20000 f518 - 1 idm (iSCSI Data Mover)
187 ffffffff8145000 265b0 30 1 sd (SCSI Disk Driver 1.578)

bash-3.2# **modinfo -i 27**
 Id   Loadaddr   Size Info Rev Module Name
 27 ffffffff7851000 17ba8 174 1 scsi_vhci (SCSI VHCI Driver 1.77)

bash-3.2# **modunload -i 27**
can't unload the module: Device busy

Similarly to load a module we can use modload command.
Let's load ip filter module.

bash-3.2# modload /usr/kernel/drv/ipf
bash-3.2# modinfo | grep -i ipf
249 ffffffffff89d4000 37cf0 165   1 ipf (IP Filter: v4.1.9)

<u>Note</u>: - The point to note here is that modload and modunload do not show any error/message in case the module is already loaded or not. So we should always check first whether a module is loaded or not and load/unload the required module.

2.   <u>Kernel Parameters:</u> UNIX provides a good flexible option to change system behavior by modifying few kernel parameters. For example: - By default UNIX occupies 60% of RAM and rest 40% is moved into swap space and this behavior is controlled by a kernel parameter called swappiness. So in this case we can modify this kernel parameter value to something else like 50% to move half of the data to swap space. Or sometimes we modify its value to 10% to increase system performance when we have high amount of RAM or physical memory available. In solaris 11, this parameter is called as swapfs_minfree.

As we know we can't make changes to the solaris kernel at runtime, we can only tune its existing parameters to improve its functionality as per our requirements.

4.3.   **Tuning Solaris Kernel**
The Oracle Solaris kernel can be tuned using any of the below techniques at runtime.

4.3.1. /etc/system file

We can modify the /etc/system file and can tune many system parameters. Since this file is read at system boot up, so the settings changed will require a system reboot to reflect. It is always recommended to take a backup of this file before making any changes to it, so that we can restore the file in case anything goes wrong accidently.

For example:- suppose we have a requirement to increase pagesize as per some application program, so we have added below lines to /etc/system file:

set max_uheap_lpsize = 0x2000
set max_ustack_lpsize = 0x2000
set max_privmap_lpsize = 0x2000
set max_shm_lpsize = 0x2000

Make sure we have taken a backup copy of the file before making the changes.
cp /etc/system /etc/system.fine

Now we need to reboot the system for the settings to take effect. Suppose we have changed some parameter to wrong value and the server is not coming up. In this case, we can restore the backup copy we had taken before making the changes by mentioning the filename at OK prompt.

ok boot -a

boot command with a argument enters into interactive mode and causes the system to ask for the name of various system boot up files. Accept the default values until the name of the /etc/system file is requested by the system. When the name of system files [/etc/system]: prompt is displayed; type the name of the good /etc/system file, or /dev/null:

Name of system file [/etc/system]: /etc/system.fine

Now our system will be booted fine without any issues.

Note:- The comment in /etc/system file starts with *, instead of #. So make sure you don't use #, any wrong changes in this file may take the system in cyclic reboot.

4.3.2.   Modular debugger (mdb) or kernel debugger (kmdb)

Module debugger or mdb is an utility for editing the live operating system kernel parameters. Also it helps to modify operating system crash dumps settings, user processes and system core at runtime. However since these settings are modified at runtime, hence these are not persistent and will vanish on reboot. To make it persistent, we need to add the changes in /etc/system file.

We can use mdb to check the process stack like pstack.

bash-3.2# ps -ef | grep tty
   root   443   431   0   Oct 08 ?   0:00 /usr/lib/saf/ttymon

bash-3.2# pstack 443
443:   /usr/lib/saf/ttymon
 feddc045 pause   ()
 080530be main   (1, 8047ddc, 8047de4) + ea
 08052f2a ???????? (1, 8047e84, 0, 8047fa0, 8047fd0, 8047eb3)

View process threads and stack using mdb.
To view different kernel parameters we use mdb command with "k" argument which opens the module debugger in debugging mode and allows us to read various kernel parameters.

bash-3.2# mdb -k

```
> ::pgrep tty
S   PID  PPID  PGID  SID  UID   FLAGS         ADDR NAME
R   443   431   431  431    0 0x4a014000 ffffffff812f8090 ttymon
> ffffffff812f8090 ::threadlist
        ADDR         PROC       LWP CMD/LWPID
ffffffff812f8090 ffffffff817c6500       0 /239
> ffffffff812f8090 ::findstack
mdb: thread ffffffff812f8090 isn't in memory
```

Modify kernel parameter using mdb

To modify a parameter using mdb, we need to run mdb in write mode by using "-w" argument with mdb command. Let us look at an example how we can modify a kernel parameter.

```
bash-3.2# mdb -kw
Loading modules: [ UNIX krtld genunix specfs dtrace uppc apix
cpu.generic ufs sockfs ip hook neti dls sctp arp usba fcp fctl nca lofs mpt
zfs nfs audiosup random md cpc crypto fcip logindmux ptm sppp ]
> ufs_WRITES/D
ufs_WRITES:
ufs_WRITES:    1
> ufs_WRITES/W 3
ufs_WRITES:    0x1        =      0x3
> ufs_WRITES/D
ufs_WRITES:
ufs_WRITES:    3
```

Similarly we can change any other parameter using mdb. By now we know how to check any kernel parameter and how to change it using mdb. Now let us look at a new feature called projects in solaris by which also we can set/modify these paramaters different for specific users to meet different application requirements on a single system.

4.3.3. Project Way to set kernel parameters from Solaris 10 onwards

From Solaris 10 onwards, we have a new feature of projects where a project id is assigned to each user by default and if you want to change any kernel parameter for a specific user then we can make changes to his/her project.

If /etc/project file is used for tuning, please make sure that you do not set values that are lower than the Solaris default values.

a.   Check project id of the required user
bash-3.2# id **-p** dbadmin
uid=101(dbadmin) gid=1(other) **projid=3(default)**

b.   Now just have a look at the available projects on our system.
bash-3.2# **cat /etc/project**
system:0::::
user.root:1::::
noproject:2::::
default:3::::
group.staff:10::::

We can also use projects –l command to list all projects alongwith paramaters set. Lets look into default proect in detail.

bash-3.2# **projects -l default**
default
      projid : 3
      comment: ""
      users : (none)

```
        groups : (none)
        attribs:
bash-3.2#
```

Now as per requirement we need to edit this project and add a new kernel parameter value. Since we will modify the project, hence we will use projmod(PROJect MODify) command.

```
bash-3.2# projmod -sK "project.max-shm-
memory=(privileged,8G,deny)" default
bash-3.2# projects -l default
default
        projid : 3
        comment: ""
        users  : (none)
        groups : (none)
        attribs: project.max-shm-memory=(privileged,8589934592,deny)
```

If you want to change this value then you can define it again like below.

```
bash-3.2# projmod -sK "project.max-shm-
memory=(privileged,2G,deny)" default
bash-3.2# projects -l default
default
        projid : 3
        comment: ""
        users  : (none)
        groups : (none)
           attribs: project.max-shm-memory=(privileged,2147483648,deny)
```

We can also achieve this task of setting an already defined parameter using prctl(controls resources assigned to an active Process) command.. Let's see how to achieve this using prctl command.

bash-3.2# **prctl -n project.max-shm-memory -i project default**
prctl: default: No controllable process found in task, project, or zone.

There is an ERROR occurred. The above error says that there is no controllable process available/running under this project id and hence it is not able to retrieve the output. Lets switch to dbaadmin user and then from another terminal run this command.

bash-3.2# su - dbadmin
$

Now from another root terminal run above prctl command. We can observe now the command is running successfully.

prctl -n project.max-shm-memory -i project default
project: 3: default
NAME   PRIVILEGE   VALUE   FLAG ACTION
RECIPIENT
project.max-shm-memory
    privileged   2.00GB   - deny   -
    system   16.0EB   max deny   -

We can also set this parameter to a new value lets say 4gb.

bash-3.2# **prctl -n project.max-shm-memory -v 4gb -r -i project default**

bash-3.2# prctl -n project.max-shm-memory -i project default
project: 3: default

```
NAME   PRIVILEGE     VALUE   FLAG   ACTION
RECIPIENT
project.max-shm-memory
privileged    4.00GB    -   deny                    -
system        16.0EB    max   deny                  -
bash-3.2#
```

In case you want to add a new project and want to make changes in the new project then you can use projadd command like below and carry out above steps.

```
bash-3.2# cat /etc/project
system:0::::
user.root:1::::
noproject:2::::
default:3::::project.max-shm-memory=(privileged,2147483648,deny)
group.staff:10::::

bash-3.2# projadd dba

bash-3.2# cat /etc/project
system:0::::
user.root:1::::
noproject:2::::
default:3::::project.max-shm-memory=(privileged,2147483648,deny)
group.staff:10::::
dba:100::::
bash-3.2#
```

4.3.4. Use of ndd command to set TCP/IP parameters

Ndd command can be used to set different tcp/ip paramters like making an Ethernet device full duplex/half duplex, or turning its auto-negotiation off, or tune its other properties. An example to make an Ethernet interface auto negotiation off can be seen below:

ndd -set /dev/bge0 adv_autoneg_cap 0

The above command sets the auto negotiation of /dev/bge0 to 0 i.e. turns off auto-negotiation.

Auto negotiation provides capability to ethernet devices to automatically adjust their transmission capacity according to the immediate connected interface(s). For example:- If a 10GBPS line connected with 100MBPS line having auto-negotiation ON, then data will be transferred with 100MBPS capability only avoiding any data loss in between

4.3.5. Modify files under /etc/default directory.

Solaris contains default system settings in /etc/default directory for different services. For example:- the default user password settings are saved in /etc/default/passwd file and if someone wants user to enter a complex password with a special digit then this can be achieved by tuning this files' parameters.

To get all the kernel and system parameters available for system tuning in solaris we can use differenet commands like getconf and adb. To view the changed parameters by users, we can view /etc/system and /etc/project file contents.

Let's list all the system variables available on our Solaris system by using –a argument with getconf.

bash-3.2# **getconf -a | more**
_CS_PATH:
/usr/xpg4/bin:/usr/ccs/bin:/usr/bin:/opt/SUNWspro/bin
_POSIX_ADVISORY_INFO: undefined
_POSIX_AIO_LISTIO_MAX: 2
_POSIX_AIO_MAX: 1
_POSIX_ARG_MAX: 4096

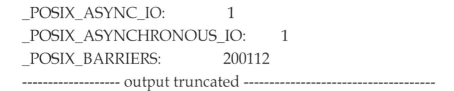

```
_POSIX_ASYNC_IO:              1
_POSIX_ASYNCHRONOUS_IO:       1
_POSIX_BARRIERS:              200112
------------------- output truncated ------------------------------------
```

The getconf command gets configuration data from our system. We can't change values returned by getconf without reconfiguring and rebooting our system.

5.   Disk Devices Administration

In this topic, we will look how to take care hardware devices on our solaris system which mainly involves various disk and storage devices connected with our system. To easily learn through device administration that we as an UNIX administrator use, I have marked the topics inside quick tips to make is short and interesting.

"**To understand Unix Device Administration**, the first thing that we should know is: how various devices are named, where they are stored and how they are referenced."

/dev --> Logical device names of devices stored in /devices
/devices --> Original device names, also called devfs.
/etc/path_to_inst file --> Contains all device names accessed by system while boot.

To administrate all the above locations, and file, we have utility or command called devfsadm in solaris.

5.1.   Understanding device names in Solaris

To understand how devices are configured in Solaris, we should know how they are named and accessed. When I look in my test system I found below partition.

bash-3.2# df -h /
File system   size used avail capacity Mounted on
/dev/dsk/c0d1s0   14G 4.6G 8.8G   34%   /

/dev is the devices directory.
Dsk is the disk device subdirectory containing block devices i.e. formatted character devices.
C0 is the logical controller number.
D1 is the disk number attached to C0 controller.
S0 is the slice/partition on the disk D1. Sometimes pX[0-4] in case of fdisk partition number.

And when I list this logical device, I observe this is a link under /devices.

bash-3.2# ls -l /dev/dsk/c0d1s0
lrwxrwxrwx 1 root   root   50 May 2 2013 **/dev/dsk/c0d1s0 ->** ../../devices/pci@0,0/pci-ide@7,1/ide@1/cmdk@1,0:a

Hence the original device name is as follows.

bash-3.2# ls -l ../../devices/pci@0,0/pci-ide@7,1/ide@1/cmdk@1,0:a
brw-r----- 1 root   sys   102, 0 Oct 8 13:19 **../../devices/pci@0,0/pci-ide@7,1/ide@1/cmdk@1,0:a**

Here ""b" is the block device, which means readable file system which is accessed block by block. This is the device that refers to file system, however in every OS, there exists a raw partition, also called character device which consists the raw data, without any knowledge of block information and hence accessed character by character.

Now let's see a quick tip how to identify raw device corresponding to a block device in Solaris.

5.2. <u>Quick Tip 8</u>: Identify raw device from block device.

a. First identify the logical block device name.

bash-3.2# **df -h /**

File system   size used avail capacity Mounted on

/dev/dsk/**c0d1s0**   14G 4.6G 8.8G 34%   /

b. Now find the actual device name under /devices.

bash-3.2# **ls -l /dev/dsk/c0d1s0**

lrwxrwxrwx 1 root   root   50 May 2 2013 **/dev/dsk/c0d1s0 ->**
../../devices/pci@0,0/pci-ide@7,1/ide@1/cmdk@1,0:a

c. Now refer the raw device by adding ",raw" in the block device name.

bash-3.2# **ls -l /devices/pci@0,0/pci-ide@7,1/ide@1/cmdk@1,0:a,raw**

crw-r----- 1 root   sys   102, 0 Nov 10 22:40 /devices/pci@0,0/pci-ide@7,1/ide@1/cmdk@1,0:a,raw

d. Now get the inode number of the raw device.

bash-3.2# **ls -i /devices/pci@0,0/pci-ide@7,1/ide@1/cmdk@1,0:a,raw**

 53477380 /devices/pci@0,0/pci-ide@7,1/ide@1/cmdk@1,0:a,raw

e. Now find all sym links pointing to this raw device.

bash-3.2# **find / -follow -inum 53477380** 2> /dev/null
/dev/rdsk/c0d1s0

/devices/pci@0,0/pci-ide@7,1/ide@1/cmdk@1,0:a,raw

Hence the raw device name is **/dev/rdsk/c0d1s0 or**
/devices/pci@0,0/pci-ide@7,1/ide@1/cmdk@1,0:a,raw**.** If you have

observed, the block device and character device name are same except the change in device driver directory name i.e. dsk is changed into rdsk. This is the beauty of Solaris device driver naming. However the correct and actual way is as shown above by going through /devices directory path.

5.3.   Quick Tip 9: What is 1,0,a meaning in the below hard disk device ?

/devices/pci@0,0/pci-ide@7,1/ide@1/cmdk@**1,0**:a,raw

cmdk --> Common Interface to Various Disk Devices
1 --> target id (t1 in case of sparc, disk id i.e. d1 in case of x86)
0 --> unit address (disk id in case of sparc, can be ignored in x86)
a --> shows first partition(i.e. s0)
,raw --> shows the raw device type i.e. character device.

On our x86 server, the above name will represent disk with d1s0 and on sparc it will be t1d0s0.

Above we have seen the device naming in case of logical SCSI drives on our server. In case of Serial Attached SCSI-2(i.e. SAS 2) storage devices, the t number is replaced with a unique WWN(world wide number in hexadecimal format) and the new device name will look like below.
cntWWNdn
For example:-
c4t**5000CCA0432D2E31**d0s0

5.4.   Quick Tip 10: Scan new hardware in solaris

To start with adding new device in solaris, we should know how to scan any new hardware/storage connected to our system in solaris in real time without rebooting the system. For this, we can use devfsadm command.

#devfsadm –Cv

By default, devfsadm tries to attach all the available devices, and "-C" option tells it to clean all dangling device links, and –v enhances the output to make it easy to understand

In linux, we have a similar command or process which is called Startudev which is responsible for this task.

Now we know how the devices are named, however the device concept will not be clear unless and until we look how we can create partitions and format the partition in solaris.

5.5.   Administrating Partitions/Slices in Solaris

Solaris provides few utilities or command which can be used to administer the disk devices and help us to create new partitions, delete available partitions, modify partitions, and to perform all other device admin tasks. These commands are as follows:

1.   Fdisk:- The utility is only available on x86/i86 based systems and not on SUN sparc servers, hence we will not discuss it in case of Solairs OS. However in linux we mostly use this utility.

2.   Format :- Format command provides a very easy interface to check and do the tasks related to partition management.

2.   Prtvtoc:- The utility is used to print the volume table of contents stored on the disk..

3.   Fmthard :- Utility used to update VTOC(volume table of contents of a hard disk partition, also this can load/unload the boot information from the disk)

Hard disk has several circular patterns which store the data, also called as Platters.

Platters (or circular disks) have magnetic media to store data on it.

First partitions are created on a raw disk, and then file system. File system creation is both a Constructive as well as destructive task. It destructs or removes the old data, and puts zero/empty spaces in the partition, thereby creating a new format partition

.

5.5.1. Format Command

We will now check how to use format command in Solaris for partition creation and management.

Format command displays all available disks on our system and allows us to create new partitions, delete exsiting partitions and relabel the disk. In brief, we will create new slices, or disk partitions using this utilitiy and then proceed further.

a.   Check available disks using format

bash-3.2# **format**

Searching for disks...

Inquiry failed for this logical diskdone

AVAILABLE DISK SELECTIONS:

    0. c0d0 <�u��µ������Lm cyl 2085 alt 2 hd 255 sec 63>

       /pci@0,0/pci-ide@7,1/ide@0/cmdk@0,0

Specify disk (enter its number): **0**

selecting c0d0

Controller working list found

[disk formatted, defect list found]

Warning: Current Disk has mounted partitions.

FORMAT MENU:
    disk   - select a disk
    type   - select (define) a disk type
    partition - select (define) a partition table
    current   - describe the current disk
    format   - format and analyze the disk
    fdisk   - run the fdisk program

Note 1:- fdisk is not available in sparc machine.
Note 2: Why t number is not shown in disk name ?
    0. **c0d0** <�u��µ�����Lm cyl 2085 alt 2 hd 255 sec 63>
       /pci@0,0/pci-ide@7,1/**ide**@0/cmdk@0,0

    ✓   *IDE harddisk ---> ide --> doesn't show T number.*
    ✓   SCSI ---> it shows **sd**
    ✓   Ssd --> shown if fiber channel disk
Also please note that Scsi is faster than IDE.

b.   Understanding Partition Table
format> p   ---> To go inside partition management.
PARTITION MENU:
    0   - change `0' partition
    1   - change `1' partition
    2   - change `2' partition
    3   - change `3' partition
    4   - change `4' partition
    5   - change `5' partition
    6   - change `6' partition
    7   - change `7' partition
    select - select a predefined table

modify - modify a predefined partition table

name   - name the current table

print - display the current table

label - write partition map and label to the disk

!<cmd> - execute <cmd>, then return

quit

partition> p --> To print current partition table.

Current partition table (original):

Total disk cylinders available: 2085 + 2 (reserved cylinders)

Part	Tag	Flag	Cylinders	Size	Blocks	
0	root	wm	265 - 2058	13.74GB	(1794/0/0)	28820610
1	swap	wu	3 - 264	2.01GB	(262/0/0)	4209030
2	backup	wm	0 - 2084	**15.97GB**	(2085/0/0)	33495525 --->

size of hard disk

Part	Tag	Flag	Cylinders	Size	Blocks	
3	unassigned	wm	0	0	(0/0/0)	0
4	unassigned	wm	0	0	(0/0/0)	0
5	unassigned	wm	0	0	(0/0/0)	0
6	unassigned	wm	0	0	(0/0/0)	0
7	unassigned	wm	2059 - 2084	203.95MB	(26/0/0)	417690
8	boot	wu	0 - 0	7.84MB	(1/0/0)	16065
9	alternates	wu	1 - 2	15.69MB	(2/0/0)	32130

> Part(partition number)

> Tag(does not have any importance, only a name)

> Flag(important till sol 9, from solaris 10 it is obsolete and have no meaning), wu – write-unmountable, wm-write-mountable

> Cylinders   (no of cylinders) -> never overlap, 100 end, start with 101(don't skip any cylinder)

> Size(to find which partitions are free)

> Blocks --> Defines the size of partition in blocks.

c.   Meaning of Slice Number

➢   0-7 are hard partitions.

➢   2nd partition ---> we will never change ---> keeps information of entire disk, not the data.

➢   From 8 ---> soft partitions.

➢   By default 7 partitions can be created.

➢   If we want to create more than 7, then we have to create soft partitions.

➢   **8 and 9th partitions can only be seen on x86, not available in sparc.**

➢   **On sparc, only solaris can be installed, on x86 any OS can be installed or dual OS.**

➢   **On SPARC, there is no MBR.**

d.   Try to tag a slice/partition.

partition> **3**

Part	Tag	Flag	Cylinders	Size	Blocks
3	unassigned	wm	0	0	(0/0/0) 0

Enter partition id tag[unassigned]: **?**
Expecting one of the following: (abbreviations ok):

unassigned	boot	root	swap
usr	backup	stand	var
home	alternates	reserved	

Enter partition id tag[unassigned]:
Enter partition id tag[unassigned]: **solaris**
`solaris' not expected.   --> we can't give our own tag.

Enter partition id tag[unassigned]:

Enter partition permission flags[wm]: ?

Expecting one of the following: (abbreviations ok):

    wm   - read-write, mountable

    wu   - read-write, unmountable

    rm   - read-only, mountable

    ru   - read-only, unmountable   ---> *can't umount, once mounted-->*

valid till sol 9, no meaning from sol 10

e.   <u>Format a new disk.</u>

First run format command and select the new disk added, then follow below steps.

format> **p**

WARNING - This disk may be in use by an application that has

       modified the fdisk table. Ensure that this disk is

     not currently in use before proceeding to use fdisk.

format> **fdisk**

No fdisk table exists. The default partition for the disk is:

 a 100% "SOLARIS System" partition

Type "y" to accept the default partition, otherwise type "n" to edit the partition table.

y

format> **p**

PARTITION MENU:

    0   - change `0' partition

    1   - change `1' partition

    2   - change `2' partition

```
     3      - change `3' partition

partition> 0
Part   Tag  Flag  Cylinders    Size        Blocks
 0 unassigned  wm    0          0     (0/0/0)      0


Enter partition id tag[unassigned]:
Enter partition permission flags[wm]:
Enter new starting cyl[0]: 1                 --> Always skip 1st cylinder -->
beneficial for adding raid, or ZFS.
Enter partition size[0b, 0c, 1e, 0.00mb, 0.00gb]: 500m
partition> p
Current partition table (unnamed):
Total disk cylinders available: 2044 + 2 (reserved cylinders)


Part   Tag  Flag  Cylinders    Size        Blocks
 0 unassigned  wm    1 - 250   500.00MB  (250/0/0) 1024000


partition> 1
Part   Tag  Flag  Cylinders    Size        Blocks
 1 unassigned  wm    0          0     (0/0/0)      0


Enter partition id tag[unassigned]:
Enter partition permission flags[wm]:
Enter new starting cyl[0]: 251
Enter partition size[0b, 0c, 251e, 0.00mb, 0.00gb]: 500m
partition> p
Current partition table (unnamed):
Total disk cylinders available: 2044 + 2 (reserved cylinders)


Part   Tag  Flag  Cylinders    Size        Blocks
 0 unassigned  wm    1 - 250   500.00MB  (250/0/0) 1024000
```

```
 1 unassigned   wm    251 - 500    500.00MB   (250/0/0) 1024000
 2   backup  wu     0 - 2043    3.99GB   (2044/0/0) 8372224


partition> 3
Part   Tag  Flag  Cylinders    Size      Blocks
 3 unassigned  wm    0        0     (0/0/0)      0


Enter partition id tag[unassigned]:
Enter partition permission flags[wm]:
Enter new starting cyl[0]: 850
Enter partition size[0b, 0c, 850e, 0.00mb, 0.00gb]: 500m
partition> p
Current partition table (unnamed):
Total disk cylinders available: 2044 + 2 (reserved cylinders)


Part   Tag  Flag  Cylinders    Size      Blocks
 0 unassigned  wm    1 - 250   500.00MB   (250/0/0) 1024000
 1 unassigned  wm    251 - 500   500.00MB   (250/0/0) 1024000
 2   backup  wu    0 - 2043    3.99GB   (2044/0/0) 8372224
 3 unassigned  wm    850 - 1099   500.00MB   (250/0/0) 1024000
 4 unassigned  wm    0        0     (0/0/0)
 5 unassigned  wm    0        0     (0/0/0)      0
 6 unassigned  wm    0        0     (0/0/0)      0
 7 unassigned  wm    0        0     (0/0/0)      0
 8    boot  wu    0 - 0    2.00MB   (1/0/0)     4096
 9 unassigned  wm    0        0     (0/0/0)      0


partition> 4
Part   Tag  Flag  Cylinders    Size      Blocks
 4 unassigned  wm    0        0     (0/0/0)      0


Enter partition id tag[unassigned]:
```

Enter partition permission flags[wm]:

Enter new starting cyl[0]: **501**

Enter partition size[0b, 0c, 501e, 0.00mb, 0.00gb]: **849e   --> Take Last cylinder number 849.**

partition> **p**

Current partition table (unnamed):

Total disk cylinders available: 2044 + 2 (reserved cylinders)

Part	Tag	Flag	Cylinders	Size	Blocks	
0	unassigned	wm	1 - 250	500.00MB	(250/0/0)	1024000
1	unassigned	wm	251 - 500	500.00MB	(250/0/0)	1024000
2	backup	wu	0 - 2043	3.99GB	(2044/0/0)	8372224
3	unassigned	wm	850 - 1099	500.00MB	(250/0/0)	1024000
4	unassigned	wm	501 - 849	698.00MB	(349/0/0)	1429504

Save Changes

To save changes, label the disk. Otherwise all changes gone.

partition> **l**

Ready to label disk, continue? **y**

Deleting 3rd Partition

partition> **3**

Part	Tag	Flag	Cylinders	Size	Blocks	
3	unassigned	wm	850 - 1099	500.00MB	(250/0/0)	1024000

Enter partition id tag[unassigned]:

Enter partition permission flags[wm]:

Enter new starting cyl[850]: **0**

Enter partition size[1024000b, 250c, 249e, 500.00mb, 0.49gb]: **0**

partition> **p**

Current partition table (unnamed):

Total disk cylinders available: 2044 + 2 (reserved cylinders)

Part	Tag	Flag	Cylinders	Size	Blocks	
0	unassigned	wm	1 - 250	500.00MB	(250/0/0)	1024000
1	unassigned	wm	251 - 500	500.00MB	(250/0/0)	1024000
2	backup	wu	0 - 2043	3.99GB	(2044/0/0)	8372224
3	unassigned	wm	0	0	(0/0/0)	0

5.5.2. Quick Tip 11: How to assign all available disk space to a slice in format?

partition> **5**

Part	Tag	Flag	Cylinders	Size	Blocks	
5	unassigned	wm	0	0	(0/0/0)	0

Enter partition id tag[unassigned]:
Enter partition permission flags[wm]:
Enter new starting cyl[0]: 1100
Enter partition size[0b, 0c, 1100e, 0.00mb, 0.00gb]: **$**   **----> to take all space remaining**
partition> p
Current partition table (unnamed):
Total disk cylinders available: 2044 + 2 (reserved cylinders)

Part	Tag	Flag	Cylinders	Size	Blocks	
0	unassigned	wm	1 - 250	500.00MB	(250/0/0)	1024000
1	unassigned	wm	251 - 500	500.00MB	(250/0/0)	1024000
2	backup	wu	0 - 2043	3.99GB	(2044/0/0)	8372224
3	unassigned	wm	850 - 1099	500.00MB	(250/0/0)	1024000
4	unassigned	wm	501 - 849	698.00MB	(349/0/0)	1429504
5	unassigned	wm	1100 - 2043	1.84GB	(944/0/0)	3866624
6	unassigned	wm	0	0	(0/0/0)	0

5.6. Taking Partition table backup

We can take existing partition table backup of the disk and store as a file on some partition of some other disk, it can help us to recover partition table in case of any emergency situation.

a.   First Identify Bootable Disk from which we need to store partition table backup

bash-3.2# df -h /

File system   size   used avail capacity Mounted on

/dev/dsk/c0d0s0   14G   8.4G   5.0G   63%   /

b.   Take Partition Table backup.

First view the partition table.

bash-3.2# **prtvtoc /dev/rdsk/c2t0d0s0** #print volume table of contents

* /dev/rdsk/c2t0d0s0 partition map

*

* Dimensions:

*   512 bytes/sector

*   32 sectors/track

*   128 tracks/cylinder

*   4096 sectors/cylinder

*   2046 cylinders

*   2044 accessible cylinders

*

* Flags:

* 1: unmountable

* 10: read-only

*

*   First   Sector   Last

* Partition Tag Flags Sector   Count   Sector Mount Directory

     0   0   00   4096 1024000 1028095

     1   0   00 1028096 1024000 2052095

2	5	01	0	8372224	8372223
3	0	00	3481600	1024000	4505599
4	0	00	2052096	1429504	3481599
5	0	00	4505600	3866624	8372223
8	1	01	0	4096	4095

Now you can re-direct this output and save the partition table backup.
bash-3.2# prtvtoc /dev/rdsk/c0d0s0 > /var/disk1.backup
bash-3.2# prtvtoc /dev/rdsk/c2t0d0s0 > /var/disk2.backup

5.7. Restoring Partition table backup

Solaris has a very nice utility called fmthard which can load the new VTOC table on any disk, either from other disk or from backup file created with prtvtoc utility.

Let's see how to restore the partition table from the partition table backup saved using prtvtoc utility.

bash-3.2# **fmthard -s /var/disk2.backup /dev/rdsk/c2t0d0s2**   ### s stands for source
fmthard: New volume table of contents now in place.
bash-3.2#

If restored from wrong file, then the complete system comes down immediately and shows 0 size in all partitions.

5.8. Device Files

As we know in UNIX/Linux, everything is a file whether we talk about a hardware device or software program. Everything is accessed via a file; it could be a character, block, text, or any other type of file.
All the devices will be accessed via the device files which are usually created during install.

For example:- disk, nic, terminal, mouse, keyboard, etc.

/dev
/dev/dsk
/dev/rdsk
/devices

> DSK contains block device files
> Rdsk contains raw device files linked to /devices
> /devices contains the original device file

5.9. Recreating device files(rm –rf /dev/dsk/* /dev/rdsk/*)

Let's do an experiment to see the power of devfsadm utility. We will remove all dsk and rdsk files and recreate them online without system reboot.

```
 bash-3.2# cd /dev/dsk/
bash-3.2# ls
c0d0p0    c0d0s0    c0d0s13   c0d0s4    c0d0s9    c1t0d0p4  c1t0d0s12
c1t0d0s3  c1t0d0s8  c2t0d0p3  c2t0d0s11 c2t0d0s2  c2t0d0s7
c0d0p1    c0d0s1    c0d0s14   c0d0s5    c1t0d0p0  c1t0d0s0  c1t0d0s13
c1t0d0s4  c1t0d0s9  c2t0d0p4  c2t0d0s12 c2t0d0s3  c2t0d0s8
c0d0p2    c0d0s10   c0d0s15   c0d0s6    c1t0d0p1  c1t0d0s1  c1t0d0s14
c1t0d0s5  c2t0d0p0  c2t0d0s0  c2t0d0s13 c2t0d0s4  c2t0d0s9
c0d0p3    c0d0s11   c0d0s2    c0d0s7    c1t0d0p2  c1t0d0s10 c1t0d0s15
c1t0d0s6  c2t0d0p1  c2t0d0s1  c2t0d0s14 c2t0d0s5
c0d0p4    c0d0s12   c0d0s3    c0d0s8    c1t0d0p3  c1t0d0s11 c1t0d0s2
c1t0d0s7  c2t0d0p2  c2t0d0s10 c2t0d0s15 c2t0d0s6
bash-3.2# rm -rf *
bash-3.2# ls
```

```
bash-3.2# cd /dev/rdsk/
bash-3.2# ls
c0d0p0    c0d0s0    c0d0s13   c0d0s4    c0d0s9    c1t0d0p4  c1t0d0s12
c1t0d0s3  c1t0d0s8  c2t0d0p3  c2t0d0s11 c2t0d0s2  c2t0d0s7
c0d0p1    c0d0s1    c0d0s14   c0d0s5    c1t0d0p0  c1t0d0s0  c1t0d0s13
c1t0d0s4  c1t0d0s9  c2t0d0p4  c2t0d0s12 c2t0d0s3  c2t0d0s8
c0d0p2    c0d0s10   c0d0s15   c0d0s6    c1t0d0p1  c1t0d0s1  c1t0d0s14
c1t0d0s5  c2t0d0p0  c2t0d0s0  c2t0d0s13 c2t0d0s4  c2t0d0s9
c0d0p3    c0d0s11   c0d0s2    c0d0s7    c1t0d0p2  c1t0d0s10 c1t0d0s15
c1t0d0s6  c2t0d0p1  c2t0d0s1  c2t0d0s14 c2t0d0s5
c0d0p4    c0d0s12   c0d0s3    c0d0s8    c1t0d0p3  c1t0d0s11 c1t0d0s2
c1t0d0s7  c2t0d0p2  c2t0d0s10 c2t0d0s15 c2t0d0s6
bash-3.2# rm -rf *
bash-3.2# ls

bash-3.2# format
Searching for disks...done
No disks found!
```

Now lets create the device files.
```
bash-3.2# devfsadm -Cv
devfsadm[1058]: verbose: symlink /dev/dsk/c0d0s0 ->
../../devices/pci@0,0/pci-ide@7,1/ide@0/cmdk@0,0:a
devfsadm[1058]: verbose: symlink /dev/dsk/c0d0s1 ->
../../devices/pci@0,0/pci-ide@7,1/ide@0/cmdk@0,0:b
devfsadm[1058]: verbose: symlink /dev/dsk/c0d0s2 ->
../../devices/pci@0,0/pci-ide@7,1/ide@0/cmdk@0,0:c
devfsadm[1058]: verbose: symlink /dev/dsk/c0d0s3 ->
../../devices/pci@0,0/pci-ide@7,1/ide@0/cmdk@0,0:d
devfsadm[1058]: verbose: symlink /dev/dsk/c0d0s4 ->
../../devices/pci@0,0/pci-ide@7,1/ide@0/cmdk@0,0:e
```

Devfsadm –Cv #### (-c – clean install --> remove unwanted device files for which no hardware is there, for example, any device removed earlier and then recreate the device files which are missing)

Now the device files are created.

5.10. Disk Name description

A device file contains metadata of disks, no user data. Metadata contains the device major number and minor number.

Major Number:- Device driver number entry in the kernel.

Minor Number:- Physical location of the device on the system.

/devices contains all the physical paths of the devices. It tells physically where the device/file is located.

```
bash-3.2# ls -l /devices/
total 34
drwxr-xr-x  2 root   sys       512 Jan 10 12:16 agpgart
crw-r--r--  1 root   sys    55,  0 Mar 31 14:16 agpgart:agpgart
drwxr-xr-x  2 root   sys       512 Jan 10 12:16 cpus
drwxr-xr-x  4 root   sys       512 Jan 10 12:16 isa
drwxr-xr-x  2 root   sys       512 Jan 10 12:16 iscsi
crw-------  1 root   sys    73,  0 Mar 31 12:38 iscsi:devctl
```

/dev/dsk contains all block device files(access by block--> if we need data then we need to access by block device). /dev/rdsk contains all the character device files (access by character).

For file system check and recovery we should take rdsk.

If you are not sure, then first use dsk path and in case of error, use rdsk.

Sometimes it takes rdsk automatically.

```
bash-3.2# ls -lL /dev/dsk/
total 0
brw-r-----   1 root    sys    102, 16 Mar 31 14:16 c0d0p0
brw-r-----   1 root    sys    102, 17 Mar 31 14:16 c0d0p1
brw-r-----   1 root    sys    102, 18 Mar 31 14:16 c0d0p2
brw-r-----   1 root    sys    102, 19 Mar 31 14:16 c0d0p3


bash-3.2# ls -lL /dev/rdsk/ | head
total 0
crw-r-----   1 root    sys    102, 16 Mar 31 12:43 c0d0p0
crw-r-----   1 root    sys    102, 17 Mar 31 14:16 c0d0p1
crw-r-----   1 root    sys    102, 18 Mar 31 14:16 c0d0p2
crw-r-----   1 root    sys    102, 19 Mar 31 14:16 c0d0p3
crw-r-----   1 root    sys    102, 20 Mar 31 14:16 c0d0p4
```

C0d0t0s0 description
C-> Controller number
T --> Target
d--> disk
s --> slice number

The 4 numbers are :
C0: bus: normally 0 unless we have multiple busses or controllers.
T0: target: mostly 0. (Sometimes also referred as LUN: logical unit number)..
D0: device: the scsi ID of the disc, usually 0-7, bigger on wide scsi
S0: slice: the disk partition. P[1-3] in case of ide disk
Let's see a sample diagram where we have four disks with following names:
C0t0d0
C0t0d1

C1t1d0
C1t1d1

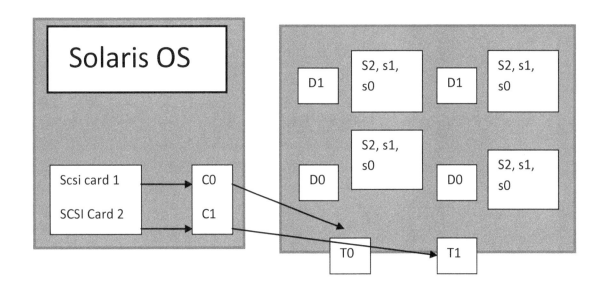

Fig. 2.1 Disk Numbering

The disks could be hard disks directly attached to the server, or any LUN id/iqn number.
LUN is the logical unit number, it could be internal or external disk id taken from storage

6.   Quick Tip 12 : How to see disk size without going into format. ?
A very handy and useful tool to check system disk drives and its size is iostat. Let's see how to use it on our server.

bash-3.2# iostat –En   ### shows _total how many disks are available and the errors on the disk_.
c0d0   Soft Errors: 0 Hard Errors: 0 Transport Errors: 0

Model: VMware Virtual Revision: Serial No: 000000000000000 Size: 17.18GB <17179706880 bytes>

Media Error: 0 Device Not Ready: 0 No Device: 0 Recoverable: 0

Illegal Request: 0

c1t0d0   Soft Errors: 0 Hard Errors: 0 Transport Errors: 0

Vendor: NECVMWar Product: VMware IDE CDR10 Revision: 1.00 Serial No:

Size: 1.57GB <1567981568 bytes>

Media Error: 0 Device Not Ready: 0 No Device: 0 Recoverable: 0

Illegal Request: 12 Predictive Failure Analysis: 0

c2t0d0   Soft Errors: 0 Hard Errors: 0 Transport Errors: 0

Vendor: VMware, Product: VMware Virtual S Revision: 1.0 Serial No:

Size: 4.29GB <4294966784 bytes>

Media Error: 0 Device Not Ready: 0 No Device: 0 Recoverable: 0

Illegal Request: 56 Predictive Failure Analysis: 0

7.   Quick Tip 13 : How to check removable media attached to system ?

bash-3.2# **rmformat**   ## removable media format

Looking for devices...

   1. Volmgt Node: /vol/dev/aliases/cdrom0
     Logical Node: /dev/rdsk/c1t0d0s2
     Physical Node: /pci@0,0/pci-ide@7,1/ide@1/sd@0,0
     Connected Device: NECVMWar VMware IDE CDR10 1.00
     Device Type: DVD Reader/Writer

8.   Quick Tip 14 : How to see all controllers attached?

Cfgadm is the configuration administration command which help us to administrate dynamically reconfigurable hardware devices attached to a solaris system.

bash-3.2# **cfgadm -al | more**

cfgadm: Configuration administration not supported: Error: hotplug service is probably not running, please use 'svcadm enable hotplug' to enable the service. See cfgadm_shp(1M) for more details.

Ap_Id	Type	Receptacle	Occupant	Condition
c2	scsi-bus	connected	configured	unknown
c2::dsk/c2t0d0	disk	connected	configured	unknown

"-al" simply lists all available configured hardware devices. We usually use this command after devfsadm to check the updated hardware devices links on the system.

9.   **Quick Tip 15 : How to see fiber channels connected ?**
bash-3.2# luxadm probe
ERROR: No Fibre Channel Adapters found.

10.   **/etc/path_to_inst file description**
bash-3.2# ls -l /etc/path_to_inst
-r--r--r-- 1 root   root   2266 Mar 31 12:38 /etc/path_to_inst

This file contains path of devices created by devfsadm.

Devfsadm ran and it modifies the system links like below:
1.   First goto /devices and add physical paths.
2.   Now creates links of dsk and rdsk
3.   Update in path_to_inst the devices; otherwise the system may not come up on reboot.

11.   **Reconfigure Reboot**
bash-3.2# touch /reconfigure
bash-3.2# init 6
updating /platform/i86pc/boot_archive

A reconfiguration boot tells the system to probe for all connected devices and build the names for them in /devices and /dev. A reconfiguration boot, performed when adding new hardware to the system, can be triggered by booting with the -r option.

ok> boot -r

12. Creating, Managing and mounting the file system

A file system for OS is a control structure of tracks, sectors, controllers, etc. For user, it is a place for IO activity. The commands that we will use during filesystem (fs) administration are as follows:

Newfs :- To create a new ufs file system

Fstyp :- To know the file system type whether ext4, etx3, etc

Fsck :- File system integrity check to correct data corruption.

Mount/Umount :- To mount/umount the partition/slice.

/etc/vfstab :- To automatically mount the partition on boot.

Df –h :- To know the usage and currently mounted file system

Fuser :- To check the users and processes(pid) running on a particular partition. Useful when we want to umount particular partition and want to know which process is using the files.

13. Types of file system

The file system can be categorized into three types depending upon how the storage is accessed or mounted.

a.   Disk based file system (ufs, zfs, cifs, Vxfs, gfs(global), mfs(memory) etc)

b.   Distributed FS(NFS)

c.   Pseudo FS(virtal fs, tmp proc directory are pseudo fs)

14.   Structure of UFS file system

We will go through ufs file system structure through a diagram. Before that let's understand few points:

14.1.   Quick Tip 16: How our OS is detected and booted from Disk ?

We usually hear that this disk is bootable and you can install your OS using this disk since this will be detected by BIOS and it will take an automatic boot from this disk. So the question is how our BIOS knows this disk is bootable and how to boot it ?

When we add 8KB of boot information on first cylinder block of a hard disk/slice then it becomes bootable.

This 8KB of information also referred to as boot block.

Hence the reason is the existence of this boot block which enables the disk to be booted. This boot block when exists on individual partition/slice, its also called as VBR or volume Boot record and when we talk about whole hard disk starting boot block its even called MBR or master boot record.

14.2.   Quick Tip 17 : When we format our 16gb pen drive, the usable space shown is less than 16gb, sometimes even around 15GB. Where does remaining space disappear?

Usually manufacturers provide 16GB or 16000MB of character/raw disk to us.
We need to format it to some usable format say fat32, ext3, ext4, etc to make it usable.
When we format the disk it reserves some space for keeping the future data information:

a.   Superblock

It contains all information of the file system like file system size and status, Label (file system and volume name), Size of the logical block, timestamp of the last update, Cylinder group size, Number of data blocks in a cylinder group, Data block information summary, File system state: clean, stable, or active, last mount point path, and cylinder group Map. To know what is cylinder group map, lets see second point below.

Hence we can say the superblock is very important for any file system integrity. If it is lost, the data can't be accessed or recovered.

b.   Cylinder Group Map

Each disk is made of different platters or circular magnetic storage portion, each platter contains few cylinders. Cylinder group map contains information of how many cylinders are free and how many are used; hence it is the one which helps us in disk defragmentation. Usually on every platter our system saves a backup superblock which contains the backup cylinder group map as well.

 Hence when we format the disk, multiple copies of superblocks containing cylinder group map are created as it is very vital to have this information in order to access the data.:-

➤   One primary cylinder group map is stored with superblock on cylinder group 0 on first platter which is also called primary super block.

➤   And few random platters are selected by OS to save another few backup copies of this superblock information so that we can recover our data in case primary superblock gets corrupted.

14.3. Quick Tip 18: How to see where backup super blocks are saved on a disk in Solaris?

a.   First get the disk name for which you want to see the superblock information.

bash-3.2# echo | **format**
Searching for disks...done

AVAILABLE DISK SELECTIONS:
    0. **c0d1** <�u��µ������n cyl 2085 alt 2 hd 255 sec 63>
       /pci@0,0/pci-ide@7,1/ide@1/cmdk@1,0
Specify disk (enter its number): Specify disk (enter its number):

b.   Now check the superblock information using the newfs command.

bash-3.2# **newfs -N /dev/dsk/c0d1s0**
Warning: 894 sector(s) in last cylinder unallocated
/dev/rdsk/c0d1s0:   28820610 sectors in **4691 cylinders of 48 tracks**,
128 sectors
     14072.6MB in 294 cyl groups (16 c/g, 48.00MB/g, 5824 i/g)
super-block backups (for fsck -F ufs -o b=#) at:
 **32, 98464, 196896, 295328, 393760, 492192, 590624, 689056, 787488,
885920,
 27921952, 28020384, 28118816, 28217248, 28315680, 28414112, 28512544,
 28610976, 28709408, 28807840**
bash-3.2#

14.4. Inodes

File system level of information is saved in superblock. However have you ever thought how our system manages to save data of our files/directories like uid/gid of our files, access/modification times, etc. So here comes the concept of inode.

The inode number is a unique number assigned to each file/directory and contains all information required to access the data stored inside a file or directory. Let's see what all saved in an inode:

➢ Type of file (Directory, file, raw disk, logical disk, link, socket, etc)
➢ Permissions (rw/ro)
➢ Number of hard links
➢ UID/GID
➢ Size in bytes
➢ Creation time, modification time and last access time

So if we conclude all information that we see by ls command in UNIX is stored inside an inode, except the filename.

Are file names saved in an inode or somewhere else ?

No, filenames are not saved by inodes. Inodes saves all other data w.r.t files/directories except filename which is saved inside the data block/storage block of a directory. To understand it better lets have a look how data managed in our disk.

➢ Directory Data block:- Save names and inodes of all files inside that directory.
➢ File Data Block:- Contains Data of the file.Let's understand the structure through a diagram below.

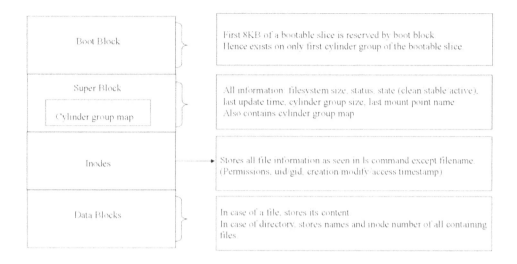

Fig. 2.2 Disk Space Allocation

15.   New file system Creation

Here we will see how to create a new file system. The first step is to check if there is any existing FS/partitions available on our disk.

a.   <u>Confirm no existing File system exists.</u>

bash-3.2# prtvtoc /dev/dsk/c2t0d0s0
* /dev/dsk/c2t0d0s0 partition map
*
* Dimensions:
*   512 bytes/sector
*   32 sectors/track
*   128 tracks/cylinder
*   4096 sectors/cylinder
*   2046 cylinders
*   2044 accessible cylinders
*

```
* Flags:
*   1: unmountable
*  10: read-only
*
*                   First    Sector   Last
* Partition  Tag Flags  Sector    Count   Sector Mount Directory
      0    0   00     4096  1024000  1028095
      1    0   00  1028096  1024000  2052095
      2    5   01        0  8372224  8372223
      3    0   00  3481600  1024000  4505599
      4    0   00  2052096  1429504  3481599
      5    0   00  4505600  3866624  8372223
      8    1   01        0     4096     4095
```

bash-3.2# df /dev/dsk/c2t0d0s0

File system   kbytes   used   avail capacity   Mounted on

df**: /dev/dsk/c2t0d0s0: not a ufs file system**

bash-3.2# **fstyp /dev/dsk/c2t0d0s0**

Unknown_fstyp (no matches)

b.   <u>Now run format and create a slice/partition on the disk using below steps.</u>

➢   Run format
➢   Select disk : 2
➢   Press P to print the current partition table.
➢   Now change the partition or create new partition/slice from the menu using n.
➢   Write the changes by labeling the disk using l

c.   Once Slice is created, we can use the slice is following ways

1.   Create UFS
2.   Create ZFS
3.   Volume
4.   Swap
5.   Crash dumps
6.   Oracle raw data
7.   Iscsi configuration

We will see how to create ufs now and other tasks we will go through in next chapters.

c.   Creating UFS on new Slice

Format it as ufs using newfs command.
bash-3.2# **newfs /dev/dsk/c2t0d0s0**
newfs: construct a new file system /dev/rdsk/c2t0d0s0: (y/n)? **y**
/dev/rdsk/c2t0d0s0:   1024000 sectors in 250 cylinders of 128 tracks, 32 sectors
     500.0MB in 16 cyl groups (16 c/g, 32.00MB/g, 15360 i/g)
super-block backups (for fsck -F ufs -o b=#) at:
 32, 65600, 131168, 196736, 262304, 327872, 393440, 459008, 524576, 590144,
 655712, 721280, 786848, 852416, 917984, 983552
bash-3.2#

Now check the file system type.
bash-3.2# **fstyp /dev/dsk/c2t0d0s0**
ufs

Now mount it on a directory, say /newfs.
 # mount /dev/dsk/c2t0d0s0 /newfs

bash-3.2# **df /dev/dsk/c2t0d0s0**

File system	kbytes	used	avail	capacity	Mounted on
/dev/dsk/c2t0d0s0	481007	9	432891	0%	/newfs

16.   Quick Tip 19 : How to see space occupied user wise in solaris ?

We can see the space occupied by different users directly by one command called quot with –a option. However the point to note is that Quot only works for ufs file system

bash-3.2# quot -a
/dev/rdsk/c0d0s0 (/):
4801976 root
3636109 oracle
316923 #1987
 778   uucp
 188   bin
 140   svctag
 121   adm
  73   noaccess
  13   lp
  11   nobody
   8   daemon
   8   postgres
   2   gdm
   2   smmsp
   2   #70001
   2   webservd

17.   FSCK a file system

FSCK or file system check is one of the most useful utility to recover a file system in case of any data corruption. Now the question is how can our file system get corrupt? So the answer is simple often we face problems with power outage and our system gets powered off immediately without killing all processes and exiting all open files, which majorly causes the file system corruption. There may be few other reasons like forcefully killing a process, umounting a partition, reducing/increasing file system size, etc which can also cause file system corruption.

bash-3.2# **fsck -y /dev/rdsk/c2t0d0s0**

** /dev/rdsk/c2t0d0s0

** Last Mounted on

** Phase 1 - Check Blocks and Sizes

** Phase 2 - Check Pathnames

** Phase 3a - Check Connectivity

** Phase 3b - Verify Shadows/ACLs

** Phase 4 - Check Reference Counts

** Phase 5 - Check Cylinder Groups

2 files, 9 used, 480998 free (14 frags, 60123 blocks, 0.0% fragmentation)

"-y" tells the OS to take yes in case of any prompt for recovery.

18.   Quick Tip 20 : Importance of lost+found directory. What happens if you remove it?

If you have observed, when we create any partition or slice, by default there exists a directory called "lost+found".

bash-3.2# ls -l

total 16

drwx------ 2 root   root   8192 Mar 31 15:43 lost+found

Why lost+found ?

It is used by fsck, it keeps metadata. FSCK command uses this directory to repair the file system.

If you remove this directory, it will be automatically re-created by our system on next reboot, however in case the partition crashes in between you may face some unexpected file system corruption.

19.   Mkfile command

Mkfile command is very useful when we need to do testing and create dummy files of required size.

bash-3.2# **mkfile** 10m file1
bash-3.2# ls -l
total 20512
-rw-r--r-- 1 root   root   0 Mar 31 15:46 abc
-rw------T 1 root   root   10485760 Mar 31 15:47 **file1**
drwx------ 2 root   root   8192 Mar 31 15:43 lost+found

20.   Mounting FS

Mount command is used to mount a file system on solaris. You need to create a directory where you mount the specific device and access its contents.

First create the directory where we will mount the new partition.
mkdir /oradb

Now mount the device on this new directory.
mount /dev/dsk/c2t0d0s0 /oradb

To see time, date when it was mounted we can use mount –v command.

bash-3.2# mount -v

/dev/dsk/c0d0s0 on / type ufs
read/write/setuid/devices/rstchown/intr/largefiles/logging/xattr/on
error=panic/dev=1980000 on Mon Mar 31 15:02:43 2014

/vol/dev/dsk/c1t0d0/1_19089-cxp9024790_1.c on /cdrom/1_19089-cxp9024790_1.c type hsfs read-only/nosetuid/nodevices/rstchown/noglobal/maplcase/rr/traildot/dev=1740002 on Mon Mar 31 15:02:51 2014

21.   /etc/vfstab file

Zfs file system by default is not dependent on this file, only ufs is dependent. However we can make zfs mount point to control via this file. We will see it in the zfs section in further chapters.

The vfstab file contains following entries to mount a file system.

#device	device	mount	FS	fsck	mount
#to mount	to fsck	point	type	pass	at boot
options					
/dev/**dsk**/c0d1s0	/dev/**rdsk**/c0d1s0	/	**ufs**	**1**	
no -					

➢   Mount device will contain the path of block or formatted device i.e. dsk path.

➢   FSCK will be done on character/raw device, hence we can see rdsk path.

➢   Fsk pass --> -,no,1,2

-      Or no   --> Don't run fsck

1   --> First priority fsck

2   --> Second priority fsck

➢   Mount options --> -(none specified take default), ro , rw, etc

22.   Quick Tip 21: Why mount at boot is set to no for root file system in vfstab file ?

Mount at boot option is set to yes or no which helps system to identify whether mount the partition automatically on system boot or not, when mountall utility is executed on system startup.

Root (/), /usr and /var file systems are not mounted from the vfstab file on system startup. This field should always be set to no for these system file systems and for virtual file systems such as /proc and /dev/fd.

23.   Quick Tip 22: Why I am not able to edit /etc/mnttab file ?

As we know /etc is mounted read write, still the file /etc/mnttab is read only.

bash-3.2# ls -l /etc/mnttab
r--r--r-- 5 root   root   895 Oct 15 05:44 /etc/mnttab

bash-3.2# chmod 744 /etc/mnttab-
chmod: WARNING: can't change /etc/mnttab

We can't edit this file even with root and force because this is made in kernel. This file is updated in real time by kernel and we can't edit it even as root since this is not on /etc, it is mounted seperatly; lets see how its mounted.

bash-3.2# df -h /etc/mnttab
File system   size used avail capacity Mounted on
mnttab   0K   0K   0K   0%   /etc/mnttab

bash-3.2# df -h /etc/
File system   size used avail capacity Mounted on

/dev/dsk/c0d1s0   14G   4.6G   8.8G   34%   /

Hence it can't be changed even by root user.

24. **Quick Tip 23** : **Find inode number and its links.**

a.   Check inode number of a file, say /etc/mnttab.

bash-3.2# ls -il /etc/mnttab
    2 -r--r--r-- 5 root   root   1101 Mar 31 16:58 **/etc/mnttab**

b.   Now find all files which have this inode number 2.

bash-3.2# **find / -inum 2 -exec ls -ild {} \;**
    2 drwxr-xr-x 26 root   root   512 Mar 31 16:35 /
    2 -r--r--r-- 5 root   root   1101 Mar 31 16:58 /etc/mnttab
    2 dr-xr-xr-x 2 root   root   144 Mar 31 17:02 /dev/fd
    2 dr-xr-xr-x 57 root   root   260032 Mar 31 17:02 /proc
    2 dr-xr-xr-x 2 root   root   2 Mar 31 17:02
/system/object/genunix
    2 drwxr-xr-x 2 root   sys   512 Mar 31 15:02 /devices
    2 dr-xr-xr-x 6 root   root   512 Mar 31 15:02 /vol
    2 drwxr-xr-x 2 root   root   1024 Mar 31 16:38 /gadha

We say that inode number is unique, but still we can see there are many
files and directories with same inode number. How is it possible ?
The inode number is unique for files or directories on a file system. On
our system there are multiple file systems or mount points , for
example:- /proc, /devices, /vol, and on each file system there can be a
single inode number exists. This is the reason we can see multiple files
with same inode number on our system which exists on different mount
points or file systems.

Questions

Q.1 Describe Hierarchy of UNIX File system ?

Q.2 Is there any difference between UNIX and Linux File system Hierarchy ?

Q.3 How you detect autofs directory or partition in Solaris ?

Q.4 Check current kernel version and our OS bit level.

Q.5 How to identify new hardware on a solaris system ?

Q.6 Check inode number of /etc/shadow file and find all its links on /etc only.

Q.7 Create partitions on small disk, and copy the same partitions with one command to another disk of same of large size.

Q.8 Check available disks and their size on your Soalris System.

Q.9 Remove /dev/dsk/* /dev/rdsk/* files and give a reconfiguration reboot.

Q.10 Boot your test system in failsafe and run fsck on root file system.

Chapter -3
Networking, Zpool/ZFS/Snapshots, Package/Patch Administration
Day - 2

1.   Networking in Unix

The first thing that comes in one person's mind after installing the Solaris OS is to enable networking on system to interact with other servers or to gain internet access.

The most useful task involves setting IP addresses and hostname along with checking the eth interfaces on the server. Hence at first we will look at these tasks on our Unix operating system which is most important when we are working on Solaris. However there are tons of tasks w.r.t. networking on this OS, which involves setting up dhcp, samba, nfs, etc servers and making their clients. Let's have a look at the basic networking first which is most important to know.

Commands:

1.   Ifconfig –a

To check status of different running interfaces and to know their IP addresses.

bash-3.2# ifconfig -a
lo0:
flags=2001000849<UP,LOOPBACK,RUNNING,MULTICAST,IPv4,VIRTUAL> mtu 8232 index 1
        inet 127.0.0.1 netmask ff000000

e1000g0:
flags=1000843<UP,BROADCAST,RUNNING,MULTICAST,IPv4> mtu 1500 index 2
    inet 192.168.2.2 netmask ffffff00 broadcast 192.168.2.255
    ether 0:c:29:80:b:95
e1000g0:1:
flags=1000843<UP,BROADCAST,RUNNING,MULTICAST,IPv4> mtu 1500 index 2
    inet 172.16.159.33 netmask ffffff00 broadcast 172.16.159.255
bash-3.2#

2.   **Dladm show-dev** (To check and display how many Network Interface Cards/NICs available on the system)

Dladm is a Data Link administration command which helps us to identify status of eth interface alongwith its characterstics.

bash-3.2# dladm show-dev
e1000g0   link: up   speed: 1000 Mbps   duplex: full
bash-3.2#

3.   **Hostname** (to see host name of our node, or to set it temporarily)
To view currently assigned hostname to the system.
bash-3.2# hostname
vsserver1

Each command provides more features when we talk about modifying the system settings. We will understand how to use them in live scenarios by looking at different tasks below. I have categorized the topics under quick tips and tasks which will help you to co-relate things and easily accomplish it as a system admin.

1.1. Quick Tip 1: Changing Hostname in Solaris

Changing hostname in Solaris is a very easy task and you need to check/do just three things to get it done.

1.   First check the currently assigned node name..

bash-3.2# cat **/etc/nodename**

vsserver1

      Modify it to new hostname, say SolarisLab1.

vi /etc/nodename → type the new hostname → SolarisLab1

2.   Now nodename is modified, however we need to mention the Ip address of this nodename in /etc/hosts so that system can resolve the IP address of this node.

Check the IP of the interface.

bash-3.2# ifconfig -a

e1000g0:

flags=1000843<UP,BROADCAST,RUNNING,MULTICAST,IPv4> mtu 1500 index 2

 inet **192.168.2.2** netmask ffffff00 broadcast 192.168.2.255

 ether 0:c:29:80:b:95

      Now edit /etc/hosts and enter the IP and new hostname.

bash-3.2# **cat /etc/hosts**

::1   localhost

127.0.0.1   localhost

192.168.2.2   SolarisLab1   loghost

3. Last step to write new hostname in the eth file. Edit the file /etc/hostname.e1000g0 (i.e. /etc/hostname.<cardname>)
(vi /etc/hostname.e1000g0 -→ write SolarisLab1

bash-3.2# cat /etc/hostname.e1000g0
SolarisLab1

4. Now to see the change run below two commands to have the changes in your current profile and to restart the service so to have new hostname in place:
bash-3.2# hostname SolarisLab1   ### To have the changes in current shell
bash-3.2#
bash-3.2# hostname
SolarisLab1
bash-3.2# **svcadm restart network**   ## restart the service so that the changes will take effect.
bash-3.2#

Now when you take another session, you can see the hostname is modified.
root@L9AHG13:~# ssh 172.16.159.33
Password:
Last login: Sun Nov 23 20:02:16 2014 from 172.16.159.1
Oracle Corporation   SunOS 5.10   Generic Patch January 2005
You have new mail.
bash
bash-3.2#
bash-3.2# **hostname**

SolarisLab1

1.2.   <u>Quick Tip 2</u>: Assigning/Changing IP address of an interface.

1.   Check the available interfaces and choose one interface where you want to assign IP address.

bash-3.2# dladm show-dev

e1000g0   link: up   speed: 1000 Mbps   duplex: full

e1000g1   link: up   speed: 1000 Mbps   duplex: full

Let's assign an IP address to second interface i.e. e1000g1.

2.   Now open the interface so that an IP can be assigned to it.

ifconfig e1000g1 plumb up

Now the device can be viewed under ifconfig –a output, however still no IP is assigned to it.

3.   Now let's assign an IP address to the interface.

bash-3.2# **ifconfig e1000g1 192.168.2.3/24**

bash-3.2# ifconfig e1000g1

e1000g1:

flags=1000843<UP,BROADCAST,RUNNING,MULTICAST,IPv4> mtu 1500 index 2

    inet 192.168.2.3 netmask ffffff00 broadcast 192.168.2.255

    ether 0:c:29:80:b:95

4.   Update /etc/hosts file with new interface IP address.

bash-3.2# cat /etc/hosts

::1   localhost

127.0.0.1   localhost

192.168.2.3   vsserver1   loghost

<u>Few things to check</u>

➤   If the interface is successfully up. If not you can try running below command:

\# ifconfig e1000g1 up

Otherwise unplumb it and plumb it again

➤   Make sure the DNS is updated.

<u>Making the IP address Permanent</u>

The IP address is plumbed and now up on the new interface. However if you want to make it permanent so that it can come up on reboot automatically then we need to create one file(/etc/hostname.interface-name) like below.

bash-3.2# cat **/etc/hostname.e1000g1**
192.168.2.3/24

1.3.   Snoop: To capture the network traffic

When we get error between two nodes and didn't get any clue which node caused the error then capturing network traffic is one of the best ways to troubleshoot where the root problem lies. Snoop is the inbuilt utility in Solaris OS which provides various options to filter and capture the network traffic going out or coming into the server.

However there are tons of options we can use with snoop, but we will look only the selected options which are used in real time to capture the packets.

Usually we need to track traffic on one IP subnet and on a specific port. So let's have a small note describing how to capture network traffic in this case.

Example :- Capture traffic from specific eth interface e1000g0 on port 10011 of 10.238.12.23.

bash-3.2# snoop -V -d e1000g0 port 10011 -o /tmp/traffic10011.pcap 10.238.12.23
Using device e1000g0 (promiscuous mode)
^Cbash-3.2#

➢ Press Ctlr+C to terminate the snoop.
➢ Now download this file /tmp/traffic10011.pcap and examine the traffic using wireshark.
➢ Port option captures all packets which on mentioned port i.e. 10011
➢ "-d" options specifies the device from which the packets are flowing.
➢ "-V" option also shows little verbose summary of each packet in readable format.
➢ 10.238.12.23 is the destination IP address.

Similarly you can run snoop to capture traffic as per your requirements. You can even specify the IP address, network or filter the traffic based on different requirements. Also note snoop is only available under solaris. I will not go into depth of this utility otherwise this will require me to have a separate chapter on this utility. The purpose of knowing different utilities in unix administration is to know what we can do, and the answer of how to do can be readily searched when the requirement arises.

Another snoop command that we should know is only snoop and snoop broadcast which will simply show all packets flowing through our system and "-v" will make the output verbose i.e. easily readable.

bash-3.2# **snoop –v**   **→ simply captures all traffic**

Using device e1000g0 (promiscuous mode)

^Cbash-3.2#

bash-3.2# **snoop -v broadcast**   **→ captures all broadcast packets**

Using device e1000g0 (promiscuous mode)

^Cbash-3.2#

1.4. Quick Tip 3: Difference between Host and Node

Host will host the application, any system or server.

Node which uses the ip address may be printer, router, etc.

2. Virtual IP in solaris

In Linux/Unix, we have a special feature by which we can assign multiple IP addresses on the same Ethernet adapter and fool our network to have multiple IP address on our node and that too in runtime without any downtime.

So get ready to add a new virtual IP address. To add a virtual IP address, we need to create virtual Ethernet device from the existing one, so that the virtual device will send the packet on the available physical device. Let's see in quick tip how to create the virtual interface and IP address online.

2.1. Quick Tip 4: Creating Temporary VIP on the fly.

First view the available interfaces and IP addresses on our node.

bash-3.2# **ifconfig -a**
lo0:
flags=2001000849<UP,LOOPBACK,RUNNING,MULTICAST,IPv4,VIRT
UAL> mtu 8232 index 1
     inet **127.0.0.1** netmask ff000000
e1000g0:
flags=1000843<UP,BROADCAST,RUNNING,MULTICAST,IPv4> mtu
1500 index 2
     inet **192.168.2.3** netmask ffffff00 broadcast 192.168.2.255
     ether 0:c:29:80:b:95

So we have only one physical interface available i.e. **e1000g0** , one
loopback interface i.e. lo0.
Hence we have only one option to choose this interface for creating a
new virtual interface.
Let's assign new IP address say **192.168.2.55.**

bash-3.2# **ifconfig e1000g0:9 plumb 192.168.2.55 up**

bash-3.2# ifconfig -a
lo0:
flags=2001000849<UP,LOOPBACK,RUNNING,MULTICAST,IPv4,VIRT
UAL> mtu 8232 index 1
     inet 127.0.0.1 netmask ff000000
e1000g0:
flags=1000843<UP,BROADCAST,RUNNING,MULTICAST,IPv4> mtu
1500 index 2
     inet 192.168.2.3 netmask ffffff00 broadcast 192.168.2.255
     ether 0:c:29:80:b:95

e1000g0:9:
flags=1000843<UP,BROADCAST,RUNNING,MULTICAST,IPv4> mtu
1500 index 2
     inet **192.168.2.55** netmask ffffff00 broadcast 192.168.2.255
bash-3.2#

That's it !!
Yes the new interface is plumbed and is up with new IP address.

However it's not permanent, if you want to make it permanent then we
need to create one file.

2.2.   Making VIP permanent

To make the new Virtual IP permanent, create one file under /etc/ with
name like hostname<cardname>.

bash-3.2# cat **/etc/hostname.e1000g0:9**
192.168.2.55 /24
bash-3.2#

To test if it has become permanent, try to restart the service and the new
IP should come up.

bash-3.2# svcadm -v restart network/physical
Action restart set for svc:/network/physical:default.
So now we are done, however it would be always a good practice if we
add this new IP address in our /etc/hosts file and on our DNS server so
that it could be available for other hosts on the network.

Few features of virtual interface in solaris

✓   256 ips can be added on a single NIC card.

✓   Different subnet Ip addresses can be added to a single nic virtual interfaces.

      bash-3.2# ifconfig e1000g0:10 plumb 152.168.2.55 up

bash-3.2# ifconfig e1000g0:10

e1000g0:10:

flags=1000843<UP,BROADCAST,RUNNING,MULTICAST,IPv4> mtu 1500 index 2

      inet 152.168.2.55 netmask ffff0000 broadcast 152.168.255.255

3.   **Quick Tip 5: How to enable ssh root login ?**

✓   Change sshd_config file and enable PermitRootLogin parameter as follows:

bash-3.2# cat /etc/ssh/sshd_config | grep -i permitroot

PermitRootLogin yes

✓   Now restart the service as follows:

bash-3.2# svcadm -v restart svc:/network/ssh:default

Action restart set for svc:/network/ssh:default.

4.   **Quick Tip 6: How to remove interface from DHCP?**

If your system is booted via dhcp, and you want to remove the dhcp configuration and want to assign static IP then you can follow below steps:

i.   First move the dhcp configuration file to some other name.

bash-3.2# mv /etc/dhcp.e1000g0 /etc/dhcp.e1000g0.bak

ii.   Now create the hostname.<interfacename> file containing the IP address or alias corresponding to new static IP address.

bash-3.2# vi /etc/hostname.e1000g0
system11
"/etc/hostname.e1000g0" 1 line, 9 characters

iii.   Now mark an entry of IP address corresponding to this alias name/hostname system11 in hosts file.
#cat /etc/hosts
192.168.2.2   system11
iv. Now restart the network service.
bash-3.2# svcadm -v restart svc:/network/ssh:default
Action restart set for svc:/network/ssh:default.

Now the new static IP is in place and the interface is removed from dhcp.

5.   ZFS (ZettaByte File System)

Just like UFS, Oracle Solaris has released its own filesystem called ZFS or zettabyte filesystem started from Solaris 10, release 2006 and above. ZFS is not only a filesystem, but also act as volume manager and allows the user to get the features of both a FS and Volume manager bundled into one.

Features of ZFS
a.   Protection against data corruption.
b.   Support for high storage capacities.
c.   Efficient data compression.

d.   Integration of the concepts of filesystem and volume management, snapshots and copy-on-write clones.

e.   Continuous integrity checking and automatic repair.

f.   RAID-Z and native NFSv4 ACLs.

5.1.   UFS Vs ZFS

The ZFS features itself tells the difference and advantages of ZFS over UFS.

Let's have a look at some of the major differences between them.

✓   ZFS can store large file system/large storage.

✓   UFS is not stable, power outage or ungraceful shutdown, it can corrupt the root fs and we need to run fsck to repair it whereas in ZFS it is not required.

✓   Less tunable options as compared to ZFS

✓   UFS dependent on /etc/vfstab and any wrong entry in this file makes the system unbootable. However ZFS is not dependent on this file by default.

✓   ZFS Snapshots are pointing time read only copy with practically zero space occupied on disk.

✓   ZFS provides features of UFS and SVM bundled into one and no additional configuration required for volume management.

ZFS provides a very simple administration. One product contains: Volume manager + FS (no need to configure svm). Mainly two commands and sub commands are enough for its administration:

1.   Zpool

2.   Zfs

3.   Zdb(optional)

✓ If filesystem gets corrupt in zfs, then zfs do automatically checkup, unless and until there are hard errors i.e. some issue in hard disk.

✓ No fsck is required in zfs because zfs does scrubbing when filesystem is ideal automatically.

✓ ZFS works on copy on write technology i.e. successful transaction will be committed, and unsuccessful will be reverted, there is no intermediate state.

✓ ZFS also provides tunable properties of filesystem like quota, reservations, etc inbuilt with zfs format.

✓ By default,. Zfs will always do the striping and hence provides fast IO operations thereby increasing the speed of user operations.

How to start with ZFS ?

Since the volume manager is combined in ZFS, hence the first step in ZFS filesystem creation is to create zpool i.e. a logical volume which contains disks/slices. Thereafter we can create filesystems from this pool space.

1. Create the pool (zpool → volume)

a. The pool can be created using the whole disk, disk slice, or a dummy file created using mkfile or dd command.

b. The block size is 128k by default in ZFS(can be increased to 1MB), whereas in ufs its 8k by default.

c. Pool name must start with a character (no number/reserved character [mirror/cache/log/spare/raidz] can be given)

2.   Once pool is created, create the filesystem in the pool.
That's it! Now everything can be handled by ZFS i.e. mounting the filesystem, mount point creation, and we can also tune it like setting quota on the particular filesystem, etc.

5.2.   ZFS Disadvantages

The performance is always increased when we use ZFS, however in some cases it could also lead to slow read write speed. As we know ZFS uses striping to save data across multiple disks added into the zpool, so imagine if we added one local disk, one disk coming from emc and some other iscsi lun. So here ZFS will try to contact each disk every time to save the data and hence it reduces the speed. In such cases, we should keep in our mind that our vdevs(virtual devices i.e. zfs created) are created with appropriate disks and if possible then we can have separate zpools of each disk from different source.

Another feature or disadvantage of ZFS is with their user and group quota. A user quota or group quota which is set on a parent file system is not automatically inherited by a descendent file system.

Other than these, you may encounter few other disadvantages, however overall when we check the feedback from various users it's noted that performance is increased in almost all cases where ZFS is used over UFS.

6.   Snapshots

Suppose your system is running fine at the moment, and you want to save the current system state, say state1. So here comes the concept of snapshot. To save this state state1 we need snapshots which can save the current system state and can help us to recover our system later on in case of any issues.

Same happens with data. Suppose you have 100 files in a directory and you want to save the current state of all the files before making modifications. Then you will create a snapshot say snap1, and now you can modify the files. Suppose after 10 days you feel everything is fine, then create another snapshot, say snap2 and make further changes. After successful testing of the changes you can remove snap1 and snap2, otherwise you have an option to revert to snap2 or snap1 state. Hence snapshot can be defined as a state of a system/data at particular point of time. The process of snapshot creation in UFS and ZFS is completely different and there are several differences that make zfs snapshots took over ufs snapshots. Let's have a look at an overview of ufs and zfs snapshots and their differences.

6.1.   Difference between UFS and ZFS snapshots

UFS snapshots are applicable on UFS filesystem whereas ZFS snapshots are carried out on ZFS filesystem. UFS snapshots were released from Solaris 8 and were considered a very good way to backup the data on a running system without any downtime. When we take UFS snapshot, the backup device should be different from the device whose backup is taken, for example:- /opt snapshot can't be created under some directory inside opt like /opt/backup is not possible, it should be on some other mount point.

- ✓   Ufs snapshots take huge space.
- ✓   UFS snapshots are not consistent/permanent across reboot
- ✓   Zfs uses inode concept and initial snapshot will be of zero size. (game of pointers)

6.2.   Quick Tip 7: ZFS snapshots Vs Hard Links

ZFS snapshot uses the concept of hard links, or pointers. Instead of copying the whole data, hard links just stores a list of all inode numbers of the files/blocks and whenever any change is made to any file, the changed file is not overwritten, however saved with a new inode number at different memory location. This is the reason initially the ZFS snapshot size is zero and it grows as we make changes in the files.

7.   How to check if ZFS configured?

As we know, the first thing we need to check in case of ZFS is zpool. Hence we can check whether our system has ZFS configured or not by checking the available zpools.

bash-3.2# **zpool list**

no pools available

Since there is no output it means no zpool is available and if no volume is available then there could be no filesystem, therefore no ZFS filesystem is configured on this system yet.

8.   Quick Tip 8: How to check block size of UFS/ZFS filesystem ?

The easiest command to check block size of ufs or zfs filesystem on our solaris system is df with g option. However there are few other commands as well. Lets check the available commands for checking the block size.

bash-3.2# **df -g /**

/   (/dev/dsk/c0d0s0   ):   **8192 block size**   1024 frag size
28383096 total blocks   10840968 free blocks 10557138 available
1712256 total files
 1492657 free files   26738688 filesys id
    ufs fstype   0x00000004 flag   255 filename length

bash-3.2# **fstyp -v /dev/rdsk/c0d1s0 | grep -i ^bsize**

bsize **8192**   shift 13   mask   0xffffe000

9.   Comparision between VxVM and ZFS

➢   VxVM or Veritas Volume Manager is another type of platform independent software suite that allows us to manage disks and perform volume manager tasks like reducing/extending partition online, adding new disks in volume without any downtime. VxVM is a proprietary volume manager introduced by Veritas(now Symantec). VxVM supports all platforms like windows, linux, and unix flavors and hence provides efficient way when we want to migrate the storage from one server type to another. VxVM also supports multipath disks and provides enhanced performance in case of Veritas Cluster.

➢   ZFS is native developed by Sun during Opensolaris project, VxVM is 3rd party utility.

➢   ZFS costs zero, VxVM costs a lot of money to get licenses. VxVM is better if you can pay for its license and have VCS cluster in place.

➢   ZFS is fully supported within our Oracle Solaris.

➢   ZFS is implemented as open-source software, licensed under the Common Development and Distribution License (CDDL), hence it can't be charged.

➢   If you don't have Veritas Cluster(VCS) installed then you can go with ZFS and achieve similar functions for Volume management with less commands and in less time, whereas in VCS you need to run a lot of commands to achieve the same task.

10.   Zpool Administration

In this section, we will see how to create zpool, what are different types of zpool, and the different operation(s) that we can perform on zpool volume. Zpool is same like Volume group in Linux, where we create a pool of disks and then create sub filesystems of required size and mount at different mount points.

10.1. What is Zpool

A zpool is a virtual storage device created by combining different vdevs(virtual devices). A virtual device can be constructed using a slice/partition, or a file, or a complete disk/drive. These block devices(slice/disk/file) can be combined in different ways to create a vdev like in RAID-0 or stripe, or in RAID-1, RAID-Z, or RAID-2Z form providing different levels of data redundancy. To get into the details of each type of these zpools, lets see the different types of zpools that can be configured on a system in next section.

10.2. Zpool Types

Depending upon how zpool is created, we have four different types of zpools that can be configured on a solaris system.

1.   <u>Basic or simple (stripe, raid 0)</u> :- As its name suggests, this type of pool simply adds new storage devices and increases the pool size without any redundancy. Just one command to achieve this task is as follows. Although its understood that we need to make required slices first.
zpool create vol0 /dev/sda1 /dev/sda2 /dev/sda3

2.   <u>Mirror pool(raid 1)</u> :- Mirror pool requires at two or more vdevs of same size. In Mirror pool, we add two vdevs(for example) of same size in redundant manner, so that the data written to vdev1 is automatically written to vdev2 and in case of disk failure of vdev1, the data can be recovered from vdev2. This type of pool has extra load on disk in write

operations, however for read operations it provide fast access as two devices are ready to serve read requests.

 # zpool create vol0 mirror /dev/sda1 /dev/sdb1

Here we have used slices on different hard drives, so that in case one disk fails the data still can be recovered. Make sure you create partitions with exact size.

3.   <u>Raid Z pool(raid 5)</u> :- This type of pool requires three or more vdevs. The parity information of one disk is stored on other available disks and in case of failure of one disk, the data can be recovered from parity information stored on other disks. However it can't offer fault tolerance in case two disks are failed. In this case, we need to go with double parity stored on disks which is also called RAID 6.

 # zpool create vol0 raidz /dev/sda /dev/sdb /dev/sdc

Here we have created one zpool with three disks sda, sbb, and sdc.

4.   <u>RaidZ2 Pool (RAID6 or RAID5 with dual parity)</u> :- It requires four or more devices to store double parity of disks. Using 4 disks in RAID with double distributed parity configuration, it provides fault tolerance for upto 2 disks.

 # zpool create vol0 raidz2 /dev/sda /dev/sdb /dev/sdc /dev/sdd

Here we have taken four disks to create RAID 5 with dual parity volume.

10.3.   Creating zpool with new disk

Till now, we have seen what is zpool and what are its different type. Let's see a practical how to create a new default zpool i.e. a stripe zpool volume.

I have added a new disk to my VM test server and upon restarting the disk is named as c2t0d0. Now lets proceed further.

1.   First create the stripe or default zpool with this new disk.
bash-3.2# **zpool create oracle c2t0d0**

2.   Now check the newly created zpool.
bash-3.2# **zpool list**
NAME   SIZE ALLOC FREE   CAP HEALTH ALTROOT
oracle 3.97G 78.5K 3.97G   0% ONLINE -

3.   We can also check Disks in zpool.
bash-3.2# **zpool status**
 pool: oracle
 state: ONLINE
 scan: none requested
config:

```
    NAME      STATE    READ WRITE CKSUM
    oracle    ONLINE    0   0    0
    c2t0d0    ONLINE    0   0    0
```

errors: No known data errors
bash-3.2#

4.   Zpool is created. Check it should now visible under mounted partitions.

bash-3.2# **df -h**
Filesystem   size used avail capacity Mounted on
/dev/dsk/c0d0s0   14G 8.4G 5.0G 63%   /
/devices   0K   0K   0K   0%   /devices
oracle   3.9G 31K 3.9G   1% /oracle

Also if we see the mount –v command output, we can see its type as zfs.

#mount –v | grep oracle

oracle on /oracle type **zfs**
read/write/setuid/devices/rstchown/nonbmand/exec/xattr/atime/de
v=2d50002 on Tue Apr 1 12:20:27 2014

10.4.   Quick Tip 9: How to check iostat activity on zpool/zfs filesystem ?

A very interesting feature of zpool is that we can check the IO activity of zpool/zfs with just one command. Lets view how to check iostat of our newly created zpool.

bash-3.2# **zpool iostat -v**

pool	capacity alloc	free	operations read	write	bandwidth read	write
----------	-----	-----	-----	-----	-----	-----
oracle	91K	1.98G	0	1	362	15.7K
c1t0d0	91K	1.98G	0	1	362	15.7K
----------	-----	-----	-----	-----	-----	-----

10.5.   Dataset and its types

Dataset refers to the collection of database tables or a single database table containing zpool configuration. ZFS dataset is saved under /etc and it's named as zpool.cache.

bash-3.2# **ls -l /etc/zfs/zpool.cache**

-rw-r--r-- 1 root   root   1160 Apr 1 12:20 /etc/zfs/zpool.cache

This dataset file contains the list of all pools which were ever created on the system. And we can see what all pools are there in this file by using below command. Please do not try to cat/more this file, use only zdb command to list its contents.

bash-3.2# **zdb | more**
oracle:
   version: 29
   name: 'oracle'
   state: 0
   txg: 4
   pool_guid: 17857179158783640165
   hostid: 114702641
   hostname: 'system11'
   vdev_children: 1
   vdev_tree:
     type: 'root'

If you remove this file, then you will not able to see the pools list in zdb command.
Let's remove this file and see the experiment result. Please don't perform this on production server ;).

bash-3.2# rm /etc/zfs/zpool.cache

Now when we run zdb command, we can't see any available pools.
bash-3.2# zdb

Let's come back to the topic. The ZFS Datasets can be of different types depending upon what we create out of the zpool.

1.   **Pool** :- A pool or zpool is the first step in setting zfs on our system. Creating a complete volume is referred to as a zpool.

2.   **Sub Filesystem** :- The filesystems create on a pool is called as sub filesystem.

3.   **Snapshot** :- The snapshot is the current state of the zfs filesystem and it can be created on a pool or a filesystem.

4.   **Clone** :- A zfs clone is created by cloning the zfs snapshot and this way we can create clones of any zfs snapshots available. However later on we can promote clone to replace the original zfs.

5.   **Volume**:- Suppose you need a logical device to create swap or dump disk, which should not be mountable and can be used as a character disk. In this case, volumes are used in ZFS. In ZFS, we can also create volumes which will refer to raw/block devices and gets saved in /dev/zvol/{dsk,rdsk}/pool directory.

We will look how to create each of these dataset types in ZFS later in this chapter one by one to understand how to create them and under which requirement we should use what type of dataset.

10.6.   Quick Tip 10 :- How to import a destroyed pool ?

Suppose someone accidently destroyed the pool like below:
1.   Destroying a zpool.
bash-3.2# zpool list
NAME   SIZE ALLOC FREE   CAP HEALTH ALTROOT
oracle 1.98G 145K 1.98G   0% ONLINE -

bash-3.2# **zpool destroy oracle**

bash-3.2# **zpool list**

no pools available

The zpool.cache file is removed as soon as all pools are destroyed.
bash-3.2# ls -ltr /etc/zfs/

2.   Now see all the deleted pools.
bash-3.2# **zpool import -D**
  pool: oracle
    id: 4434552831298521491
  state: ONLINE (DESTROYED)
action: The pool can be imported using its name or numeric identifier.
config:

     oracle   ONLINE
       c1t0d0   ONLINE

3.   Now import the destroyed pool as follows. There could be
multiple destroyed pools as seen in last step, make sure to use correct
name.
bash-3.2# **zpool import -Df oracle**

Now you can list and see the pool with zpool list command. The pool is
successfully imported and mounted.

10.7.   Creating Sub filesystem
Now let's create few filesystems under the oracle pool we have created
earlier. Here we will see the other command usage i.e. zfs , how to create
filesystem and then list it using this command.

1.   First check the available pools and filesystems under the pool.
bash-3.2# **zpool list**
NAME   SIZE ALLOC FREE   CAP HEALTH ALTROOT
oracle 3.97G 91K 3.97G   0% ONLINE -

bash-3.2# **zfs list -r oracle**
NAME   USED AVAIL REFER MOUNTPOINT
oracle   91K 3.91G   31K /oracle

2.   Now lets create few other filesystems under this pool named 'linux', sap, solaris,, and aix.
bash-3.2# **zfs create oracle/linux**
bash-3.2# zfs create oracle/sap
bash-3.2# zfs create oracle/solaris
bash-3.2# zfs create oracle/aix

3.   List and see the newly created filesystems.
bash-3.2# zfs list -r oracle
NAME   USED AVAIL REFER MOUNTPOINT
oracle   248K 3.91G   34K /oracle
oracle/aix   31K 3.91G   31K /oracle/aix
oracle/linux   31K 3.91G   31K /oracle/linux
oracle/sap   31K 3.91G   31K /oracle/sap
oracle/solaris   31K 3.91G   31K /oracle/solaris

If we check df output, we can see these filesystems are automatically mounted.
bash-3.2# **df -h | grep -i oracle**
oracle   3.9G 34K 3.9G   1%   /oracle
oracle/linux   3.9G 31K 3.9G   1% /oracle/linux

---

oracle/sap	3.9G	31K	3.9G	1%	/oracle/sap
oracle/solaris	3.9G	31K	3.9G	1%	/oracle/solaris
oracle/aix	3.9G	31K	3.9G	1%	/oracle/aix

This is it, now we have 4 file systems created in oracle pool within few seconds.

10.8.   Understanding Space occupied in a pool

You may be confused how zpool and zfs manages space under each file system and pool as we can see above that each file system of the pool is showing the same space occupied and available.

To understand which pool occupies how much space lets create a file of 500MB under ZFS file system /oracle/linux, and see how it shows the occupied space.

bash-3.2# cd /oracle/linux/
bash-3.2# mkfile 500m file1
bash-3.2# ls -ltr
total 851333
-rw------T 1 root   root   524288000 Apr 1 12:40 file1
bash-3.2# df -h | grep -i oracle

oracle	**3.9G**	**39K**	**3.5G**	**1%**	**/oracle**
oracle/linux	**3.9G**	**500M**	**3.5G**	**11%**	**/oracle/linux**
oracle/sap	3.9G	31K	3.5G	1%	/oracle/sap
oracle/solaris	3.9G	31K	3.5G	1%	/oracle/solaris
oracle/aix	3.9G	31K	3.5G	1%	/oracle/aix

bash-3.2#

In the above output of df, its clear that /oracle/linux is occupying 500MB of space, but other file systems are still showing available space as 3.5G which is false since 500MB is already occupied by file system /oracle/linux.

A better way is to check pool space instead of file system to get an idea how much space is still left on the volume.

bash-3.2# zfs list -r oracle
```
NAME            USED  AVAIL  REFER  MOUNTPOINT
oracle          501M  3.42G   39K   /oracle
oracle/aix       31K  3.42G   31K   /oracle/aix
oracle/linux    500M  3.42G  500M   /oracle/linux
oracle/sap       31K  3.42G   31K   /oracle/sap
oracle/solaris   31K  3.42G   31K   /oracle/solaris
```

So in this section, we have learned that the actual space occupied should be seen in a pool, and not in the file system otherwise high usage on one file system can bring operations on all file systems down.

10.9.   Quick Tip 11: How to see zpool command history ?

Sometimes we need to check out the history of all commands related to zpool , say w.r.t the oracle pool or any other keyword then Oracle Solaris provides an option for this also. However you always have unix/linux commands available like grep which can be used in case you don't remember this command.

bash-3.2# **zpool history oracle**
History for 'oracle':
2014-04-01.12:20:57 zpool create oracle c2t0d0
2014-04-01.12:35:59 zfs create oracle/linux

2014-04-01.12:36:02 zfs create oracle/sap
2014-04-01.12:36:07 zfs create oracle/solaris
2014-04-01.12:36:37 zfs create oracle/aix

10.10. ZFS Quota

ZFS Quota can be set on any ZFS filesystem, which sets a upper limit on the amount of space that can be used on that filesystem. In case someone tries to store a file larger than quota space then it will throw an error and the user need to contact administrator or root user to increase the quota.

Quota must be more than refer(or used) space as seen in zfs list.

bash-3.2# **zfs list -r oracle**
NAME   USED AVAIL **REFER** MOUNTPOINT
oracle   500M 3.42G   39K   /oracle
oracle/aix   31K 3.42G   31K   /oracle/aix
oracle/linux   500M 3.42G **500M** /oracle/linux
oracle/sap   31K 3.42G   **31K** /oracle/sap
oracle/solaris   31K 3.42G   31K   /oracle/solaris
bash-3.2#

To view the current quota of all pools and filesystem we can use below command.

bash-3.2# **zfs get quota**
NAME   PROPERTY VALUE SOURCE
oracle   quota   none default
oracle/linux quota   none default
oracle/test quota   none default
bash-3.2#

We can also mention the required ZFS to get its quota.

bash-3.2# **zfs get quota oracle/solaris**

NAME	PROPERTY	VALUE	SOURCE
oracle/solaris	quota	none	default

To see all properties that can be set on a zfs filesystem. We can use zfs get command.

bash-3.2# **zfs get all oracle/linux | more**

NAME	PROPERTY	VALUE	SOURCE
oracle/linux	type	filesystem	-
oracle/linux	creation	Tue Apr 1 12:35 2014	-
oracle/linux	used	500M	-
oracle/linux	available	3.42G	-
oracle/linux	referenced	500M	-
oracle/linux	compressratio	1.00x	-
oracle/linux	mounted	yes	-
oracle/linux	quota	none	default
oracle/linux	reservation	none	default
oracle/linux	recordsize	128K	default

1   -→ read only
2   default → r/w
3   local → tuned property

bash-3.2# **zfs get all oracle/linux | grep -i quota**

oracle/linux	quota	none	default
oracle/linux	refquota	none	default

10.10.1.   Setting quota

In this section we will see the command how to set quota on a filesystem.

To set the quota we can use "zfs set" command with quota option like below.

bash-3.2# **zfs set quota=100m oracle/solaris**

Now lets see the quota limit using zfs get command.

bash-3.2# zfs get all oracle/solaris | grep -i quota

oracle/solaris	**quota**	**100M**	**local**
oracle/solaris	refquota	none	default

We can also observe quota when we see the output of zfs list command by checking the AVAIL disk space on a filesystem whose pool size is greater than ZFS filesystem size in this command output.

bash-3.2# **zfs list -r oracle**

NAME	USED	AVAIL	REFER	MOUNTPOINT
oracle	500M	3.42G	39K	/oracle
oracle/aix	31K	3.42G	31K	/oracle/aix
oracle/linux	500M	3.42G	500M	/oracle/linux
oracle/sap	31K	3.42G	31K	/oracle/sap
oracle/solaris	**31K**	**100M**	**31K**	**/oracle/solaris**

10.10.2.   Removing quota

We have seen how to set quota on the filesystem, however we should know how can we remove the quota, or increase its limit in ZFS. So let us have a look at the command how can we remove the quota from the ZFS.

1.   First lets create a sample zfs and see the quota currently applied.

bash-3.2#**zfs create oracle/test**

bash-3.2# **zfs get quota**

NAME   PROPERTY VALUE SOURCE

oracle   quota   none   default

oracle/linux quota   none   default

oracle/test quota   none   default

2.   So as seen in above command, no quota or none quota is applied currently. Lets set a quota of 100MB .

bash-3.2# **zfs set quota=100M oracle/test**

bash-3.2# **zfs get quota**

NAME   PROPERTY VALUE SOURCE

oracle   quota   none   default

oracle/linux quota   none   default

oracle/test   quota   100M   local

bash-3.2# **df -h | grep -i oracle**

oracle   2.0G   33K   1.4G   1%   /oracle

oracle/linux   2.0G   500M 1.4G   27%   /oracle/linux

oracle/test   100M   0M   100M   90%   /oracle/test

3.   Now let's come to main part of removing the quota from the newly created zfs oracle/test.

As we have seen above while setting quota, default quota allocated is none, hence to remove quota we need to set it back to none.

bash-3.2# **zfs set quota=none oracle/test**

bash-3.2# **zfs get quota**

```
NAME          PROPERTY VALUE SOURCE
oracle      quota   none  default
oracle/linux quota    none  default
oracle/test  quota   none  local
bash-3.2#
```

```
bash-3.2# df -h /oracle/test
Filesystem        size  used  avail capacity  Mounted on
oracle/test       2.0G  90M   1.4G   7%    /oracle/test
```

The quota is now removed from the filesystem and it is again set to none i.e. no quota. However as we can see above the AVAIL space plus USED space is less than 2GB because it subtracts the used space by other filesystems on the same pool.

10.11. Delete ZFS Filesystem

Deleting ZFS is very easy by using the keyword destroy. For example lets delete a ZFS oracle/solaris.

bash-3.2# **zfs destroy oracle/solaris**

bash-3.2# **zfs list -r oracle**

```
NAME          USED  AVAIL  REFER  MOUNTPOINT
oracle      500M 3.42G  39K  /oracle
oracle/aix    31K 3.42G   31K  /oracle/aix
oracle/linux  500M 3.42G  500M  /oracle/linux
oracle/sap    31K 3.42G   31K  /oracle/sap
```

10.12. Quick Tip 12: How to see help of zfs commands ?

bash-3.2# **zpool help**

unrecognized command 'help'

usage: zpool command args ...

where 'command' is one of the following:

    create [-fn] [-o property=value] ...
        [-O file-system-property=value] ..

Zfs help

10.13. Increasing zpool size

The zpool size can be increased without any downtime and loss of data. Hence there is no risk in growing the zpool size.

```
-bash-3.2# zpool add oracle c2t1d0s2
-bash-3.2# zpool list oracle
NAME    SIZE ALLOC  FREE   CAP  HEALTH  ALTROOT
oracle  4.45G  500M  3.96G   10%  ONLINE  -
-bash-3.2#
-bash-3.2#
-bash-3.2# zpool status oracle
  pool: oracle
 state: ONLINE
  scan: none requested
config:
     NAME       STATE    READ WRITE CKSUM
     oracle     ONLINE    0    0    0
      c2t0d0    ONLINE    0    0    0
      c2t1d0s2 ONLINE     0    0    0
```

errors: No known data errors

-bash-3.2#

We can't take out any hard disk from the stripe pool.

10.14. Replace a disk in zpool

Let's create a mirror pool i.e RAID 1 pool and then replace a faulty disk from this pool at runtime without any downtime and with one single command.

a. First lets create a stripe or mirror pool named "test" with two disks.

-bash-3.2# zpool create -f test c2t0d0s0 c2t0d0s1

b.   Now to replace one disk we can simply mention the failed disk name followed by new disk name. We can see faulty disk in red color, also the new disk should be of same size as of old disks.

-bash-3.2# zpool replace -f test c2t0d0s1 c2t0d0s3

10.15. <u>Quick Tip 13</u>: How to delete all partition table on a disk ?

A very quick hack to bring your system down, or making it unusable is to put zero or null in your partition/disk vtoc table.

Simply use fmthard command and put /dev/null or /dev/zero on your raw/character device of the disk, on second slice as it contains the partition table.

-bash-3.2# **fmthard -s /dev/null /dev/rdsk/c2t0d0s2**

fmthard: New volume table of contents now in place.

Note:- Please don't use such command on any server, after above command the disk will become unusable.

10.16. RAID-1 Zpool

To create a mirror zpool, or a RAID-1 zpool, we can use below zpool command with mirror keyword and the two devices of same size.

```
# zpool create datapool mirror <firstdevice> <second_device>
```

Lets have a look at an example where we have created two slices of same size and then creating a zpool named datapool.

```
-bash-3.2# zpool create -f datapool mirror c2t0d0s0 c2t0d0s1

-bash-3.2# zpool list
NAME      SIZE ALLOC  FREE   CAP HEALTH  ALTROOT
datapool  496M 78.5K  496M   0% ONLINE  -
oracle2   984M 135K   984M   0% ONLINE  -

-bash-3.2# zpool status
  pool: datapool
 state: ONLINE
  scan: none requested
config:

    NAME         STATE    READ WRITE CKSUM
    datapool     ONLINE    0   0    0
      mirror-0   ONLINE    0   0    0
        c2t0d0s0 ONLINE    0   0    0
        c2t0d0s1 ONLINE    0   0    0

errors: No known data errors
```

pool: oracle2
state: ONLINE
 scan: none requested
config:

```
    NAME        STATE    READ WRITE CKSUM
    oracle2     ONLINE    0    0    0
     c2t1d0s0   ONLINE    0    0    0
     c2t1d0s1   ONLINE    0    0    0
```

10.17. Detach disk from Pool

To detach a disk from zpool, we can simply use detach keyword followed by zpool name and diskname.

-bash-3.2# **zpool detach datapool c2t0d0s0**

-bash-3.2#

-bash-3.2# zpool status datapool

 pool: datapool
state: ONLINE
 scan: none requested
config:

```
    NAME        STATE    READ WRITE CKSUM
    datapool    ONLINE    0    0    0
     c2t0d0s1   ONLINE    0    0    0
```

errors: No known data errors

10.18. Mirroring the existing pool

Zpool provides flexible options to add, remove disks from existing pool by simply executing a single command. A new disk can be attached to an existing pool in mirror at runtime by simply executing a single command with attach keyword.

-bash-3.2# **zpool attach -f datapool c2t0d0s1 c2t0d0s0**
-bash-3.2#

11.   ZFS Snapshot

A snapshot is a read only copy of the filesystem or partition at a point of time. Initially snapshots don't consume any new space and simply maintains a record of all inode numbers of the existing data. However the snapshot size keeps on growing when the changes are made to original data.

11.1.   Features of ZFS snapshots

a.   The snapshot ideally consumes zero space on pool at the time of creation.

b.   Since it works on inode concept, hence ideally a snapshot is created on the same pool, because inode reference can't be made on other disk/slice.

c.   A ZFS snapshots can persist across server reboots and hence reliable for data recovery until and unless there is some hardware issue on disk.

d.   A zfs snapshot can be created of complete zpool or of a specific filesystem under a zpool.

11.2. Check all snapshots

To check all snapshots configured on our system we can use simple zfs list command or even add –t snapshot to see only the snapshot list.

```
-bash-3.2# zfs list -t snapshot
no datasets available
```

11.3. Create new snapshot

A new snapshot can be created by using keyword snapshot followed by zpool and filesystem name. For example lets create a snapshot of data filesystem under zpool named datapool.

```
-bash-3.2# zfs snapshot datapool/data@snap1_Tuesday

-bash-3.2# zfs list -t snapshot
NAME                    USED  AVAIL  REFER  MOUNTPOINT
datapool/data@snap1_tuesday    0    -  10.0M  -

-bash-3.2# zfs list -r datapool
NAME                    USED  AVAIL  REFER  MOUNTPOINT
datapool           10.3M  454M  35K  /datapool
datapool/data         10.0M  454M 10.0M  /datapool/data
datapool/data@snap1_tuesday     0    -  10.0M  -
datapool/myora          31K  454M  31K  /datapool/myora
datapool/oracle         31K  454M  31K  /datapool/oracle
datapool/solaris        31K  454M  31K  /datapool/solaris
-bash-3.2#
```

11.4. Quick Tip 14: Where snapshot is stored ?

You might be thinking where the snapshot is stored and how it is accessed. The answer is simple, under the same zpool, it is hidden inside .zfs directory.

```
-bash-3.2# cd /datapool/data

-bash-3.2# ls -al
total 20493
drwxr-xr-x  2 root    root        3 Apr  1 14:54 .
drwxr-xr-x  6 root    root        6 Apr  1 14:53 ..
-rw------T  1 root    root    10485760 Apr  1 14:54 file1

-bash-3.2# cd .zfs
bash-3.2# ls -altr
dr-xr-xr-x  2 root    root        2 Dec 17 17:04 snapshot
```

As we can see above this hidden directory is even not visible under ls with "-a" option, however we can browse into this directory by typing cd.

11.5. Same inode number concept in snapshot.

Let's see how snapshots contain the same data by referencing the same inode numbers.

```
-bash-3.2# ls -ail
total 20490
     4 drwxr-xr-x  2 root    root        3 Apr  1 14:54 .
     4 dr-xr-xr-x  3 root    root        3 Apr  1 14:56 ..
     8 -rw------T  1 root    root    10485760 Apr  1 14:54 file1
```

```
-bash-3.2# ls -il /datapool/data/
total 20487
      8 -rw------T  1 root    root    10485760 Apr  1 14:54 file1

-bash-3.2# pwd
/datapool/data/.zfs/snapshot/snap1_tuesday
```

So here we can see the same inode numbers of the files under the filesystem and the snapshot. Hence we can say that same data is referenced in snapshot, and that's why their size is practically 0 on creation. When we change this file, then the new data is written with new inode number and hence the size of snapshot increases.

11.6. Deleting snapshot

We can delete the snapshot in a similar manner as we do for zfs filesystems by using the destroy keyword.

```
-bash-3.2# zfs list
NAME                      USED  AVAIL  REFER  MOUNTPOINT
datapool                  10.3M  454M   35K  /datapool
datapool/data             10.0M  454M  10.0M  /datapool/data
datapool/data@snap1_tuesday    0    -  10.0M  -
datapool/myora              31K  454M   31K  /datapool/myora
datapool/oracle             31K  454M   31K  /datapool/oracle
datapool/solaris            31K  454M   31K  /datapool/solaris
oracle2                    135K  952M   32K  /oracle2
oracle2/firstpart           31K  952M   31K  /oracle2/firstpart
```

-bash-3.2# zfs destroy datapool/data@snap1_tuesday

```
-bash-3.2# zfs list
NAME            USED  AVAIL  REFER  MOUNTPOINT
datapool        10.3M  454M   35K   /datapool
datapool/data   10.0M  454M  10.0M  /datapool/data
datapool/myora   31K   454M   31K   /datapool/myora
datapool/oracle  31K   454M   31K   /datapool/oracle
datapool/solaris 31K   454M   31K   /datapool/solaris
oracle2         135K   952M   32K   /oracle2
oracle2/firstpart 31K  952M   31K   /oracle2/firstpart
```

11.7. ZFS restore(with same inode number)

Zfs also provides an option to do data restore or rollback with same inode numbers and hence restoring this data will not occupy any new space.

-bash-3.2# zfs rollback datapool/solaris@newsnapshot

Otherwise if you copy data from zfs snapshot to the filesystem then this data will use unix cp command and the data will be copied with new inode numbers and hence more space will be taken.

12. Package Administration

Solaris provides a very easy way to do package administration by using some commands prefixed with pkg and the usage of these commands are pretty simple.

Package Administration Commands

Some commands prefixed with pkg and the usage of these commands are pretty simple we can manage new or existing packages on our solaris system. However five of them are the most important utilities as they provide almost all required options which are usually required for basic package management.

- Pkginfo :- Lists all packages installed on system.
- Pkgadd :- Installs new software package.
- Pkgrm :- Removes existing package from system.
- Pkgchk :- Checks the installed package details.
- Pkgtrans :- Translate a package directory to datastream or vice versa.

We will check what these commands do in the next sections.

12.1. Two formats of package

A Package that we install is of two types either directory format or, data stream format i.e. a single file type.

Any software we want to install. Two format:

1. Directory Format (also called File system format) :- Can have multiple files and directories.
2. Data Stream :- We can combine several packages into a single file and this is called data stream.

12.2. Types of Package

In Solaris, a package is either related to the operating system, or a package provided by various other software organizations also called third party software/package for different hardware or software functions.

Hence depending upon the source of package and its usage, we can divide a package into two different types.

a.   OS related package (starts with SUNw or Sun FreeWare-SFW)
b.   Third party package starts with any other name.

For example:- In pkginfo output, we can see different types of packages.

Operating System Related Package

system   SFWgawk   gawk - pattern scanning and processing language
system   SFWncur   ncurses - new curses library

Third Party package

system   BRCMbnxe   Broadcom NetXtreme II 10GbE NIC Driver
system   CADP160   Adaptec Ultra160 SCSI Host Adapter Driver
fds   EABpython   Python for the EAB FDS environment.
application INITTOOL   Navisphere Initialization Wizard

12.3.   Check if any package is installed

Now we will look the above commands' usage and learn how to do package management in solaris. To check all installed packages on our solaris system we can use pkginfo command.

bash-3.2# **pkginfo | grep -i zip**

system   SUNWbzip   The bzip compression utility
system   SUNWgzip   The GNU Zip (gzip) compression utility
system   SUNWzip   The Info-Zip (zip) compression utility

system   SUNWzlib   The Zip compression library
bash-3.2#

The details of a specific package can be viewed with "-l" option.
bash-3.2# **pkginfo -l SUNWzip**

```
  PKGINST:  SUNWzip
    NAME:  The Info-Zip (zip) compression utility
 CATEGORY:  system
    ARCH:  i386
  VERSION:  11.10.0,REV=2005.01.08.01.09
  BASEDIR:  /
   VENDOR:  Sun Microsystems, Inc.
     DESC:  The Info-Zip (zip) compression utility
   PSTAMP:  sfw10-patch-x20100616081238
 INSTDATE:  Jan 31 2013 15:20
  HOTLINE:  Please contact your local service provider
   STATUS:  completely installed
    FILES:      6 installed pathnames
             2 shared pathnames
             2 directories
             4 executables
           772 blocks used (approx)
```

12.4. Adding Package

To add a new package in Solaris, we can use pkgadd command .
bash-3.2# pkgadd SUNWoptdir
pkgadd: ERROR: no packages were found in </var/spool/pkg>
By default, our system looks for new package in /var/spoolpkg
directory.
To install a package from current directory, we can use below command.
bash-3.2# **pkgadd -d . SUNWoptdir**

You can also mention the path of the package instead of dot, i.e. current directory.

Processing package instance <SUNWoptdir> from </var/tmp/soft/packages>

Solaris Test Package (opt)(all) 11.10.0,REV=3009.09.08.16.34
Copyright 2007 Sun Microsystems, Inc. All rights reserved.
Use is subject to license terms.

12.5.   Removing Package

To remove a package we can simply use pkgrm command.

bash-3.2# **pkgrm SUNWoptdir**

The following package is currently installed:
   SUNWoptdir Solaris Test Package (opt)
        (all) 11.10.0,REV=3009.09.08.16.34

Do you want to remove this package? [y,n,?,q] y

12.6.   **Quick Tip 15: Check what is there in Package**

Now we know how to see all installed package, list package details, add or remove a new package. Not only this, oracle solaris also provides an option to check what is there in a package means what all files/directories which will be installed by the package.
We can use pkgchk command with –l or –v options to get these details.

bash-3.2# **pkgchk -l SUNWoptdir**
Pathname: /opt/packages/bin

Type: directory
Expected mode: 0755
Expected owner: root
Expected group: sys
Referenced by the following packages:
    SUNWoptdir
Current status: installed

Pathname: /opt/packages/bin/testfile.sh
Type: regular file
Expected mode: 0555
Expected owner: root

bash-3.2# **pkgchk -v SUNWoptdir**
/opt/packages/bin
/opt/packages/bin/testfile.sh

12.7.   Transform Directory package into a single file.

Earlier we have discussed that there are two types of packages, one is directory format, and the other one is datastream format. In this section we will see the command how we can transform the directory package into a datastream format.

The command used is pkgtrans, and then option "-s" is used which will instruct pkgtrans command to convert the directory package into stream package rather than filesystem package, then we will mention the source directory containing packages followed by the name of new datastream package.

bash-3.2# **pkgtrans -s /var/tmp/soft/packages/**
/var/tmp/soft/mypack.pkg

The following packages are available:
  1 SUNWoptdir   Solaris Test Package (opt)
          (all) 11.10.0,REV=3009.09.08.16.34
  2 SUNWusrdir   Solaris Test Package
          (all) 11.10.0,REV=3009.09.08.16.34

Select package(s) you wish to process (or 'all' to process
all packages). (default: all) [?,??,q]:
Transferring <SUNWoptdir> package instance
Transferring <SUNWusrdir> package instance

Now by using above command we have made a single .pkg file named
/var/tmp/soft/mypack.pkg from a directory which contained two
packages.

12.8.   Quick Tip 16: Check which packages are there in pkg file.

Now suppose you want to check what all packages contained in a pkg
file, so we can use head command to view this information.
bash-3.2# **head -5 ./mypack.pkg**
PaCkAgE DaTaStReAm
SUNWoptdir 1 76
SUNWusrdir 1 76
# end of header
BASEDIR=/opt/packages

To install this pkg file, use pkgadd command with –d option and mention the path of the package.

bash-3.2# **pkgadd -d ../mypack.pkg**

The following packages are available:
  1 SUNWoptdir   Solaris Test Package (opt)
          (all) 11.10.0,REV=3009.09.08.16.34
  2 SUNWusrdir   Solaris Test Package
          (all) 11.10.0,REV=3009.09.08.16.34

13.   Patch Administration

Till now we have seen package administration is solaris, however there are much more features available in this operating system that needs to be explored. Package is a new software that we want to install, however a patch refers to the modification/improvement in an existing package that is released by companies for bug fixing.

Suppose you have installed a package and after some time you found its behaving abnormally, hence you will raise ticket towards oracle, and oracle will provide a patch for bug fixing. Solaris 10 OS patches are now available by Tuesday closest to 17th of each month. However in big companies they used to run patch updates each quarter or by every six months because this is not possible to run patch updates every month.

13.1.   Check installed patches

Before installing any new patch, we must be aware what patches are already applied on our system , so that already installed patch can be avoided. To check installed patches, we can use patchadd command with –p option to print all patches available.

-bash-3.2# **patchadd -p | more**

Patch: 125096-15 Obsoletes: Requires: Incompatibles: Packages:
SUNWocfd SUNWkvm SUNWcar SUNWcakr SUNWcsu SUNWcsr
SUNWcnetr SUNWckr SUNWcsd SUNWo
s86r SUNWperl584core SUNWperl584usr SUNWesu SUNWxwdv
SUNW1394 SUNW1394h SUNWgssc SUNWkrbr SUNWkrbu SUNWbip
SUNWtftp SUNWrcmdc SUNWtnetc SUNWrcmd
r SUNWrcmds SUNWscpr SUNWscpu SUNWaac SUNWaccr
SUNWaccu SUNWaudd SUNWad810 SUNWadpu320 SUNWagp
SUNWagph SUNWamd8111s SUNWamr SUNWcslr SUNWbtool
SUNWtoo SUNWapct SUNWib SUNWarc SUNWarcr SUNWrsg
SUNWhea SUNWgssdh SUNWgssk SUNWipoib SUNWmdr
SUNWmdu SUNWintgige SUNWipc SUNWipfh SUNWpapi SUNW
ippcore SUNWipplr SUNWipplu SUNWas

We can also grep a single patch for which we want to see the
information. In case output is displayed, then this patch is already
installed.

-bash-3.2# **patchadd -p | grep -i 140388**

Patch: 144501-19 Obsoletes: 118736-02 120045-01 120086-02 122184-03
122409-01 122829-02 124238-01 125168-01 125365-03 125415-01 125550-01
125567-02 126259-03 126261-02 126318-01 126656-02 127738-02 127999-01
128001-01 128327-01 136890-01 138080-01 138090-01 138111-01 138129-01
138240-01 138262-03 138292-01 138294-

13.2. Add new patch

Now we have checked all available patches, and the required patch is
not yet installed, we can go ahead and install the newly downloaded
patch using the patchadd command simply without any option.

-bash-3.2# **patchadd 123456-01**
Validating patches...

Loading patches installed on the system...

13.3. Remove a patch

Similar to patchadd, we also have a command available to remove the existing installed patch from our system. Pkgrm command can be used to remove the existing installed patch and the usage is simple just like the pkgadd command.

#patchrm patch_name

13.4. Quick Tip 17: How to know whether a patch requires a reboot or not?

Usually a patch which (a) don't make any changes in kernel or kernel modules, or (b) which doesn't update complete system environment doesn't require a reboot to implement.

The best practice to determine whether it requires system reboot or not is to go inside patch directory and check readme file for the instructions.

14. Quick Tip 18: Disable IP forwarding in Solaris?

IP forwarding allows our source system to forward the requests to the next DNS server in case the query IP/server is not directly reachable from the source node. In Solaris, by default IP forwarding is enabled, which means if someone queries google.com and it is reachable from my solaris box then my system will route the packet to the nearest gateway and the next server in network from here it can reach google.com. if we disable Ip forwarding then this packet is not delivered to next gateway or server for further query and the packet is rejected.

To protect our server from unwanted traffic, some critical nodes usually disable IP forwarding on the system. To achieve this we can use below command and disable IP forwarding at runtime.

#ndd -set /dev/ip ip_forwarding 0

This command can be added in any runlevel script to achieve this task on system boot.

Questions

1. What is hostname and IP address ?
2. How can you capture network packets between two nodes ?
3. How to assign multiple IPs to the same interface ?
4. Add the new virtual IP address permanently to the system.
5. How to check ssh service status on the system ?
6. How we can create a ZFS snapshot ?
7. What is meant by zpool ?
8. What is ZFS and how can you create it ?
9. How to add and remove a package?
10. How to delete a ZFS snapshot ?

15.   Quick Tip 19: How to mount/umount all ZFS partitions in one go?

To mount all zfs partitions in one go use "zfs mount -a" command.

-bash-3.2# **zfs mount -a**

-bash-3.2# **df -h**

Filesystem	size	used	avail	capacity	Mounted on
/dev/dsk/c0d0s0	14G	8.4G	5.0G	63%	/
/devices	0K	0K	0K	0%	/devices
ctfs	0K	0K	0K	0%	/system/contract
proc	0K	0K	0K	0%	/proc

```
mnttab           0K   0K   0K   0%   /etc/mnttab
swap            2.0G 1.0M 2.0G  1%   /etc/svc/volatile
objfs            0K   0K   0K   0%   /system/object
sharefs          0K   0K   0K   0%   /etc/dfs/sharetab
fd               0K   0K   0K   0%   /dev/fd
swap            2.0G 188K 2.0G  1%   /tmp
swap            2.0G 44K  2.0G  1%   /var/run
datapool        464M 35K  243M  1%   /datapool
datapool/data   464M 10M  243M  4%   /datapool/data
datapool/myora  464M 31K  243M  1%   /datapool/myora
datapool/oracle 464M 31K  243M  1%   /datapool/oracle
datapool/solaris 464M 210M 243M 47%  /datapool/solaris
oracle2         952M 32K  952M  1%   /oracle2
oracle2/firstpart 952M 31K 952M 1%   /oracle2/firstpart
```

<u>For un mounting</u>
Similar to mount options, for umounting we can use "unmount -a"
option with zfs command.
-bash-3.2# zfs unmount -a

16.   <u>Quick Tip 20</u>: ZFS: changing default mount point while creation or after creation.

In zfs,we can change the mount point as per our requirements to any directory/path.

```
bash-3.2# zpool list
NAME    SIZE ALLOC FREE  CAP HEALTH ALTROOT
datapool 496M 221M 275M  44% ONLINE -
oracle2  984M 141K  984M  0% ONLINE -
```

```
bash-3.2# zfs list -r oracle2
NAME            USED  AVAIL  REFER  MOUNTPOINT
oracle2         141K  952M   32K    /oracle2
oracle2/firstpart  31K  952M  31K  /oracle2/firstpart
```

bash-3.2# **zfs set mountpoint=/mysolaris oracle2/firstpart**

```
bash-3.2# zfs list -r oracle2
NAME            USED  AVAIL  REFER  MOUNTPOINT
oracle2         152K  952M   32K    /oracle2
oracle2/firstpart  31K  952M  31K  /mysolaris
```

<u>Setting mount point while Creating ZFS</u>
bash-3.2# **zfs create -o mountpoint=/oracle oracle2/mydata**
bash-3.2#
```
bash-3.2# zfs list -r oracle2
NAME            USED  AVAIL  REFER  MOUNTPOINT
oracle2         198K  952M   31K    /oracle2
oracle2/firstpart  31K  952M  31K  /mysolaris
oracle2/mydata     31K  952M  31K  /oracle
```

17.   **Quick Tip 21**: **Resolve problem with ZFS pool version.**
Sometimes when we import zpool from one system to another, it gets corrupted or started showing error while importing. For this to work, we need to upgrade the pool version.

a.   <u>Check the ZFS pool.</u>
-bash-3.2# zpool upgrade -v | more
This system is currently running ZFS pool version 29.

The following versions are supported:

VER DESCRIPTION

--- --

1 Initial ZFS version
2 Ditto blocks (replicated metadata)
3 Hot spares and double parity RAID-Z
4 zpool history
5 Compression using the gzip algorithm
6 bootfs pool property
7 Separate intent log devices
8   Delegated administration

b.   <u>Upgrade the pool after importing.</u>

-bash-3.2# **zpool upgrade**

This system is currently running ZFS pool version 29.

All pools are formatted using this version.

Zpool import <pool_name>

Zpool export <pool_name> can be used to migrate pools between solaris systems.

Chapter -4
SMF, NFS and AutoFS
Day 3

1.   Boot Design Overview

The most important thing to understand how operating system works is to know how it boots, and what all files a server uses while booting. Also during boot, what all options provided and what is the difference in booting when we talk about sparc and x86 boxes.

Let's have a look at the boot process diagram to understand how our OS boots up.

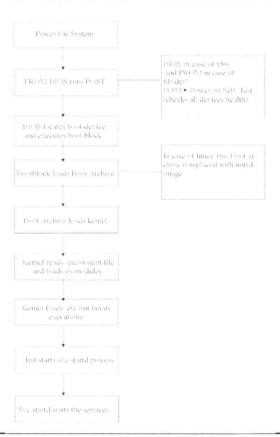

As seen above the boot process is quite simple. A user presses power button and the system is started, the control is sent to ROM where BIOS i.e. Basic Input output system is loaded. The BIOS runs a POST i.e. Power on self test which check all hardware devices attached to the system. Now this BIOS send the control to GRUB in case of x86 systems, otherwise to OK prompt which is already on ROM in case of sparc systems. This ROM(sparc), or GRUB(x86) will now checks the boot device and runs the boot block.

This boot block contains address of the boot archive and kernel. First the boot archive is loaded in RAM on which kernel is loaded. This kernel checks /etc/system file and load/change the kernel modules defined. After kernel is loaded; control is given to /etc/init which loads the runlevel scripts and then control is given to svc.startd process which loads all SMF services.

Quick Points to note
➢   X86 provides BIOS, sparc provides ok prompt.
➢   Failsafe Mode → used for troubleshooting purpose.
➢   Sparc Servers → provides eeprom command to change boot parameters while system is running.
➢   Fdisk → exclusively available for x86 only since it support dual boot and dual labeled disks. Useful for changing active partition, and for converting disk from efi to smi.
➢   Failsafe in sparc machine:- ok> boot –F failsafe
Failsafe in x86 box can be taken by choosing appropriate option from GRUB menu.

1.1.   Difference between failsafe and single user mode
The first question when we learn solaris after linux is what is this failsafe mode and how come its different from single user mode. Failsafe mode is an additional mode provided by Solaris OS to simplify the troubleshooting and maintenance of our OS.

✓　A single user mode boots the system with limited services and uses the real disk available on the system for booting/mounting root filesystem.

However failsafe mode boots the system from mentioned ramdisk (the miniroot) which provides enough tools for recovery and aims to provide a facility for administrators to recover the bad system.

✓　Since failsafe mode uses RAM disk, it is first suitable option when our root filesystem needs fsck or any task needs to be done on umounted root filesystem. Since the system will be booted from ramdisk, hence it will not prompt for root password, and this option can be used to crack forgotten root password.

1.2.　How to see boot archive files?

The boot archive is a subset of a root(/) file system which contains all of the kernel modules, driver.conf files, and necessary configuration files of /etc

The files in the boot archive are read by the kernel before the root file system is mounted and is necessary to load kernel on the disk. Once the root file system is mounted, boot archive is discarded by the kernel from memory and the I/O is performed against the root device.

bash-3.2# bootadm list-archive
etc/rtc_config
etc/system
etc/name_to_major
etc/driver_aliases
etc/name_to_sysnum
etc/dacf.conf
etc/driver_classes
etc/path_to_inst
etc/mach
etc/cluster/nodeid
etc/devices/devid_cache

etc/devices/mdi_scsi_vhci_cache
etc/devices/mdi_ib_cache
etc/devices/pci_unitaddr_persistent
kernel
platform/i86pc/biosint
platform/i86pc/kernel
platform/i86pc/ucode/GenuineIntel
platform/i86pc/ucode/AuthenticAMD
platform/i86hvm
boot/solaris/bootenv.rc
boot/solaris/devicedb/master
boot/acpi/tables
bash-3.2#

1.3.   Checking boot menu entries

We can check the boot menu list by using the same bootadm command, and can update the same also.

-bash-3.2# bootadm list-menu
The location for the active GRUB menu is: /boot/grub/menu.lst
default 0
timeout 10
0 Oracle Solaris 10 8/11 s10x_u10wos_17b X86
1 Solaris failsafe
-bash-3.2#

Other options supported by this command are as follows:
bootadm update-archive [-vn] [-R altroot [-p platform>]]
     bootadm list-archive [-R altroot [-p platform>]]
     bootadm set-menu [-R altroot] key=value
     bootadm list-menu [-R altroot]

2. Where kernel is located in Solaris ?

In Solaris sparc server, kernel is located under /platform/'uname -m' directory. The full path of kernel location is as follows:

/platform/'uname -m'/kernel/sparcv9/unix
/platform/'uname -m'/kernel/sparcv9/genunix

Genunix is the kernel binary generated from the common source code on all hardware platforms, however unix binary is specific to the hardware on which kernel is running. In x86, the genunix generated lies under /kernel and the unix named kernel file exists in /platform/i86pc/kernel/.

3. Init Runlevels

Init is the first process started by the kernel and it starts the services based on the runlevel type i.e. which runlevel 1,2,3,4,5 or 6. A system can be booted in one runlevel and this runlevel defines what all services it will load.

Till Solaris 9, runlevel was controlled by /etc/inittab file. An entry is made in inittab file with initdefault which is scanned only when init is initially invoked on system startup.

cat /etc/inittab | grep –I initdefault
is:3:initdefault:

In tha above entry, 3 is the default runlevel of our system in which it gets booted on startup. Now we can change is:3 to any other runlevel number we want.

Init runlevels define the group of scripts/services that are loaded in run level2 as defined in /etc/rc2.d/ directory. For example:- init 2 will load below services.

```
bash-3.2# ls /etc/rc2.d/
K05appserv        README          S42ncakmod
S81dodatadm.udaplt
K06mipagent     S05vmware-tools   S47pppd          S89PRESERVE
K15imq          S10lu          S70uucp           S94ncalogd
K16apache       S20sysetup      S72autoinstall   S96fdslic
K27boot.server  S40llc2        S73cachefs.daemon  S98deallocate
bash-3.2#
```

S are the startup scripts and K defines the Kill scripts. The S scripts are started when system enters into this runlevel and the K scripts/services are killed. The different runlevels in Solaris are numbered from 0 to 6.

init 6 or init 0   → Reboot
Init s/S   → Single User Mode. No critical file system available.
     Useful when wrong entry in vfstab.
Init 1   → Same as "init s", only difference is that available file system will be mounted.
Init 2   → All services are running except nfs/network resource and GUI.
Init 3   → Full multiuser
Init 4   → Reserved
Init 5   → Shutdown and poweroff
Init 6   → Reboot

However with solaris 10 Init runlevel is not defined in inittab, it is controlled by smf(service management facility). In Solaris 10, instead of runlevels, oracle has created the services' group under SMF and provides a group of services together and these different groups are called as different milestones.

So overall the purpose remained the same. In init runlevels we define different scripts/services under a directory and in Solaris these scripts/services are grouped under milestone which is further controlled by SMF. However it increased the complexity of OS working, but it provides fast service startup as compared to traditional linux like init runlevel startup.

Based on what services are started in which milestone, we can relate the init run levels with provided milestones in Solaris 10. Solaris defines three such milestones, which roughly relate to the traditional Solaris/linux runlevels:

svc:/milestone/single-user   >> init S
svc:/milestone/multi-user   >> init 2
svc:/milestone/multi-user-server   >> init 3
none   >> ok> boot –m milestone=none
all   >> svcadm milstone all

4.   Quick Tip 1: Two securities on console.

We can maintain dual level of security on our system console.
4.1.   By changing default password Admin/Admin and setting it to some complex password.
4.2.   By assigning console in different network as of server. Now ping –s <broadcast_ip> → will get list of all systems connected in the network and can get the SC IP. Its good to have Ip in private network

We can configure our Serial console from our solaris server by installing a package called RSC which will provide console commands on OS. For example:- Trace ip, change ip/password of console from our OS.

5.   Quick Tip 2: How to login and quit SC console?

The first basic tip when dealing with our system console is to know how we can login to the console and leave its session. It looks like dummy question, but when we work on production server, sometimes it takes time to identify how to take/leave the console session.

Oracle has different hardware models available in market. For each hardware family, the method to access console differs slightly. LOM or Lights out manager is the first console family released by Solaris to provide server remote access and thereafter different console versions are released.

Let's have a look at different console available and the way to access them.

- ➢ LOM (Lights Out Manager)
- ➢ ALOM (Advanced Lights Out Manager)
- ➢ ILOM (Integrated Lights Out Manager)
- ➢ ELOM (Embedded Lights Out Manager)
- ➢ RSC (Remote Serial Console)
- ➢ XSCF (eXtended System Control Facility)

5.1. How to login into console?

5.1.1. LOM and ALOM can be accessed by using below command.
Sc> console –f   ### forcefully take the console for writing/command input.
Ok>

5.1.2. ILOM and ELOM console can be invoked using below command.
-> start /SP/console
Are you sure you want to start /SP/console (y/n) ? y
Serial console started. To stop, type #.

ILOM also provides GUI interface to check hardware status. To check its GUI interface, simply type the IP address of the ILOM console port in the browser.

In case of a Blade server, first we need to start the cli mode for the blade.
 -> cd /CH/BL2/SP/cli
/CH/BL2/SP/cli

-> start
Are you sure you want to start /CH/BL2/SP/cli (y/n)? y
Password:

5.1.3. Login to console from RSC.
To reach to server console from RSC, we can use the command
"console".
rsc> console
Console session already in use.

If the console is busy or already in use, then we need to reset the console
and clear any open sessions: From the rsc prompt run resetsc:
rsc> resetrsc

5.1.4. Login into console from XSCF
As defined by its name, XSCF provides extended system control facility
and provides one or more domains attached to the XSCF.
To login into console from XSCF, we must know in which domain we
want to login.
To see all the domains on a server:

XSCF> showdomainstatus -a
DID Domain   Status
00   Running
01   Running
02   -
03   -
If we want to login into domain 0 :
XSCF> console -d 01
Here "-d" mention the domain number.

5.2.   Exit from System to Console
Just press . followed by hash to leave the console.
#.

6.   Controlling legacy services in Solaris.

Legacy services are the old services(used prior to solaris 10) which are stored and controlled from script files saved inside /etc/rc*.d/ directory where * represents the runlevel. Solaris makes a list of these services under SMF, however executes them from same script files. Lets have a look at these script files where they are stored.

Script Files
The separate scripts for each service are saved under a directory named rc*.d under /etc where * represents the runlevel or equivalent milestone.

bash-3.2# ls -l /etc/ | grep -i rc[0-9].d
drwxr-xr-x 2 root   sys   512 May 2 2013 rc0.d
drwxr-xr-x 2 root   sys   512 May 2 2013 rc1.d → Scripts will be called on init 1.
drwxr-xr-x 2 root   sys   512 May 2 2013 rc2.d
drwxr-xr-x 2 root   sys   512 May 2 2013 rc3.d

These scripts are referred by a single script file called /etc/rc[0-3], where [0-3]corresponding to the respective runlevel.

Services Scripts Links in /etc/rc
-bash-3.2# ls -ld /etc/rc*
lrwxrwxrwx 1 root   root   11 Jan 10 12:11 /etc/rc0 -> ../sbin/rc0
drwxr-xr-x 2 root   sys   512 Mar 12 15:46 /etc/rc0.d
lrwxrwxrwx 1 root   root   11 Jan 10 12:11 /etc/rc1 -> ../sbin/rc1
→ *This script file /sbin/rc1 is called by init process which will then call each and every script inside /etc/rc1.d directory. Lets have a look at these runlevel control(RC) scripts.*

Runlevel control scripts:

```
-bash-3.2# ls -ld /sbin/rc*
-rwxr--r--  3 root    sys         1983 Jan 22  2005 /sbin/rc0
-rwxr--r--  1 root    sys         2242 Jan 22  2005 /sbin/rc1
-rwxr--r--  1 root    sys         2536 Jan 22  2005 /sbin/rc2
-rwxr--r--  1 root    sys         2567 Jan 22  2005 /sbin/rc3
-rwxr--r--  3 root    sys         1983 Jan 22  2005 /sbin/rc5
-rwxr--r--  3 root    sys         1983 Jan 22  2005 /sbin/rc6
-rwxr--r--  1 root    sys         5125 Jan 22  2005 /sbin/rcS
```

These files are responsible for handling the linux legacy services.

7.   System Shutdown

As a linux administrator we should know how to bring down our system gracefully and if its not killing the processes gracefully then how we can bring them down forcefully. Oracle Solaris provides various commands for giving graceful shutdown and for forceful shutdown of our system.

7.1.   Graceful Shutdown

For giving graceful shutdown to our system, Oracle Solaris provides below two utilities.
➢   Init (runlevels s,0,1,5,6)
➢   Shutdown (runlevels s,0,1,5,6)

a.   Shutdown command notifies users and gives grace period of 60 minutes to save data. We can also customize the notification and time. Shutdown also sends the broadcast message.
b.   We can cancel the shutdown command but not init command.

7.2. Immediate Shutdown (Ungraceful)

Sometimes graceful shutdown is not successful due to some hanged processes and we may need to go with forceful or ungraceful shutdown. Graceful shutdown executes the kill scripts and then shuts the system, however immediate shutdown simply frees up system memory and shut the system down without closing the processes gracefully and hence is not recommended in general day to day practice. However in emergency situations, we can use these commands for immediate shutdown.

We can use below commands for immediate shutdown.
➢ Halt
➢ Poweroff
➢ Reboot (to restart the system forcefully without running kill scripts)

Let's see few command examples we can use for graceful shutdown.

init 5 (to poweroff our solaris system gracefully)
shutdown –y –g 600 –I 6 "Please save your jobs. System gets rebooted in few minutes."

In above shutdown command:
–y (yes to send the broadcast message)
 –g grace-period(in sec.)
 –I init-state
"this message sent as broadcast message"

8. SMF (Service Management Facility)

Service Management Facility (SMF) is a new feature introduced with Solaris 10 operating system which creates a unified model of all services and the service management is done through the new SMF interface replacing init.d scripts.

> Started from Solaris 10 onwards.
> Till Solaris 9, only legacy services were there.
> But in Solaris 10, almost 95% services are controlled by SMF and only 5% are legacy.
> SMF maintains, monitors and restarts system services automatically and helps to auto heal the system breakdown.
> SMF maintains and displays clear dependencies and hence it is easier to check and troubleshoot the process startup.
> SMF allows system to start various services in parallel.

8.1. Starting Legacy Service Vs SMF service

In Solaris, for managing SMF services we have few commands like svcs, and svcadm, where svcadm allows us to restart/enable/disable the SMF services. However the legacy service start/stop procedure remains the same as done in old servers by running the initiation script with argument start/stop or restart.

How to start Legacy service?
/etc/init.d/<service> start/stop/restart

How to start SMF service?
Svcadm –v <enable>/disable/restart/refresh <service_name>

8.2. Advantages of SMF over legacy services

1. Provides parallel service startup
2. Auto service restart can be monitored by using Solaris fault manager alongwith SMF.
3. Fast service startup done on server reboot makes the system to boot up fast.
4. Service status can be checked with one command (svcs –a | grep –I service_name)
5. Check the dependencies of the service. (svcs –l <service>)

6.   Troubleshoot the service by dependencies and log file. (svcs –xv <service>)

7.   Centralized repository for services (/etc/svc/repository.db -→ read it with svccfg, or svcprop). System always takes backup of this file.

8.   Daemon which starts SMF -→ svc.startd and svc.configd is responsible for its editing.

-bash-3.2# ps -ef | grep -i svc
    root   9   1   0 16:36:46 ?   0:01 /lib/svc/bin/svc.startd
    root   11   1   0 16:36:46 ?   0:04 /lib/svc/bin/svc.configd

-bash-3.2# cat /etc/inittab | grep -i svc

smf::sysinit:/lib/svc/bin/svc.startd   >/dev/msglog 2<>/dev/msglog </dev/console

            That is why solaris 10 boots up fast.

9.   Services can be enabled and disabled temporarily. In legacy services, rename S script to some other name, example:- svcadm –v disable –t telnet. (-t for temporary disable)

-bash-3.2# svcadm -v disable -t telnet

svc:/network/telnet:default temporarily disabled.

10.   Configuration files are written in XML.

11.   We can migrate legacy service into smf. Can't convert smf service to legacy.

8.3.   Quick Tip 3: How to know if a service is managed by SMF or its legacy?

To know if a particular service is managed by SMF, we can simply look this into svcs command output by looking at FMRI and State.

-bash-3.2# svcs -a | more
STATE   STIME   FMRI(fault management resource identifier)
legacy_run   16:36:56 lrc:/etc/rcS_d/S50sk98sol
legacy_run   16:36:56 lrc:/etc/rcS_d/S80ChSysSetup

```
legacy_run    16:36:56 lrc:/etc/rcS_d/S81NetConfigSetup
legacy_run    16:37:03 lrc:/etc/rc2_d/S10lu
legacy_run    16:37:03 lrc:/etc/rc2_d/S20sysetup
legacy_run    16:37:03 lrc:/etc/rc2_d/S40llc2
legacy_run    16:37:24 lrc:/etc/rc3_d/S84appserv
legacy_run    16:37:24 lrc:/etc/rc3_d/S97emcmonitor
disabled      16:36:46 svc:/system/metainit:default
disabled      16:36:46 svc:/network/ipfilter:default
online        16:36:48 svc:/system/scheduler:default
```

FMRI shows the category of the service.

The FMRI lrc shows that it's a legacy service and svc denotes this is smf managed service. Similarly legacy_run is the method used for managing services via /etc/init.d/, and for SMF managed services, it will show the status whether it's disabled/online/offline.

8.4. Different states of SMF services.

SMF services have different states depending on whether its running, or is stopped, or in faulty state i.e. not able to start.

1)   Online → Service is up and running

2)   Disabled → Service is not enabled and not running.

3)   Offline → Service is up but not running. (Most probably the problem with dependencies)

4)   Maintenance -→ Service is up but not running. (Problem with the config file of the service. We need to edit the config file. Then stop and start)

5)   Degraded Mode → (still no improvement)

6)   Uninitialized → (service is up but not running. Two problems:- dependencies and config files error)

8.5.   Quick Tip 4: How to get process id of a SMF service ?

We know that we can see the status of the service, however sometimes we need to know the pid or process id of the process to troubleshoot the issues with the running service like high memory usage, or to check if the correct arguments have been passed. To check the pid we can simply use –p argument with svc command.

-bash-3.2# svcs -p svc:/network/ssh:default
STATE   STIME   FMRI
online   16:37:03 svc:/network/ssh:default
         16:37:03   621 sshd

8.6.   Where are files stored for SMF services?

Each SMF service is managed by creating xml files containing the service details how to start/stop it. As a unix/linux administrator we should know where these files are stored and what they contain.

-bash-3.2# cd /var/svc/profile/
-bash-3.2# ls
generic_limited_net.xml   inetd_services.xml   ns_files.xml
ns_none.xml   prophist.SUNWcsr
generic_open.xml   inetd_upgrade.xml   ns_ldap.xml
platform_i86pc.xml   upgrade.app.20130131152753
generic.xml   name_service.xml   ns_nis.xml
platform_none.xml   upgrade.app.20130131161034
inetd_generic.xml   ns_dns.xml   ns_nisplus.xml
platform.xml

Usually generic.xml contains all the services that are started with system.
   93   <service name='network/ssh' version='1' type='service'>
   94   <instance name='default' enabled='true'/>
   95   </service>

8.7. SVCS commands.

SVCS is a very useful command available to manage SMF services, so we should know the power of this command. What all we can look with this command, and how to manage different services using this command.

1.   List all online, offline and maintenance services.
#**svcs**
online   14:16:43 svc:/application/autoreg:default
online   14:16:48 svc:/system/webconsole:console
online   14:18:42 svc:/milestone/network:default
online   14:18:42
svc:/application/management/storagemgmtd:default
online   14:19:06 svc:/network/physical:default
maintenance   14:22:44
svc:/application/management/hwmgmtd:default

2.   List all services including disabled.
bash-3.2# **svcs -a** | grep -i disabled | head
disabled   14:16:16 svc:/system/device/mpxio-upgrade:default
disabled   14:16:16 svc:/system/metainit:default
disabled   14:16:16 svc:/network/ipsec/ike:default
disabled   14:16:16 svc:/network/ipsec/manual-key:default
disabled   14:16:16 svc:/network/ipfilter:default

At first we should know the difference between svcs and svcs –a command. The svcs does not show disabled services since we need to deal with online services by default. So to see all services including those which are disabled we need to run command svcs with "-a" argument.

3.   Display all available information regarding a service.
bash-3.2# **svcs -l ssh**
fmri   svc:/network/ssh:default
name   SSH server
enabled   true

state   online
next_state   none
state_time   January 17, 2015 02:16:33 PM IST
logfile   /var/svc/log/network-ssh:default.log
restarter   svc:/system/svc/restarter:default
contract_id 60
dependency   require_all/none svc:/system/filesystem/local (online)
dependency   optional_all/none svc:/system/filesystem/autofs (online)
dependency   require_all/none svc:/network/loopback (online)
dependency   require_all/none svc:/network/physical (online)
dependency   require_all/none svc:/system/cryptosvc (online)
dependency   require_all/none svc:/system/utmp (online)
dependency   require_all/restart file://localhost/etc/ssh/sshd_config
(online)

4.   List process id associated with the service.
We have already seen it above, however lets have a look at it again.

        bash-3.2# **svcs -p ssh**
STATE   STIME   FMRI
online   14:16:33 svc:/network/ssh:default
        14:16:33   498 sshd

        Lets see its ptree how this process is initiated and its child
processes.
        bash-3.2# ptree -a 498
1   /sbin/init
 498 /usr/lib/ssh/sshd
  975 /usr/lib/ssh/sshd
   976 /usr/lib/ssh/sshd
    1038 -sh
     1043 bash
      1214 ptree -a 498
bash-3.2#

5.   See all dependencies of the service which needs to be online.
bash-3.2# **svcs -d ssh**
STATE   STIME   FMRI
online   14:16:17 svc:/network/loopback:default
online   14:16:26 svc:/system/cryptosvc:default
online   14:16:28 svc:/system/filesystem/local:default
online   14:16:31 svc:/system/utmp:default
online   14:16:32 svc:/system/filesystem/autofs:default
online   14:19:06 svc:/network/physical:default
bash-3.2#
To make ssh online, we need to bring all above services online.

6.   See what all services getting impacted by this service.
bash-3.2#
bash-3.2# **svcs -D ssh**
STATE   STIME   FMRI
online   14:16:30 svc:/milestone/ multi-user-server:default
bash-3.2#
If ssh is disabled, the above service multi-user-server:default can't be started.

7.   Troubleshooting SMF service startup.
Sometimes few services fail to start and we need deeper troubleshooting to identify why the service is not getting started. For this, oracle solaris provides a very powerful option "-x". "-v" simply makes the output more easily readable.

bash-3.2# **svcs -xv**
svc:/application/management/hwmgmtd:default (Sun Server Hardware Management Agent)
 State: maintenance since January 17, 2015 02:22:44 PM IST
Reason: Restarting too quickly.

See: http://sun.com/msg/SMF-8000-L5

See: /var/svc/log/application-management-hwmgmtd:default.log

Impact: This service is not running.

8.8.   Quick Tip 5: How to restore the repository?

The repositories are stored in /etc/svc directory with names repository*.
A repository in Solaris stores all available services on a system and
during system install it imports service manifesto into the database and
never call the manifesto again.

Let's look at different repositories available on my system.

-bash-3.2# ls -l /etc/svc/repo*

lrwxrwxrwx 1 root   root   31 Apr 1 16:36 /etc/svc/repository-
boot -> repository-boot-20140401_163651

-rw------- 1 root   root   4107264 Apr 1 10:52 /etc/svc/repository-
boot-20140401_105235

-rw------- 1 root   root   4107264 Apr 1 11:35 /etc/svc/repository-
boot-20140401_113539

-rw------- 1 root   root   4111360 Apr 1 13:54 /etc/svc/repository-
boot-20140401_135416

-rw------- 1 root   root   4117504 Apr 1 16:36 /etc/svc/repository-
boot-20140401_163651

lrwxrwxrwx 1 root   root   42 Jan 10 12:11 /etc/svc/repository-
manifest_import -> repository-manifest_import-20130131_162400

-rw------- 1 root   root   3885056 Jan 31 2013 /etc/svc/repository-
manifest_import-20130131_152753

Whenever we perform any system task, our system takes the backup of
old repository. However sometimes during major activities we should
take and keep one repository backup with us separately.

Manifest(repository-manifest) backup is taken by the system when xml
changes occur. Simlarly in case of normal service change occurs, the
system takes backup of boot repository(repository-boot).

Few situations when should we restore the repository.
1.   Repository corrupts on boot and the services unable to start.
2.   In case we want to revert SMF to some specific backup file (for restoring database file)
3.   To revert to previous boot state.

To restore the repository we can use restore_repository command found in /lib/svc/bin directory. When you run this command, it will automatically show available repositories and we can enter the repository which we want to restore.

-bash-3.2# **/lib/svc/bin/restore_repository**

See http://sun.com/msg/SMF-8000-MY for more information on the use of
this script to restore backup copies of the smf(5) repository.
If there are any problems which need human intervention, this script will
give instructions and then exit back to your shell.
Note that upon full completion of this script, the system will be rebooted using reboot(1M), which will interrupt any active services.

The following backups of /etc/svc/repository.db exist, from oldest to newest:
manifest_import-20130131_152753
manifest_import-20130131_161034
manifest_import-20130131_161852
manifest_import-20130131_162400
boot-20140401_105235
boot-20140401_113539
boot-20140401_135416
boot-20140401_163651

The backups are named based on their type and the time what they were taken. Backups beginning with "boot" are made before the first change is made to the repository after system boot. Backups beginning with "manifest_import" are made after svc:/system/manifest-import:default finishes its processing. The time of backup is given in YYYMMDD_HHMMSS format.

Please enter either a specific backup repository from the above list to restore it, or one of the following choices:

CHOICE	ACTION
boot	restore the most recent post-boot backup
manifest_import	restore the most recent manifest_import backup
- seed-	restore the initial starting repository (All customizations will be lost, including those made by the install/upgrade process.)
-quit-	cancel script and quit

Enter response [boot]: -quit-
Exiting.

Once you enter the required repository and press return the utility will restore the required repository.

9.   Inetd Services

-bash-3.2# **inetd**
inetd is now an smf(5) managed service and can no longer be run from the
command line. To enable or disable inetd refer to svcadm(1M) on
how to enable "svc:/network/inetd:default", the inetd instance.

The traditional inetd command line option mappings are:
    -d : there is no supported debug output

-s : inetd is only runnable from within the SMF
-t : See inetadm(1M) on how to enable TCP tracing
-r : See inetadm(1M) on how to set a failure rate

To specify an alternative configuration file see svccfg(1M) for how to modify the "start/exec" string type property of the inetd instance, and modify it according to the syntax: "/usr/lib/inet/inetd [alt_config_file] %m".

For further information on inetd see inetd(1M).
-bash-3.2#
-bash-3.2#
-bash-3.2# **inetadm**
ENABLED STATE   FMRI
enabled   online   svc:/application/x11/xfs:default
disabled disabled   svc:/application/x11/xvnc-inetd:default
enabled   online   svc:/application/font/stfsloader:default

9.1.   Quick Tip 6: How to block/unblock all inetd services in one go?

Inetd is responsible to start Internet standard services when a system boots. Till Solaris 9 it is managed by a daemon called inetd, however now it is also managed through SMF. However we have some commands through which we can manage all inetd services altogether instead of handling the services separately.

Inetd services uses clean text to transfer the data, like telnet, ftp etc so usually system administrators block these services to make the system more secure.

To block all inetd services in one go, we can use the command netservices limited.

bash-3.2# svcs -a | grep -i ftp
online   16:40:33 svc:/network/ftp:default

bash-3.2# netservices limited
restarting syslogd
restarting sendmail
restarting wbem
dtlogin needs to be restarted. Restart now? [Y] y
restarting dtlogin

bash-3.2# svcs -a | grep -i ftp
disabled   16:39:52 svc:/network/ftp:default

Unblock the service back.
-bash-3.2# **netservices open**
restarting syslogd
restarting sendmail
restarting wbem
dtlogin needs to be restarted. Restart now? [Y] no
dtlogin not restarted. Restart it to put it in open-mode.
-bash-3.2#
-bash-3.2# svcs -a | grep -i ftp
online   1:25:24 svc:/network/ftp:default

10.   NFS (Network File System)

NFS(Network File system) originally developed by Sun microsystems in 1984 is a distributed filesystem which can be shared over network to multiple locations with different read/write permissions. NFS uses the Remote Procedure Call (RPC) method of communication between nodes and mounts the remote location to behave as if its local disk space.

NFS allows us to share information between different architecture systems. The node which shares its resources is known as NFS server and the node which uses these resources is known as NFS client.

Quickly check if our machine is nfs server or client?

To check if our node is NFS server or not, we can use showmount command with "-e" option that prints all shared filesystems.

```
-bash-3.2# showmount -e
showmount: system11: RPC: Program not registered
-bash-3.2#
```

In case of above error, it shows no directory is shared by our node, and hence this is not NFS server. You can also check its service must be disabled.

```
-bash-3.2# svcs -a | grep -i nfs
disabled        1:25:23 svc:/network/nfs/server:default
online          1:25:22 svc:/network/nfs/status:default
online          1:25:22 svc:/network/nfs/nlockmgr:default
online          1:25:22 svc:/network/nfs/cbd:default
online          1:25:22 svc:/network/nfs/mapid:default
online          1:25:22 svc:/network/nfs/client:default
online          1:25:24 svc:/network/nfs/rquota:default
```

As we can see nfs/client is enabled, hence we can mount remote directories on our system.

Let's enable the NFS server service.
```
-bash-3.2# svcadm enable svc:/network/nfs/server:default
-bash-3.2# svcs -a | grep -i nfs
disabled        2:45:21 svc:/network/nfs/server:default
online          1:25:22 svc:/network/nfs/status:default
online          1:25:22 svc:/network/nfs/nlockmgr:default
online          1:25:22 svc:/network/nfs/cbd:default
online          1:25:22 svc:/network/nfs/mapid:default
online          1:25:22 svc:/network/nfs/client:default
online          1:25:24 svc:/network/nfs/rquota:default
```

The service is not enabled, we need to share some directory first to enable the service.

10.1. Temporary Sharing in NFS

Let's create a directory say /mydata_saket and share it.

-bash-3.2# **share /mydata_saket**

-bash-3.2# svcs -a | grep -i nfs

online	**1:25:22**	**svc:/network/nfs/status:default**
online	1:25:22	svc:/network/nfs/nlockmgr:default
online	1:25:22	svc:/network/nfs/cbd:default
online	1:25:22	svc:/network/nfs/mapid:default
online	1:25:22	svc:/network/nfs/client:default
online	1:25:24	svc:/network/nfs/rquota:default
online	2:48:49	svc:/network/nfs/server:default

-bash-3.2# **showmount -e**

export list for system11:

/mydata_saket (everyone)

-bash-3.2# **exportfs -v**

share -F nfs

-          /mydata_saket rw ""

Now we can also mount this directory on our node.

-bash-3.2# mount 192.168.1.5:/April /mount

-bash-3.2#

#df –h

192.168.1.5:/April   8.1G   4.0G   4.1G   50%   /mount

#mount -v

192.168.1.5:/April on /mount type nfs remote/read/write/setuid/devices/rstchown/xattr/dev=4e40002 on Wed Apr 2 02:54:13 2014

Let's try to create some files.
-bash-3.2# touch kk kkk
touch: cannot create kk: Permission denied
touch: cannot create kkk: Permission denied

For this we need to modify permissions of this share on the NFS server.
bash-3.2# chmod o+w /April/

Now you will able to write.

10.2. See NFS exports of other machines

To see NFS shares of other server we can mention the Ip address of the NFS server alongwith showmount command.

-bash-3.2# **showmount -e 192.168.1.5**
export list for 192.168.1.5:
/April (everyone)

-bash-3.2# dfshares 192.168.1.5 ### only on solaris
RESOURCE   SERVER ACCESS   TRANSPORT
192.168.1.5:/April   192.168.1.5 -

Whenever we share/unshared any partition on our NFS server, the OS maintains this list under sharetab file which is updated run time.

-bash-3.2# cat /etc/dfs/sharetab
/mydata_saket   -   nfs   rw
/mydata2   -   nfs   root=192.168.1.5:192.168.1.12

-bash-3.2# unshare /mydata2

-bash-3.2# cat /etc/dfs/sharetab
/mydata_saket   -   nfs   rw

10.3. Permanent Sharing

To do permanent sharing, we need to enter the directory to share under dfstab file.

bash-3.2# **vi /etc/dfs/dfstab**
share /mydata_saket
share -o root=access /mydata2
share -o root=192.168.1.5:192.168.1.12 /mydata3

-bash-3.2# **shareall**

-bash-3.2# **showmount -e**
export list for system11:
/mydata_saket (everyone)
/mydata2   (everyone)

10.4. Hard Mount Vs Soft Mount

When we mount a share on our system, it provides an option whether to mount this partition as soft mount or hard mount. Hard mount, by default, assumes the NFS server to be available always and can cause issues like slow booting when the server is not available.

When we don't mention this in mount option, then by default out systems mounts any share as hard mount. Similarly, entry in /etc/vfstab is also hard mount by default.

Now to mount it as soft mount, we need to specify this in our vfstab file.

192.168.1.10:/oradb - /myoradb nfs - yes **soft,bg**

We can also mount the partition by mentioning the soft mount option with mount command.

bash-3.2# mount -o soft,bg localhost:mydata /saket
bash-3.2# df -h /saket
Filesystem   size   used avail capacity Mounted on
localhost:mydata   14G   4.6G   8.8G   34%   /saket
bash-3.2#

Soft option tells for doing the soft mount. "bg" is for background. NFS keeps on checking the server, and whenever the server is available it gets mounted. When server is not available, put the request in background. Best option to give in real time and avoid unnecessary system usage.

Few points to note:
➢	Soft mount, mounts the filesystem on demand.
➢	Soft mount umounts the idle filesystem.
➢	Autofs is soft mount by default.
➢	Till Solaris 9, NFS ver. 3 was used. From Solaris 10, NFS version 4 is used.
➢	Till NFS v3, it was considered as a stateless protocol; however NFSv4 is a statefull server.
➢	Statefull protocol allows NFS client to lease a file lock from the NFS server for a certain period of time, say. X seconds. It renews the lock with after the X seconds period has expired whereas stateless server is a simple protocol which doesn't create any lock.

## 10.5.	How to identify NFS version ?
To know the highest version of nfs used by the system, we can use nfsstat command and grep the version.

-bash-3.2# **nfsstat | grep -i version**
Version 2: (0 calls)
Version 3: (0 calls)
Version 4: (167 calls)
Version 4: (397 operations)

Version 2: (0 calls)

Here we can see how many calls/operations made on which NFS version by our system. Also it tells that NFS versions 2,3 and 4 are supported by our system.

10.6. Change NFS version.

When we configure our node as NFS server, we can modify NFS version which we want to use in order to serve client requests. And moreover, we can also mention NFS version to use when our node behaves like a NFS client.

-bash-3.2# **vi /etc/default/nfs**
\# Sets the maximum version of the NFS protocol that will be registered
\# and offered by the server. The default is 4.
\#NFS_SERVER_VERSMAX=4

\# Sets the minimum version of the NFS protocol that will be used by
\# the NFS client. Can be overridden by the "vers=" NFS mount option.
\# The default is 2.
\#NFS_CLIENT_VERSMIN=2

<u>32 clients can access the server at a time.</u>
\# Set connection queue length for the NFS over a connection-oriented
\# transport. The default value is 32 entries.
\# Equivalent to -l.
NFSD_LISTEN_BACKLOG=32

<u>Max. 16 clients can access a single particular directory at once.</u>
\# Maximum number of concurrent NFS requests.
\# Equivalent to last numeric argument on nfsd command line.
NFSD_SERVERS=16

You can find many other options that we can set in this file.

10.7. New Features of NFS Version 4

To understand the differences better, let's have a look in a tabular format below.

NFS V4	NFS v3
Statefull server a. Client will not panic. b. Mount automatically if server is available.	Stateless server :- in case server is not reachable, then client will hang, or go in panic mode. How to troubleshoot. Mount –v Umount <hanged partitions>
Improved security	
Firewall support	
Delegated administration:- we can configure delegated client and forward nfs requests to another server. Just like slave nfs server. Also NFS client can borrow a part of the filesystem from server and can work on it in its local cache with little communication to the NFS server increasing performance.	

10.8.   Quick Tip 7: How to umount all remote shares vs all mountpoints ?

To umount all remote shares.
umountall –r
To umount all filesystems including zfs, or any other optional filesystem.
umountall

11.   Autofs

Autofs as its name says, auto filesystem which means when we go into a filesystem mount point, it becomes automatically mounted, and when it is not used for some time, it is automatically umounted to save network bandwidth. Autofs is a utility which can mount different network file systems on demand when they are accessed or referenced.

➢   NFS Client side utility.
➢   Mount on demand and umount the idle filesystem. Default idle timeout is 10 minutes.
➢   Generally autofs is implemented for user home directories.
➢   /net is a special map in Solaris which automatically mounts all available network shares when accessed through it.

Depending upon how the share is accessesed, mounted, we have two types of MAPs which can be created. A MAP or mapfile contains option how the remote filesystem is accessed on our system and with what options. So we can have two types of MAP files.

Map files:
1.   Special Map
2.   Direct and Indirect Map

11.1.   Special Map

/net is a special map. The ips get automatically mounted when accessed through this special map.
#cat /etc/auto_master
+auto_master
/net   -hosts   -nosuid,nobrowse
/home   auto_home   -nobrowse

-bash-3.2# **cd /net/192.168.1.141**
-bash-3.2# pwd
/net/192.168.1.141
-bash-3.2# ls
avishek srt   test2
-bash-3.2# **showmount -e 192.168.1.141**
export list for 192.168.1.141:
/srt   (everyone)
/test2 (everyone)
/avishek (everyone)

To unshare the NFS shares
unshare /oradb
unshareall

11.2. Direct or Indirect Map

-bash-3.2# **vi /etc/auto_master**
/-   /etc/auto.dir
~
/- is the reserved key for direct map.

#vi /etc/auto.dir
/mydir1 192.168.1.12:/vikram/

#automount –v

Direct maps will be mounted under / and hence these are less flexible.
Hence mostly we see people using indirect map for better flexibility.

#df –h
192.168.1.12:/vikram 8.1G 4.0G 4.1G 50%   /mydir1

InDirect Map
When we mount a network location to any sub directory on our system then it is called as indirect map. For defining indirect map, we need to first define mapfile name in the master file.

```
-bash-3.2# cat /etc/auto_master
#
# Copyright 2003 Sun Microsystems, Inc.  All rights reserved.
# Use is subject to license terms.
#
# ident "@(#)auto_master      1.8    03/04/28 SMI"
#
# Master map for automounter
#
+auto_master
/net        -hosts        -nosuid,nobrowse
/home       auto_home     -nobrowse
/myautofs   auto_my                          #### here file with path is
given
```

Create Map and insert entries
```
-bash-3.2# cat /etc/auto_my
d1     192.168.1.12:/vikram
```

Create the directories for autofs
```
-bash-3.2# mkdir –p /myautofs/d1
```

```
-bash-3.2# automount -v
automount: no mounts
automount: no unmounts
```

Now restart service so that this mount point can be moiunted when accessed.
```
-bash-3.2# svcadm restart autofs
```

11.3. Quick Tip 8: How to change idle timeout in autofs ?

-bash-3.2# **cat /etc/default/autofs | grep -i timeout**
#AUTOMOUNT_TIMEOUT=600
We can uncomment and modify this value to any value which we want.
By default it is 10 minutes when this entry is not available.

12. Quick Tip 9: How to remove restriction from console of only root login?

To remove the restriction of only root login in Solaris, edit below file.
-bash-3.2# **cat /etc/default/login | grep -i console**
# If CONSOLE is set, root can only login on that device.
CONSOLE=/dev/console
Hash above line and now root will be able to login.

13. Quick Tip 10: Steps to convert efi(zfs format) label to smi(default solaris ufs) label.

Run format with extended functionality.
-bash-3.2# **format -e**

partition> **p**
Current partition table (original):
Total disk sectors available: 8372189 + 16384 (reserved sectors)

Part	Tag	Flag	First Sector	Size	Last Sector
0	usr	wm	256	3.99GB	8372189
1	unassigned	wm	0	0	0
2	unassigned	wm	0	0	0
3	unassigned	wm	0	0	0
4	unassigned	wm	0	0	0
5	unassigned	wm	0	0	0
6	unassigned	wm	0	0	0
7	unassigned	wm	0	0	0
8	reserved	wm	8372190	8.00MB	8388573

partition> l
[0] SMI Label
[1] EFI Label
Specify Label type[1]: **0**
Warning: This disk has an EFI label. Changing to SMI label will erase all current partitions.
Continue? **y**
You must use fdisk to delete the current EFI partition and create a new Solaris partition before you can convert the label.
partition> **q**

FORMAT MENU:
    disk   - select a disk
    type   - select (define) a disk type
    partition - select (define) a partition table
    current   - describe the current disk
    format   - format and analyze the disk
    fdisk   - run the fdisk program
    repair   - repair a defective sector
    label   - write label to the disk
    analyze   - surface analysis
    defect   - defect list management
    backup   - search for backup labels
    verify   - read and display labels
    inquiry   - show vendor, product and revision
    scsi   - independent SCSI mode selects
    cache   - enable, disable or query SCSI disk cache
    volname - set 8-character volume name
    !<cmd>   - execute <cmd>, then return
    Quit

format> **fdisk**

Total disk size is 2047 cylinders
        Cylinder size is 4096 (512 byte) blocks

                         Cylinders
    Partition Status   Type   Start End Length   %
    ========= ======   ============ ===== === ======
===

WARNING: no partitions are defined!

SELECT ONE OF THE FOLLOWING:
   1. Create a partition
   2. Specify the active partition
   3. Delete a partition
   4. Change between Solaris and Solaris2 Partition IDs
   5. Exit (update disk configuration and exit)
   6. Cancel (exit without updating disk configuration)
Enter Selection:

Partition 1 has been deleted.

Now create a partition with 100%. And label it.

Questions
   1. How to boot the system in single user mode from system shell
       and from ok prompt?
   2. How to shutdown the system immediately?
   3. How to check list of legacy services on our system?
   4. What do you mean if a SMF service is in maintenance mode?
   5. How to check and mount a remote NFS share?
   6. How to check autofs maps available on our system?

Chapter -5
User and Core file Administration
Day 4

1.   User Management

In this section, we will see how to manage users under our Oracle solaris OS, for example:- how to create new users, how to modify user settings, how to delete users, how to lock/unlock users, what are groups and how to assign groups to different users, etc. The user management can be carried out by using different utilities under solaris, either we can use GUI tools, or command line tools. Let us have a look at these different ways of administrating users on our solaris box.

1.1. Through CLI or Command line.

a.   Useradd Command: This command is used to add a new user to our system.
 # useradd -md /export/home/u1 u1
-m is used to make directory, and –d specifies the destination path of home dir.
U1 is the username with which new user is created.

To see id of the new user created we can use id command.
# id -a u1
uid=102(u1) gid=1(other) groups=1(other)
"-a" is used to see all groups assigned to the user.

b.   Usermod Command
Similar to useradd, usermod allows us to modify user settings with ease. The options for both useradd and usermod almost remains the same, for

example "-s" is used to define/change the user login shell, "-d" is used to define default home directory where user lands after login, etc.

Let's see the details of user u1 created before. We can use finger command to see any local or remote user details.

bash-3.2# finger u1
Login name: u1
Directory: /export/home/u1   Shell: /bin/sh
Never logged in.
No unread mail
No Plan.
bash-3.2#

Now we can modify its settings with usermod.

bash-3.2# usermod -d "/var/tmp/" -s "/bin/bash" u1

bash-3.2# finger u1
Login name: u1
Directory: /var/tmp/   Shell: /bin/bash
Never logged in.
No unread mail
No Plan.
bash-3.2#

c.   Userdel Command
Userdel utility is used to delete the existing user from the system. This command can be used in two ways.

1.   # userdel u1 :- Simply removes the user account from the system and the user can no more access the system from its login.
bash-3.2# userdel u1
bash-3.2#

2.   # userdel –r u1 :- Removes user account alongwith its home directory contents.

bash-3.2# useradd -md /var/tmp/hello u1

bash-3.2# ls -l /var/tmp/hello
total 6
-rw-r--r-- 1 u1   other   136 Jan 17 22:02 local.cshrc
-rw-r--r-- 1 u1   other   157 Jan 17 22:02 local.login
-rw-r--r-- 1 u1   other   174 Jan 17 22:02 local.profile

bash-3.2# userdel -r u1

bash-3.2# ls -ld /var/tmp/hello
/var/tmp/hello: No such file or directory
bash-3.2#

1.2   Edit the configuration files.

We can also change user settings, login information, etc by directly editing the configuration files on our Solaris host, however this is not at all recommended, since in case you introduce any error by mistake in any of the configuration files, then it can make your complete system unusable and the users may not able to login.

However as a unix administrator we should know how to edit and change the user configuration from these files. There are few different configuration files that save the created users information and settings how these new users are created. These configuration files are as follows:

a.   /etc/passwd :- Saves the list of users and their id, group id, shell, etc.

The /etc/passwd contains one entry in each line for every user of the system. The fields are separated by a colon (:) symbol. Total seven fields as follows.

dbadmin:x:101:1:DBA Adminstrator:/home/dbadmin:/bin/sh

dbadmin: It is username used when user logs in. It should be between 1 and 32 characters in length.
x: Indicates that encrypted password is stored in /etc/shadow file.
101 (User ID or UID): Each user must be assigned a user ID (UID).
1: Group ID (GID): The primary group ID (stored in /etc/group file)
DBA Adminstrator: This is comment field allows us to add extra information about the users such as user's full name, phone number etc.
/home/dbadmin : The absolute path of user's home directory where the user will be in when they log in. If this directory does not exists then users dropped to root directory /
/bin/sh: The absolute path of the login shell which will be assigned when user logs in.

b.   /etc/shadow :- Stores mainly user password's md5 sum to authenticate user password and few other user information.

dbadmin:$md5$mjsj577C$$a2S7FB/GClD4VBNTdpKQJ/:16397:0:99999:7:::

Solaris uses SUN MD5 algorithm alongwith shadow password technology to encrypt the password and save the corrosponding key in /etc/shadow file. The password can't be decrypted back from the unique MD5 key.

Shadow password technology makes the password invisible i.e. we can only see *** on screen when entering password while login to the system.

Let's have a look at the different fields of this entry in shadow file.

dbadmin: the unique username which is used when user logs in.
:$md5$mjsj577C$$a2S7FB/GClD4VBNTdpKQJ/: The MD5 sum of our encrypted password.
16397: Days since Jan 1, 1970 that password was last changed
0: Minimum number of days required between password changes i.e. the number of days left before the user is allowed to change his/her password
99999: Maximum number of days the password is valid (after that user is forced to change his/her password)
7: Number of days before password expiry that user is warned about his/her password must be changed
Password Inactive : The number of days after password expires that account is disabled
Password Expires : days since Jan 1, 1970 that account is disabled i.e. an absolute date specifying when the login may no longer be used

a.   /etc/group:- List of all groups exist on the system and contained users. We will discuss this file under user groups later in this chapter.
b.   /etc/default/passwd :- As its name suggests, this file is used to set options for new user password which applies whenever anyone resets the user password.
  i.   Maximum days the password remains valid
 ii.   Minimum days the password remains valid
iii.   The number of days before the password becomes invalid so that the user is warned
iv.   The minimum characters a password must contain

c.   /etc/default/login :- A very important file that contains all default user login options which gets applied for every user. The different options available under this file are as follows
1.   Whether Root login allowed only at the console terminal. (CONSOLE)

2. File size limit (ULIMIT)
3. User's value for umask (UMASK)
4. Maximum number of login attempts permitted (MAXTRYS).
5. Number of failed login attempts allowed. (LOGFAILURES)

Few other options are also available like DISABLETIME (Number of seconds to sleep after a failed login), PASSREQ (Password requirement on logins either yes or no), etc.

1.3 <u>Quick Tip 4</u>: Add a new user by changing system configuration files.

First we should know what all files and directories got modified when a new user is added in order to add the user by modifying the configuration files. Whenever we add a new user, system adds a new userid, password, creates the home directory, and assigns a primary group id to the user.

1. First add the new user to /etc/passwd file to create the user.
\# vi /etc/passwd
\#\#\# Open passwd file and goto last line by pressing :$
\#\#\# Now copy(press yy) the last line and paste(press p) it back.
dbadmin:x:101:1::/home/dbadmin:/bin/sh
dbadmin:x:101:1::/home/dbadmin:/bin/sh

Now edit the last line and change it like below.

dbadmin:x:101:1::/home/dbadmin:/bin/sh

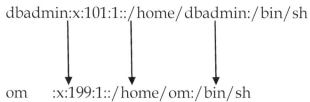

om   :x:199:1::/home/om:/bin/sh

"om" is the new username we want to add, 199 is the new unique userid allocated to this new user, and /home/om is the default home directory for this user.

Now we have this new user created, you can watch this new user and corresponding details with id command.

bash-3.2# id -a om
uid=199(om) gid=1(other) groups=1(other)
bash-3.2#

2.   However to login, we need to assign some password to this user. For this lets open /etc/shadow file and copy paste one line here also.
dbadmin:$md5$mjsj577C$$a2S7FB/GClD4VBNTdpKQJ/:::::::

om:$md5$mjsj577C$$a2S7FB/GClD4VBNTdpKQJ/:::::::

Here on user now have the password same as of dbadmin user. In case you want to assign some other password, then you can re-assign the password using passwd command.

3.   Now we have userid and password available, however the home directory assigned is still not created. Hence we need to create the home directory for this user.
mkdir /home/om

4.   Now everything is in place and the user om can login to his home directory. However the profile files are still missing and the user will not get default environment variables values in place. By default unix has all default profile files placed inside /etc/skel directory which gets copied whenever a new user is created. So lets copy all files from this directory to new user directory.
bash-3.2# cp -r /etc/skel/. /home/om/
bash-3.2# ls -al /home/om
total 48
drwxr-xr-x 2 root   root   388 Jan 22 20:02 .
drwxrwxrwt 8 root   sys   665 Jan 22 20:02 ..
-rw-r--r-- 1 root   root   144 Jan 22 20:02 .profile

```
-rw-r--r--  1 root    root        136 Jan 22 20:02 local.cshrc
-rw-r--r--  1 root    root        157 Jan 22 20:02 local.login
-rw-r--r--  1 root    root        174 Jan 22 20:02 local.profile
bash-3.2#
```

After copying we need to change the permissions and ownership of this directory.
```
# chown om:1 /home/om; chmod 755 /home/om
```

And now try to login with om user and password of dbadmin and you will see you are successfully logged in without any issue.
```
$ su – om
Password:
Oracle Corporation    SunOS 5.10    Generic Patch  January 2005
$ pwd
/home/om
```

1.4 SMC Tool

SMC or Solaris Management Console is a GUI tool which also provides an option of user administration for local as well as remote systems. It uses high resources, and hence rarely used by system administrators, as a consequence, with Solaris 11 oracle has removed this feature from server operating system versions. To run SMC on our Solaris 10 box, simply run smc command like below.
```
bash-3.2# smc &
[1] 5680
bash-3.2# Java Accessibility Bridge for GNOME loaded.
```

Now it will open a GUI like below where you can browse and manage our system.

1.5   Webmin tool

Webmin is another web based system configuration cum administration tool which helps us to manage the system efficiently in less time. The advantage of this tool over other tools available on the systems is that it is a open source tool for system administration, which is by default installed in Solaris 10.

The webmin tool is now also supported on windows, which makes it a better option compared to other tools. By using webmin tool, we can configure operating system internal operations like user management, disk quota, services or configuration files, as well as modify and control open source apps, such as the Apache Webserver, PHP or MySQL.

You need to setup webmin tool before starting it for first time. Now lets have a look how we can setup this tool for the first time.

webminsetup
Login name (default root):
Web server port (default 10000):
Use SSL? [y,n,?,q]

```
**********************************************************************
*        Welcome to the Webmin setup script, version 1.580      *
**********************************************************************
```

Webmin is a web-based interface that allows Unix-like operating systems and common Unix services to be easily administered. Installing Webmin in /usr/sfw/lib/webmin ...

```
**********************************************************************
```

Webmin uses separate directories for configuration files and log files.

Just press enter on every option asked and the system will automatically configure the tool for initial startup and will show a message in end like below.

Attempting to start Webmin mini web server..
..done

```
**********************************************************************
```

Webmin has been installed and started successfully. Use your web browser to go to
  http://SolarisLab1:10000/
and login with the name and password you entered previously.

Now open the url http://SolarisLab1:10000/ to access the webmin tool screen. At first time it will prompt you to change the default password which is root and the root login password of your system.

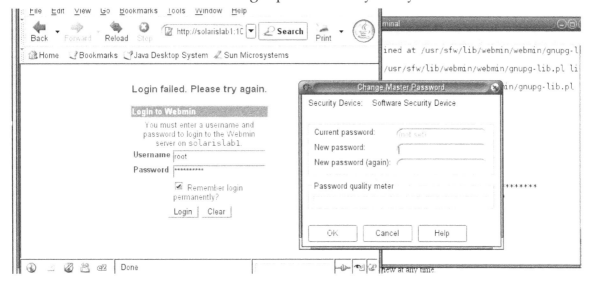

Once you change the default password, you can see the webmin tool main screen page. On left side panel, you can see different options that can be configured or changed using this tool.

These are the tools that are by default available in Oracle Solaris and we should be aware of their working and how to check them. I am not going in detail for these tools, otherwise it will take one more chapter. In case you want to learn more about this tool, then you need to open and explore this on your system, or any test server.

2.   User Administration

Till now we have seen how to administrate the users on our system, however there are few concepts that need to be cleared with user management in Solaris.

2.1   UIDs

Unix or unix like operating systems assign a unique value called user identifier (UID) to identify different users on the system. These UIDs are used to identify different users and the type(system, root, or normal) of user. A Solaris kernel only understands UIDs, and gives permissions based on user id, the passwd file just maps username to userid so that our system can query for uid based on username also.

UIDs

Root or Super User (0)
System Users (0-99)
Login Users (from 100 to 60000)
Nobody User (60001)
Noaccess User(60002)

The maximum value for a UID in 32 bit Solaris OS is 2^{32} i.e. 2147483647. However, the UIDs over 60000 do not have full utility and are considered incompatible with some Solaris OS features. So always avoid using any UID over 60000 so that it can be compatible with earlier versions of Solaris operating system.

2.2   User Add Template File

Solaris also provides a very nice feature where we can create Template files to customize default user add options. We can have a template file containing all setting of a new user to be added like gid, home dir, etc.

1.   The first thing to check is whether any default user add profile exists or not.
bash-3.2# ls -l /usr/sadm/defadduser
/usr/sadm/defadduser: No such file or directory

No template right now. Don't create it with vi editor.

---

2. Create the default template using command useradd.

```
bash-3.2# useradd -D
group=other,1  project=default,3  basedir=/home
skel=/etc/skel  shell=/bin/sh  inactive=0
expire=  auths=  profiles=  roles=  limitpriv=
defaultpriv=  lock_after_retries=
bash-3.2#
bash-3.2# ls -l /usr/sadm/defadduser
-rw-r--r--  1 root    root      286 Apr  2 09:39 /usr/sadm/defadduser
```

3. Define the template parameters.

```
bash-3.2# vi /usr/sadm/defadduser
defgroup=100
defgname=java
defparent=/mysolaris
defskel=/etc/skel
defshell=/bin/bash
```

4. Now create the user, it will assign the default parameters defined.

```
-bash-3.2# useradd -m u2
-bash-3.2# grep u2 /etc/passwd
u2:x:40100:100::/mysolaris/u2:/bin/bash
```

Now we have default template file created, which is referred by system whenever any new user is added. We can see above the new user named u2 has assigned default id, shell, group and skel directory which is defined in this file.

2.3   Tune Password requirements

To tune password requirements, check the parameters in etc/default/passwd file.

```
-bash-3.2$ vi /etc/default/passwd
```

MAXWEEKS=
MINWEEKS=
PASSLENGTH=6
#NAMECHECK=NO ## user and password name can't be same.

We have many options to define password strength and password expiry related options in this file. I am not going into detail, as it is already discussed and further the options are very simple like minimum and maximum weeks of time when the password remains valid, and what is minimum password length, etc.

2.4 Quick Tip 4: Locking and unlocking password.

1. Check if password is locked or expired.
-bash-3.2# passwd -sa
root   PS
daemon   NL
bin   NL
sys   NL
adm   NL
lp   NL
uucp   NL

2. Lock users.
-bash-3.2# passwd -sa | grep -i user123
user123   PS

-bash-3.2# passwd -l user123
passwd: password information changed for user123

-bash-3.2# passwd -s user123
user123   LK

-bash-3.2# grep user123 /etc/passwd /etc/shadow

/etc/passwd:user123:x:40099:1::/oracle2/user123:/bin/sh
/etc/shadow:user123:*LK*$md5$EZQgMJgK$$E.XNK4B7GfUwy99sZlht
50:16162::::::

3. Now unlock user again.
-bash-3.2#passwd –u user123

-bash-3.2# passwd -sa | grep -i user123
user123   PS
The above commands are also used when the user gets locked on the system.

2.5   Modify user settings

We can modify any user setting using usermod command and the options are similar that of useradd command. Lets see an example to move the user home directory from one path to another path using this command.

-bash-3.2# usermod -md /mysolaris/user123 -l user123 u1
64 blocks
Data is also moved, because it renames the directory alongwith path.

-bash-3.2# grep -i u1 /etc/passwd
-bash-3.2# grep -i user123 /etc/passwd
user123:x:40099:1::/mysolaris/user123:/bin/sh

2.6   Quick Tip 6: Analyzing SU Logs to identify failed/successful login attempts.
-bash-3.2# **tail /var/adm/sulog**
SU 04/02 00:03 + ??? root-oracle
SU 04/02 01:03 + ??? root-oracle
SU 04/02 02:03 - ??? root-oracle
+ for successful and – for unsuccessful login attempt.

2.7   Quick Tip 7: Check List of users exist in our system.

The different ways to check for available users on our system is as follows:

1.   Cat /etc/passwd
2.   Command listusers (only on unix).

bash-3.2# listusers

noaccess   No Access User
8nobody   NFS Anonymous Access User
nobody4   SunOS 4.x NFS Anonymous Access User
oracle
saket

3.   By using logins command.

bash-3.2# logins

root   0   root   0   Super-User
daemon   1   other   1
adm   4   adm   4   Admin
uucp   5   uucp   5   uucp Admin
gdm   50   gdm   50   GDM Reserved UID
postgres   90   postgres   90   PostgreSQL Reserved UID
saket   100   root   0

2.8   Quick Tip 8: How to identify login shell of users?

An easy way to identify login shell of users is by using ps command to look for pts processes and then spot the login shell process.

-bash-3.2# ps -ef | grep -i pts
   root 6002 5996   0 08:32:05 pts/1   0:00 -bash
   root 3161 3158   0 02:44:17 pts/4   0:00 -bash -c   unset DT;
DISPLAY=:0;   /usr/dt/bin/dtsession_res -mer
   root 6045 6042   0 08:38:13 pts/5   0:00 bash
   root 1982 1976   0 00:06:33 pts/2   0:01 –bash
if – is in front of shell, then it's a login shell.

Another way to know the login shell is to look the value of SHELL environment variable.

bash-3.2# echo $SHELL

/sbin/bash

3.   Groups

Every user has some groups assigned based on which the user gains the privileges assigned to that particular group. Usually a user can have two types of groups assigned.

a.   Primary Group :- Each user can have only one primary group assigned which is referenced in passwd file.

b.   Secondary Group:- The users can be added in different secondary groups as per the requirement and these groups exists in /etc/group file.

Now for group administration, adding, modifying, removing users from group we can use below commands:

1.   Usermod :- To add/modify primary or secondary group of a user. The command w.r.t groups can be used in two variants :

#usermod –g java user123   #### To change primary group to java

#usermod –G oracle, sap,dp user123   #### To add oracle,sap,dp as secondary groups for user user123

2.   Groupadd :- Add new groups to the system.

3.   Groupmod :- Modify existing groups from the system.

4.   Groupdel :- Delete existing groups.

All groups of our system are defined in /etc/group file. Lets have a look at this file.

bash-3.2# cat /etc/group

root::0:

other::1:root

bin::2:root,daemon

sys::3:root,bin,adm
adm::4:root,daemon

We can also use few commands to query different groups on our system which reads this file and displays the result.

-bash-3.2# groups user123
other

-bash-3.2# groups
root other bin sys adm uucp mail tty lp nuucp daemon

Now lets add a new group.

bash-3.2# groupadd -g 299 oracle199
UX: groupadd: oracle199 name too long.

bash-3.2# groupadd -g 399 oracle9
bash-3.2# tail -2 /etc/group
oracle199::299:
oracle9::399:

As we can see a new group is added with 399 group id or gid. Also one extra group added with name oracle199. So lets remove this group.

bash-3.2# groupdel oracle199

bash-3.2# tail -2 /etc/group
oracle-new::199:
oracle9::399:

As we can see the group oracle199 is now deleted. Now suppose we want to rename oracle9 group to dba9 name. For this we can use groupmod command.

bash-3.2# groupmod -n dba9 oracle9
bash-3.2# tail -1 /etc/group
dba9::399:

In similar fashion we can perform group add, delete, or modify operations.

3.1   Difference between primary and secondary group.

The first question arises after knowing the primary and secondary groups in unix is, what is the difference between them. A user gets the same set of permissions whether he/she is a member of primary or secondary group then where the difference arises when we talk about primary and secondary groups. To know the difference lets have a look at features of primary/secondary groups.

➢   A new file/directory created by any user gets group ownership of primary group.
➢   All Group(s) are found in the /etc/group file. A user can swap its primary group with secondary group by using newgrp command.

Changing from primary group to secondary group
$ newgrp other
$ id -a
uid=40099(user123) gid=1(other) groups=1(other),100(java)
$ newgrp java
$ id -a
uid=40099(user123) gid=100(java) groups=1(other),100(java)

4. **Quick Tip 9: Restrict all users' access to our system.**

a.   Create the file /etc/nologin.

\# touch /etc/nologin

b.   We can put message in /etc/nologin to show the message to each user when they are not allowed to login.

\# echo "Access Restricted. Upgrade activity ongoing. Please access system after 3AM IST" >> /etc/nologin

After testing please remove this file nologin, otherwise you may end up with nologin problem.

5. **Quick Tip 10: Killing all login sessions.**

Suppose you want to kill all login sessions, then you can check and kill all login session processes.

Specify shell name and kill their process
-bash-3.2# pkill -9 bash
-bash-3.2# pkill -p sh

For example:- I have killed all sh named processes and you can see my session is killed.

bash-3.2# pkill -9 sh
Connection to 172.16.159.33 closed by remote host.
Connection to 172.16.159.33 closed.
root@L9AHG13:~#

6. **Profile Files**

When you login to your system, suppose you want that a new song gets automatically played, or few new environment variables gets loaded, or a different login shell is loaded. As a user you can't make changes in system files like /etc/passwd, etc, however still you can achieve these tasks by taking into account a profile file.

A profile file is just like a script file that gets executed automatically after user logs into his account or whenever system boots up depending upon which profile file we are talking about. There are several profile files available in our system and we will discuss them in the next section.

6.1 Public or system-wide

Public or system-wide profile file is the one which gets executed whenever our system gets booted and hence in this file we can set those parameters which needs to be applied on complete system. For example:- we want to setup new environment variable, say ORACLE_HOME=/opt/oracle to be available for all users, then we can define this in this file and test by rebooting our system.

➤ /etc/profile :- Applicable for root and all other users.

For example:-
echo 'ORACLE_HOME=/opt/oracle; export ORACLE_HOME' >> /etc/profile
init 6 ### reboot the system
After reboot, check the new environment variable.
bash-3.2# env | grep -i oracle
ORACLE_HOME=/opt/oracle
bash-3.2#

6.2 Private or User-defined

Private or user defined profile file is the one which gets executed whenever the user logs into his account. Since the scope of this file is limited to user account only, hence this is called as private or user defined profile file.

a. $HOME/.profile

$HOME is the environment variable which points to home directory of the user. So the .profile needs to be created inside the home directory of the user.

b.   Command to check/load profile file :- source .profile

We can load the existing profile file using the source command and refer this file.

a.   Enter something in the profile file
        bash-3.2# echo 'echo "welcome to solaris lab"' >> $HOME/.profile

a.   Logout and login again
        bash-3.2# exit
Connection to 172.16.159.33 closed.
root@L9AHG13:~# ssh 172.16.159.33
Password:
Last login: Wed Jan 28 18:06:11 2015 from 172.16.159.1
Oracle Corporation   SunOS 5.10   Generic Patch   January 2005
You have new mail.
welcome to solaris lab
#

Hence we can see above the file is executed on the user login and the message got printed. Similarly you can enter any command/script that you want to execute whenever you login.

7   Magic Directory

Unix or Linux has a directory /etc/skel which is called as Magic directory.

➤   /etc/skel

It's called magic directory since whatever placed into this will be copied to new user home directory. In other words, this is the directory which is copied as new user home directory and whatever placed in this directory will be copied to the home directory of any new user created.

```
bash-3.2# ls -ltr /etc/skel/
total 6
-rw-r--r--  1 root    sys        174 Jun 28  2011 local.profile
-rw-r--r--  1 root    sys        157 Jun 28  2011 local.login
-rw-r--r--  1 root    sys        136 Jun 28  2011 local.cshrc
bash-3.2#
```

7.1   Quick Tip 11: Include a script/command to be placed in each user's home directory.

I think now you must have got the trick how to achieve this task after knowing the magic directory. So you can keep the script file in the magic directory and that will be copied in every new user home directory. Lets see this in action.

a.   First place the file say hello.txt.
```
# touch /etc/skel/hello.txt
# echo "welcome" >> /etc/skel/hello.txt
```

b.   Now add any new user with home directory created(-md option) and check by logging with this user if you are getting this new file inside the user's home directory.

bash-3.2# useradd -m -d "/tmp/hello" hello

bash-3.2# su - hello
Oracle Corporation   SunOS 5.10   Generic Patch   January 2005
$ ls
hello.txt   local.cshrc   local.login   local.profile
$ cat hello.txt
"welcome"

7.2   Quick Tip 12: Lock users on specific failed login attempts

Suppose as a system administrator you want to lock system after 3 failed login attempts by any user. To accomplish this task, you need to modify two files.

a. First enable lock on retries by enabling parameter in /etc/security/policy.conf.

-bash-3.2# vi /etc/security/policy.conf
LOCK_AFTER_RETRIES specifies the default account locking policy for local
user accounts (passwd(4)/shadow(4)). The default may be overridden by
a user's user_attr(4) "lock_after_retries" value.
YES enables local account locking, NO disables local account locking.
The default value is NO.
#
#LOCK_AFTER_RETRIES=NO
Change it to:
LOCK_AFTER_RETRIES=YES

b.   Now check /etc/default/login for maximum retries allowed.

bash-3.2# cat /etc/default/login | grep -i retries

---

login will wait after RETRIES failed attempts or the PAM framework returns
RETRIES determines the number of failed logins that will be
will be locked if failed logins equals or exceeds RETRIES.
#RETRIES=5
bash-3.2#

If it's commented, by default any user will be locked after three failed attempts.

c.   Now enter wrong password, then you will see the account has been locked.
-bash-3.2# ssh 0 -l user123
Password:
Password:
Password:
Permission denied (gssapi-keyex,gssapi-with-mic,publickey,keyboard-interactive).
-bash-3.2# passwd -s user123
user123   LK

7.3   Quick Tip 13: Restricting su to limited users
Suppose you want to restrict su command usage to limited users. We need to make root as a role, and then make the users member of the root user role whom we want to grant su access.

a. First check root is a user or role.
-bash-3.2# **cat /etc/user_attr**
adm::::profiles=Log Management
lp::::profiles=Printer Management
postgres::::type=role;profiles=Postgres Administration,All
root::::auths=solaris.*,solaris.grant;profiles=Web Console
Management,All;lock_after_retries=no;min_label=admin_low;clearance= admin_high

b.   As of now root is a user and not a role. Now let's create the root user as a role.

-bash-3.2# **usermod -K type=role root**
UX: usermod: root is currently logged in, some changes may not take effect until next login.
-bash-3.2# cat /etc/user_attr
adm::::profiles=Log Management
lp::::profiles=Printer Management
postgres::::type=role;profiles=Postgres Administration,All
root::::**type=role**;auths=solaris.*,solaris.grant;profiles=Web Console Management,All;lock_after_retries=no;clearance=admin_high;min_label
=admin_low

c.   Now even we know the root password, we can't su to root unless we are into a root user role.
-bash-3.2# **usermod -R root user123**
-bash-3.2# **cat /etc/user_attr | grep -i root**
root::::type=role;auths=solaris.*,solaris.grant;profiles=Web Console Management,All;lock_after_retries=no;clearance=admin_high;min_label
=admin_low
user123::::type=normal;roles=root
-bash-3.2# roles user123
Root

d. Now we can see the access has been restricted.
-bash-3.2# su - u2
Oracle Corporation   SunOS 5.10   Generic Patch   January 2005
-bash-3.2$ su -
Password:
Roles can only be assumed by authorized users
su: Sorry
-bash-3.2$

e. Now convert back root user as a individual instead of role.

-bash-3.2# **rolemod -K type=normal root**

UX: rolemod: root is currently logged in, some changes may not take effect until next login.

-bash-3.2# cat /etc/user_attr

root::::**type=normal**;auths=solaris.*,solaris.grant;profiles=Web Console Management,All;lock_after_retries=no;clearance=admin_high;min_label =admin_low

user123::::type=normal;roles=root

8   Process Management and Scheduler

Unix provides many commands to monitor the system running processes and manage them. There are several commands available and we will discuss few of them which are mostly used by system administrators and in the same form we use these commands so that it become easier for you to deal with process management.

8.1   Process management Commands

Now we will see the mainly used different process management commands.

1.   <u>Ps –ef</u> :- We know that ps command prints active processes running on the system. Without any option it will only display the processes of the user running this command which is not so useful when we talk about complete system process checkup. To see all processes running on the system we will use this command with "-ef" option where –e displays all running processes, and –f shows full listing of the process. You can easily grep any process from the output.

```
bash-3.2# ps -ef | more
   UID  PID  PPID  C  STIME TTY      TIME CMD
   root   0   0  0  Jan 28 ?        0:16 sched
   root   4   0  0  Jan 28 ?        0:00 kmem_task
```

          root   1   0   0   Jan 28 ?   0:00 /sbin/init

UID → User name who started process, here it is root.
PID → Process id of this process.
PPID → Parent process id, which process initiates this process.
C → CPU consumed by the process for scheduling. Obsolete now, hence no value is displayed.
STIME → Start time or process. If more than 24hrs, time is displayed in days or months.
TTY → From which terminal process is started. ? in case no terminal is used to start process.
TIME → Total execution time of the process.
CMD → Command/Script which is running.

2.   Whodo (which user is doing what – only in unix)
Whodo displays a list of logged in users along with the commands/utilities they are running at that point of time. "-l" is used to see long list which displays all options, not just name and command of these users.

bash-3.2# whodo -l
 8:48pm up 1 day(s), 2 hr(s), 44 min(s) 1 user(s)
User   tty   login@ idle JCPU PCPU what
root   pts/1   Wed 6pm   whodo -l

3.   Prstat (equivalent to top in linux)
Prstat is one of the most powerful command when we talk about solaris. Its just like top command in linux. However many of the administrators don't how to use it efficiently. Here we will see how to use this efficiently to manage the processes on our Solaris system.

View memory and CPU consumption by different users along with high CPU consuming processes.

We will use prstat command with "-a" which will display report about users also, about how much cpu and memory is consumed by each user.

By default the output is sorted by CPU consumption, high cpu consuming process will be on top and low cpu consuming process are in the last. You can press return/enter to see remaining processes.

bash-3.2# **prstat -a**

PID	USERNAME	SIZE	RSS	STATE	PRI	NICE	TIME	CPU	PROCESS/NLWP
PID	USERNAME	SIZE	RSS	STATE	PRI	NICE	TIME	CPU	PROCESS/NLWP
17194	root	3904K	3068K	cpu0	59	0	0:00:00	0.2%	prstat/1
655	root	7684K	4568K	sleep	59	0	0:02:15	0.2%	vmtoolsd/1
980	noaccess	156M	120M	sleep	59	0	0:01:51	0.1%	java/18
600	root	24M	13M	sleep	59	0	0:01:27	0.1%	Xorg/1
17199	om	2248K	1232K	sleep	59	0	0:00:00	0.0%	mail/1
17198	om	1488K	936K	sleep	59	0	0:00:00	0.0%	sh/1
17196	om	2896K	964K	sleep	59	0	0:00:00	0.0%	cron/1
996	root	9040K	2432K	sleep	59	0	0:00:02	0.0%	sendmail/1
527	root	3944K	1936K	sleep	59	0	0:00:01	0.0%	syslogd/11
327	daemon	2836K	1060K	sleep	59	0	0:00:00	0.0%	rpcbind/1
150	root	3744K	2112K	sleep	59	0	0:00:00	0.0%	picld/5
194	root	2324K	756K	sleep	59	0	0:00:00	0.0%	iscsi-initiator/2

NPROC	USERNAME	SWAP	RSS	MEMORY	TIME	CPU
41	root	79M	76M	19%	0:04:23	0.5%
1	noaccess	150M	119M	30%	0:01:51	0.1%
1	gdm	9740K	14M	3.6%	0:01:30	0.1%
4	om	2128K	5692K	1.4%	0:00:00	0.1%
1	smmsp	1476K	4828K	1.2%	0:00:00	0.0%
6	daemon	6588K	5288K	1.3%	0:00:00	0.0%

Total: 54 processes, 204 lwps, load averages: 0.02, 0.02, 0.01

By using this command, you can get the pid of the process as per your requirement and then you can take required action on that process.

4.   Ptree
Process tree is printed. It is useful when we want to know the topmost process in tree quickly.
-bash-3.2# ptree 1982
1975 /usr/lib/ssh/sshd
  1976 /usr/lib/ssh/sshd
    1982 -bash
      8556 ptree 1982

5.   Pstop :- Stops the process and releases its resources.

6.   Prun:- Invokes the stopped process(by pstop) again.

7.   Kill :- To kill a process by using process id.
The kill command is mostly used by us as system administrators to kill a process forcefully. The syntax of kill command is as follows :
Kill <–signal number/name> <PID>

Forcefully kill a process. (signal number 9)
root@L9AHG13:~# ps -ef | grep -i ncsvc
root   4515   1 0 18:22 ?   00:00:00 [ncsvc]
root   6788 4542 0 18:47 pts/5   00:00:00 grep --color=auto -i 4515

root@L9AHG13:~# kill -9 4515

root@L9AHG13:~# ps -ef | grep -i ncsvc
root   6790 4542 0 18:48 pts/5   00:00:00 grep --color=auto -i ncsvc

    As we can see above the process is killed rightaway. If you run kill without any argument, it will pass stop signal number 15 which will gradually kill the process and many of the times it is not able to kill the process. In this case we need to use signal number 9 to forcefully kill the process.

HUP Signal (signal number 2)
Another useful signal is HUP (or Hang UP) which is a safe signal and asks process to stop, re-read configuration files, and run again. This signal is used when we want to reload the process safely. Lets see an example:-

bash-3.2# ps -ef | grep -i syslog
   root   527   1   0   Jan 28 ?   0:01 /usr/sbin/syslogd

bash-3.2# kill -HUP 527

bash-3.2# ps -ef | grep -i syslog
   root   527   1   0   Jan 28 ?   0:01 /usr/sbin/syslogd

The point to note above is that the same process is hanged and ran again, i.e. why no process id change. There is no harm in running this command. Sometimes a process takes high memory/CPU usage then we need to run this command to test if it becomes normal.

Other signals include number 15 which is default and asks the process to end itself. One more signal is -2 which kills the process leading to loss of data(same as pressing ctrl+c when the process is running).

8.   Killall
Killall command is another version of kill command which by default send the kill signal to all running processes because of which it is usually called on system shutdown to kill all running programs which are not exited by user.

9.   Pkill :- To kill the process by using process name.
We rarely use this command as it kills all processes matching the name passed with this command.
bash-3.2# ps -ef | grep -i syslog
    root   527   1   0   Jan 28 ?   0:01 /usr/sbin/syslogd
bash-3.2# pkill syslog
bash-3.2# ps -ef | grep -i syslog
    root 18868   1   0 23:33:34 ?   0:00 /usr/sbin/syslogd
See the process id and time is changed. It means the process was killed by the command, however in Solaris this will run again as per cron scripts scheduled.

10.   Jobs
 To see running and stopped commands by the current user in the current session. The scope of this command is very limited. Lets see an example.

vi abc
Press ctrl+Z to stop this process.

#top
Again press ctrl+z to stop this process and send to background as well.

Now check the commands stopped by the user and waiting to be killed permanently or to run again.
bash-3.2# jobs -pl
[1]- 18284 Stopped (tty output)   vi abc
[2]+ 18285 Stopped (tty output)   top

Fg :- To bring a process to foreground which is working in background.

Now suppose you want to run the first job again then you need to bring this job in foreground.
fg %1

Now this will open the vi editor with abc file. Similarly you can bring the other job to foreground.

Bg :- To send a foreground process to background.

Similarly suppose you want to send a job to background and wants it to be in running state, then you can use command bg %1. This will send the job in background in running state.

11.   Pgrep
 Finds/greps a process by its name.
bash-3.2# pgrep -l vi
 9400 vi
Greps exact process name.

8.2   Quick Tip 14: How to print current process id?
Echo $$ → Prints current process id.

bash-3.2# echo $$
1182
bash-3.2# ps -ef | grep -i 1182
        root 1182 1131   0 18:26:42 pts/1   0:00 bash

To get the process id of the current process is very useful when we create scripts, to save the process ids of the different actions taken in the script.

8.3   Quick Tip 15: How to pause a process and make its resources available for some time. ?
Sometimes there are multiple process running simultaneously and slowing the processing of the priority actions or processes. In this case, there may be a requirement to pause few high cpu/memory consuming process for some time and then resume it later on. We can achieve this task by using below technique or commands.

➤ Get the process id of the process you want to pause.
-bash-3.2# ps -f
```
   UID  PID  PPID  C  STIME TTY       TIME CMD
   root  8567  1982  0 12:33:02 pts/2    0:00 ps -f
   root  1982  1976  0 00:06:33 pts/2    0:01 -bash
```
-bash-3.2#

Suppose you want to pause a process with process id 1982 which corresponds to bash shell.

➤ Run pstop command with process id to pause this process.
-bash-3.2# **pstop 1982**
Above command hangs 1982 process id and the terminal will become not responding since bash process is paused.

Now this will temporarily pauses the process and releases the resources.

➤ To resume the process execute prun command with process id from another terminal.
bash-3.2# **prun 1982**

You will see the first session will be active again.

9 Crontab

Cron or crontab is a job scheduling utility in Unix or Linux using which we can schedule any task/command/script at any specific time of the day/month/year.

This utility is very useful and almost used in every other server to schedule the maintenance/backup jobs in real time. Now lets have a look how to use this utility and what all needs to be checked to confirm if this utility is working fine.

Every utility has a daemon or process which is responsible for its working. Similarly cron utility also has a process called cron which should be online, or in running state to make crontab function.

Process required to be online for cron job.
bash-3.2# **svcs -a | grep -i cron**
online   16:36:57 svc:/system/cron:default

Now since the cron process is online, it means any script/command scheduled with cron will be executed at mentioned time. Now we need to learn how to see existing cron entries and how to make new entry to schedule any cron job.

9.1   List Crontab file

We can list crontab file data by using crontab command with –l argument.
#crontab –l
You may not see any data unless any job is already defined on your system.
For example:- On my system, following crontab exists for root user.
bash-3.2# crontab -l
#ident "@(#)root   1.21   04/03/23 SMI"
#
The root crontab should be used to perform accounting data collection.
#
#
10 3 * * * /usr/sbin/logadm
15 3 * * 0 /usr/lib/fs/nfs/nfsfind
30 3 * * * [-x /usr/lib/gss/gsscred_clean] &&
/usr/lib/gss/gsscred_clean

Similarly I can see cron of any other user say, "om" like below.

bash-3.2# crontab -l om

crontab: can't open your crontab file.
bash-3.2#

Since om user has not scheduled any job, so there is no crontab file and hence it is showing above error.

9.2   Edit crontab file

We have seen how to look different crontab entries for different users. Now we will learn the main part i.e. how to edit our crontab file and schedule a job.
Edit cron file
#crontab –e

In case you are not getting appropriate editor to write then exit from crontab edit command and export below variables first and then run command "contab –e" to edit your crontab.
#export EDITOR=vi
#export TERM=vt100

Now lets see how to put entries in crontab file to schedule different jobs. The crontab file consists of lines with six fields each. The fields are separated by spaces or tabs. The first five fields are integer patterns that specify the following:

minute (0-59),
hour (0-23),
day of the month (1-31),
month of the year (1-12),
day of the week (0-6 with 0=Sunday).

And the sixth field is the command/script we want to execute at the mentioned time calculated by first five fields.

Example 1: Schedule a backup script /opt/oracle/backup.sh at 11PM every Sunday.

0   23   *   *   0   /opt/oracle/backup.sh

0 → 0th minute of every hour
23 → 23rd hour of a 24 hour day.
*→ Every day of the month.
*→ Every month of the year
0→ Only on Sunday

Example 2: Greet all logged in users every 2 mins with message "Good day !!"

*/2 * * * * echo 'Good day !!' | wall

Now exit from the crontab editor. You will see a message will be broadcasted every 2 minutes like below.

Broadcast Message from root (???) on SolarisLab1 Thu Jan 29 07:24:00...
Good Day !!

9.3   Quick Tip 16: What is the difference between Cron and Crontab?

Cron is the utility/process, and crontab is the file responsible for scheduling jobs via cron. We can also say crontab command manages the cron file.

Cron → Daemon responsible for executing scheduled jobs.
Crontab → Command which maintains /etc/crontab file responsible for scheduling the jobs.

9.4   Remove Crontab file

a.   The recommended way is to use crontab command.
bash-3.2# crontab -r user123

b.   Another way is to remove the crontab file of user directly from path.
bash-3.2# rm /var/spool/cron/crontabs/om

9.5   Disabling cron for a particular user
bash-3.2# **vi /etc/cron.d/cron.deny**
Mention the username, lets say user123 and then try to do crontab –e. It will not allow.

bash-3.2# crontab -l user123
crontab: you are not authorized to use cron. Sorry.

9.6   Allow crontab for only few users
Allow crontab for only specified users, deny all other users.

Mention the list of users in below file.
bash-3.2# **vi /etc/cron.d/cron.allow**

All other users whose name is not present in this file will not be allowed to access cron.

10   Swap Management
Swap is a part of disk space that acts like virtual ram which is used to fake the microprocessor that more ram is available. Suppose you want to run a program which requires minimum 2gb ram, and your system has only 1.5GB or ram, in this case you can add swap and make the program believe that your total physical memory is equal to ram plus swap space.

Let's see how we can manage the swap space on our solaris system.

a.   Swap –l :- Lists already configured swap devices.

```
bash-3.2# swap -l
swapfile        dev  swaplo blocks  free
/dev/dsk/c0d0s1    102,1     8 4209016 4209016
```

10.1   Quick Tip 17: How to calculate swap size in Solaris?

In swap –l output we can see the swap size in blocks. You can get the exact size by converting these blocks into MB.

4209016 Blocks = 4209016*512 Bytes

Swap Size in MB = 4209016*512/1024/1024 = 2055 MB ~ 2GB Swap.

10.2   Why swap is required?

The swap space configured on any Solaris system is used by various application alongwith the crash dump. A crash dump is the data collected by system in case a process hangs and causes system crash so that the root cause of system crash can be analyzed from this crash dump later.

By default solaris uses swap for managing application by making the system capable of running more applications alongwith high memory requirement applications. Also swap is used to store the crash dump, however its not recommended since this may get deleted on system reboot and our purpose remains unaddressed if crash dump is not available.

By default, swap device is configured for storing crash dump. We will see in next section how to change this.

bash-3.2# **dumpadm**

    Dump content: kernel pages
     Dump device: **/dev/dsk/c0d0s1 (swap)**
Savecore directory: /var/crash/localhost

Savecore enabled: yes
Save compressed: on

The swap can be analyzed using SCAT(solaris crash dump analyzing tool),or by using mdb tools.

10.3   Check Swap

We had seen how to check swap devices, now we will see how to check total swap available and how to know the free swap available.

Swap –s :- To check the total size of the swap available.

bash-3.2# swap -s
total: 197604k bytes allocated + 58720k reserved = 256324k used, 2060260k available
bash-3.2#

You can also use top command.
bash-3.2# top | head
load averages: 0.00, 0.01, 0.00   11:52:54
54 processes: 52 sleeping, 1 zombie, 1 on cpu

Memory: 400M real, 19M free, 252M swap in use, 2009M swap free

10.4   Add swap

We can add swap anytime on our Solaris system in runtime. The swap can be added by using hard disk device, or even by using some file. However the swap space created via file is not recommended as its not safe and can cause real time issues if deleted by mistake.

To add additional swap, we can use swap command with argument a i.e. swap-a.

Swap Addition using different devices
We can add swap area into our solaris system by using any of the following devices or methods.
1.   Disk Slice
2.   File (created with mkfile) :- not recommended as it can be deleted accidently.
3.   Zfs Volumes (different from pool)

Let us have a look at these different ways one by one.

10.4.1 Using Slice/disk
Create a disk slice for swap area and then perform below steps.
bash-3.2# **swap -a /dev/dsk/c2t4d0s0**
bash-3.2#
bash-3.2# **swap -l**
swapfile   dev swaplo blocks   free
/dev/dsk/c0d0s1   102,1   8 4209016 4209016
/dev/dsk/c2t4d0s0   30,320   8 1023992 1023992

To Make it permanent.
Make an entry in vfstab
/dev/dsk/dev/dsk/c2t4d0s0   -   -   swap -   no

10.4.2 Using file
Create a file of required size, lets say 500mb using mkfile or dd command.
bash-3.2# **mkfile 500m /var/swap1**
bash-3.2#

Now add the swap area.
bash-3.2# **swap -a /var/swap1**

Check the increased swap

```
bash-3.2# swap -l
swapfile          dev  swaplo blocks   free
/dev/dsk/c0d0s1    102,1    8 4209016 4209016
/var/swap1          -       8 1023992 1023992
```

10.4.3 Using ZFS volume

A ZFS volume just represents a block device which can be used as a swap area, and since this type of volume doesn't have any mount point, it differs from a zfs filesystem. A ZFS volume has following characterstics.

1.   Is a Dataset just like filesystem.
2.   No mountpoint
3.   Can be used to add swap or collecting crash dump.

To list available ZFS volumes.
```
bash-3.2# zfs list -t volume
no datasets available
```

Create new ZFS volume
```
bash-3.2# zfs create -V 200m oracle2/myswap
```

```
bash-3.2# zpool list
NAME     SIZE ALLOC  FREE   CAP HEALTH ALTROOT
datapool 496M 221M 275M   44% ONLINE -
oracle2  984M 313K 984M    0% ONLINE -
```

```
bash-3.2# zfs list -t volume
NAME           USED  AVAIL  REFER  MOUNTPOINT
oracle2/myswap 207M  952M   16K   -
```

Add this volume as swap area.
```
bash-3.2# swap -a /dev/zvol/dsk/oracle2/myswap
bash-3.2#
```

```
bash-3.2# swap -l
swapfile          dev  swaplo blocks   free
/dev/dsk/c0d0s1    102,1     8 4209016 4209016
/var/swap1           -       8 1023992 1023992
/dev/zvol/dsk/oracle2/myswap 181,1     8 409592 409592
```

To make it permanent, you need to enter this device path in /etc/vfstab
file and create an entry for new swap area.

10.5   Remove Swap

To delete the swap area we can use swap –d command.
bash-3.2# swap -d /dev/dsk/c2t4d0s0

Make sure to remove entry from /etc/vfstab file otherwise this may
cause problems later on.

11   Crash Dump/Core File Management in Solaris

Whenever any major issue occur on our solaris system which lead to
system crash, the system dumps memory data to the dump device so
that it can be investigated later which process(es) were killed which led
to system crash. In this case, the memory data is copied to the dump
device, which is called as crash dump.

However sometimes the issue occurs with some process and it crashes,
however it may not lead to system crash. In this case a core dump is
generated which is memory data of the process which got terminated
abnormally.

11.1   Crash Dumps in Solaris

Whenever complete system crash occurs, a crash dump is generated. The
core file will be generated thereafter from this crash dump inside the

savecore directory. So we will first see how to configure the crash dump device and how to check/modify its settings.

Check the dump settings on the system.
bash-3.2# **dumpadm**
    Dump content: kernel pages
     Dump device: /dev/dsk/c0d0s1 (swap)
Savecore directory: /var/crash/localhost
  Savecore enabled: yes
   Save compressed: on
Currently only kernel pages will be dumped to the device. However we should change it to all, so that every information can be dumped.
bash-3.2# **dumpadm -c all**
    Dump content: all pages
     Dump device: /dev/dsk/c0d0s1 (swap)
Savecore directory: /var/crash/localhost
  Savecore enabled: yes
   Save compressed: on

In case a fatal system error, the system dumps all its physical memory data to the dump device. After dump completes, system will reboot.

During reboot, OS checks dump data and its process savecore creates core files for analysis.
Check the core files using mdb core files.

However as of now, dump device is referenced to swap space, and it should not be swap since the swap data is removed on system reboot. Hence we should change it to some disk device.

bash-3.2# **dumpadm -d /dev/dsk/c2t2d0s0**
    Dump content: all pages
     Dump device: /dev/dsk/c2t2d0s0 (dedicated)
Savecore directory: /var/crash/localhost

Savecore enabled: yes
  Save compressed: on

Dump device should be double than RAM to dump all data.

Save core directory specifies the path on running system where the system generates the core file from crash dump on reboot after system crash.

bash-3.2# dumpadm -s /mysolaris
Dump content: kernel pages
Dump device: /dev/dsk/c0d1s1 (swap)
Savecore directory: /mysolaris
Savecore enabled: yes
Save compressed: on
bash-3.2#
The crash dump settings are saved in a file called dumpadm.conf.

bash-3.2#
bash-3.2# cat /etc/dumpadm.conf
#
dumpadm.conf
#
Configuration parameters for system crash dump.
Do NOT edit this file by hand -- use dumpadm(1m) instead.
#
DUMPADM_DEVICE=/dev/dsk/c2t2d0s0
DUMPADM_SAVDIR=/mysolaris/
DUMPADM_CONTENT=all
DUMPADM_ENABLE=yes
DUMPADM_CSAVE=on
bash-3.2#

11.2   Generating crash dump

Till now, we have configured crash dump settings where to dump the data and what all data needs to be dumped from physical memory in case of process crash. To test if crash dump is working fine, we need to crash some process and generate the crash dump.

bash-3.2# **savecore -L**

savecore: dedicated dump device required

Above error occurs if you havn't defined dedicated device i.e. the dump device is still swap.

Lets now change the dump device to disk partition.

bash-3.2# **dumpadm -d /dev/dsk/c2t2d0s0**
    Dump content: all pages
     Dump device: /dev/dsk/c2t2d0s0 (dedicated)
Savecore directory: /mysolaris
  Savecore enabled: yes
   Save compressed: on

Below command may crash the system also. So avoid using on production servers.

bash-3.2# **savecore -L**

dumping to /dev/dsk/c2t2d0s0, offset 65536, content: all
 0:06 100% done
100% done: 262031 pages dumped, dump succeeded
savecore: System dump time: Wed Apr 2 16:58:45 2014

savecore: Saving compressed system crash dump in
/mysolaris//vmdump.0
savecore: Decompress the crash dump with
'savecore -vf /mysolaris//vmdump.0'

---

bash-3.2# du -sh /mysolaris//vmdump.0
 321M /mysolaris//vmdump.0

11.3   Generate Core files from Dump

Now we have crash dump file with us, and we can now uncompress it to generate the core file.

bash-3.2# **savecore -vf /mysolaris//vmdump.0**
savecore: System dump time: Wed Apr 2 16:58:45 2014
savecore: not enough space in /mysolaris/ (423 MB avail, 1036 MB needed)

It seems /mysolaris partition doesn't have enough free space available. Lets mention some other path and run the utility again.

bash-3.2# **savecore -vf /mysolaris//vmdump.0 /var**
savecore: System dump time: Wed Apr 2 16:58:45 2014

savecore: saving system crash dump in /var/{unix,vmcore}.0
Constructing namelist /var/unix.0
Constructing corefile /var/vmcore.0
 0:40 100% done: 262031 of 262031 pages saved
7566 (2%) zero pages were not written
0:40 dump decompress is done
bash-3.2# file /var/unix.0
/var/unix.0: ELF 64-bit LSB executable AMD64 Version 1, statically linked, not stripped, no debugging information available
bash-3.2# file /var/vmcore.0
/var/vmcore.0:   SunOS 5.10 Generic_147441-25 64-bit Intel live dump from 'system11'

11.4   Core File Configuration

Whenever the application/process gets panic, it generates the core dump followed by core file generation.

When there is problem in some process and the system remains stable, it dumps the process data which is stored in memory/RAM in the form of core file.

To see/change core file pattern, we can use coreadm command.

bash-3.2# **coreadm**
   global core file pattern:
    global core file content: default
     init core file pattern: core
     init core file content: default
       global core dumps: disabled
    per-process core dumps: enabled
    global setid core dumps: disabled
per-process setid core dumps: disabled
    global core dump logging: disabled

bash-3.2# cat /etc/coreadm.conf
#
coreadm.conf
#
Parameters for system core file configuration.
Do NOT edit this file by hand -- use coreadm(1) instead.
#
COREADM_GLOB_PATTERN=
COREADM_GLOB_CONTENT=default
COREADM_INIT_PATTERN=core
COREADM_INIT_CONTENT=default
COREADM_GLOB_ENABLED=no
COREADM_PROC_ENABLED=yes
COREADM_GLOB_SETID_ENABLED=no

COREADM_PROC_SETID_ENABLED=no
COREADM_GLOB_LOG_ENABLED=no

Core files are analyzed to identify why application is terminated and what is the issue. We will see how to change above options to generate core file as per our requirement after next section.

11.5   Generate Core files by killing a process abnormally.

Let us have a look how the core files are generated and how to change core file related options. Open two terminals of your test server and do the following tasks to generate a sample core file.

a.   First Terminal
vi abc

b.   Second terminal
bash-3.2# **ps -ef | grep -i vi**
root 9400 9235 0 20:33:42 pts/6   0:00 vi abc
root 6072   1 0 08:38:23 ?   0:32 /usr/java/bin/java -
Dviper.fifo.path=/var/run/smc898/boot.fifo -Xmx128m -Dsun.s

bash-3.2# **pgrep -l vi**
 9400 vi

c.   Kill the process and ask to generate core file by passing argument 8.
bash-3.2# **kill -8 9400**
bash-3.2#

d.   Again on first terminal
We will get below message:
Arithmetic Exception (core dumped)
bash-3.2#

e.   The core files will be generated in the same directory where the process is started. As we can see below the core file is generated in / where we have started the process.

bash-3.2# **ls -ltr | grep -i core**
-rw-------   1 root   root   2882380 Apr 2 20:37 core
bash-3.2# **pwd**
/

Another Example to generate core file
bash-3.2# zsh
system11# echo $$ ### Gets current process id (of the shell in this case)
9416

system11# ps
  PID TTY   TIME CMD
 9417 pts/6   0:00 ps
 9416 pts/6   0:00 zsh
 9235 pts/6   0:00 bash
 9231 pts/6   0:00 bash

system11# kill -8 9416
Arithmetic Exception (core dumped)

Now here we can see the old core file is overwritten which is the default behavior.
To overcome this behavior we need to change the core file pattern and its default location. We will use the commands as discussed earlier to achieve this task. Always remember not to edit coreadm or dumpadm config files, use commands only.

11.6   Change name pattern and location of core file

bash-3.2# mkdir /mycore

%f → which application
%u → which user
%p-→ which process id

bash-3.2# coreadm -g /mycore/core.%f.%u.%p –e global

bash-3.2# coreadm
   global core file pattern: /mycore/core.%f.%u.%p
   global core file content: default
    init core file pattern: core

bash-3.2# cat /etc/coreadm.conf
Do NOT edit this file by hand -- use coreadm(1) instead.
#
COREADM_GLOB_PATTERN=/mycore/core.%f.%u.%p
COREADM_GLOB_CONTENT=default

Generate core file and check.
bash-3.2# zsh
system11# ps
  PID TTY   TIME CMD
 9295 pts/7   0:00 bash
 9498 pts/7   0:00 zsh
 9499 pts/7   0:00 ps
 9299 pts/7   0:00 bash
system11#
system11# kill -8 9498
Arithmetic Exception (core dumped)
bash-3.2#

bash-3.2# ls -ltr /mycore/
total 7920
-rw-------   1 root   root   4039692 Apr 2 20:56 core.zsh.0.9498

11.7   Gcore(core of a specific process) generation

Gcore generates the core file of the mentioned process by copying the physical memory data to the core file. Sometimes this is useful in case the process is behaving abnormally to analyze the situation, otherwise gcore generation is done very rarely.

bash-3.2# zsh
system11# echo $$
9507

system11# gcore 9507
gcore: core.9507 dumped

system11# ls -l core.9507
-rw-r--r-- 1 root   root   4039717 Apr 2 20:57 core.9507
system11# pwd

12   Quick Tip 18: How to find block size in UFS and ZFS ?

We can get the block size by using df command with g option which will print entire filesystem information.

bash-3.2# **df -g /mysolaris/**
/mysolaris   (oracle2/firstpart):   **131072** block size   512 frag size
 1949696 total blocks   1949279 free blocks 1949279 available   1949294 total files
 1949279 free files   47513623 filesys id
   zfs fstype   0x00000004 flag   255 filename length

```
bash-3.2# df -g / /mysolaris/ /etc/mnttab
/            (/dev/dsk/c0d0s0   ):     8192 block size      1024 frag size
28383096 total blocks   10679782 free blocks 10395952 available
1712256 total files
 1492108 free files    26738688 filesys id
    ufs fstype     0x00000004 flag        255 filename length

/mysolaris       (oracle2/firstpart ):    131072 block size      512 frag
size
 1949696 total blocks   1949279 free blocks  1949279 available     1949294
total files
 1949279 free files    47513623 filesys id
    zfs fstype     0x00000004 flag        255 filename length

/etc/mnttab      (mnttab       ):    512 block size      512 frag size
    0 total blocks       0 free blocks     0 available       1 total files
    0 free files    79167489 filesys id  /mnttab
   mntfs fstype      00000000 flag         64 filename length
```

In ZFS, there is one more way to get the block size.

```
bash-3.2# zfs get all pool oracle2 | grep size
cannot open 'pool': dataset does not exist
oracle2  recordsize      128K          default
```

13   Quick Tip 19: How to identify amount of RAM in Solaris?

As an administrator you should know how to get physical memory of your solaris system. Instead of checking other command, the best way to get the RAM is to use prtconf command.

```
bash-3.2# prtconf -pv | grep -i mem
Memory size: 1024 Megabytes
```

Questions

1.   How to add a user mentioning shell, comment, and home directory path?
2.   How to lock and unlock a user?
3.   How to logout a user forcefully by killing its session?
4.   What is the role of System and User Profile File?
5.   What do you mean by magic directory is solaris?
6.   How we can check crontab file of a user oracle?
7.   What is swap and how can you see free swap of our system?
8.   How will you verify device where crash dump gets saved?

Chapter -6
Solaris Zones and Volume Manager
Day 5

1.   Virtualization in Solaris

With Solaris 10 onwards, Oracle provides a very nice feature to deploy different operating systems into it and allows us to run multiple types and versions of operating systems inside one high end server, just like virtual machines. Solaris OS behaves as base OS, and we can install different operating systems in it, just like guest OS and boot all of them together.

These different Operating systems deployed under base operating system are also called zones. Oracle officially calls it as Oracle Solaris Containers. These containers or zones act just like a separate operating system and serves the purpose of virtualization in Solaris.

We will see different type of containers or zones in the next sections and their benefits.

2.   Understanding Zones

Sometimes few programs conflict and they can't be run on same server, for them to run we need separate servers. We may not able to deploy multiple servers for such small programs, so the best and recommended way is to use solaris containers or zones. A zone can be created with very less memory or cpu usage, however it depends how and which zone we will create.

2.1. Check Available Zones

To check zones in the system, we can list zones using zoneadm command. "civ" options displays all zones even which are in configured state and in verbose form, nicely formatted.

bash-3.2# zoneadm list -civ
  ID NAME   STATUS   PATH   BRAND   IP
   0 global   running   /   native shared

No zone installed on the node yet. Global zone is the core/physical Solaris system on which we are working. It is always named as global zone with id 0.

2.2. Zone Features

A zone provides virtual OS services to individual applications and users. Useful for conflicting applications requires to be installed on separate operating systems.

When we install Solaris 10, it will by default install this OS under Global zone with id 0. We can create multiple non global zones. Each non global zone can have separate configuration. Zones are used to utilize the system resources effectively.

Each zone exists with separate process and file system space. These oracle solaris containers have some fantastic properties, some of which are listed below.

➢   Security:- From global zone only we can check the local zones. From local zone, we can't reach to global zone. Local zones remains separate and global zone remains secure.

>   Isolation:- Each application/zone is separate from the other.

>   Virtualization :- Multiple zones with multiple different version of solaris can co-exist and hence providing virtualization.

>   Granularity :- A single node can consist of whole different operating systems into itself.

>   Transparency :- We can check which zones are running, stopped or still not configured.

2.3.   Two Types of Zones

The zones or oracle containers can be of two types.

>   Global :- Default zone of the main system on which we install further containers. This zone is used for system admin activities. Id=0, name=global

>   Non-global:- No disk management is available(format command shows no disks). it can't act as NFS server(only as nfs client) . Zone ID is not equal to 0 and can change on boot, name=any name.

2.4.   Quick Tip 1: Installing a package on only Global Zone.

Suppose you only want to change global zone and want this package should not be installed on any containers inside this. We can restrict the package so that it will be installed only in global zone by passing G argument with pkgadd command.

#pkgadd –G <package_name>
(Now the package will be installed on only global zone)

#pkgadd –d <pkgname>
(By default, the package will install the package on all zones)

2.5. Zone Daemons

Zone daemons are the services that must be running on our base system so that the zones can function properly. We will see the different processes that control how the zones work and which are responsible for correct functioning of the zones.

✓   <u>Zoneadmd</u> :- Responsible for managing zone id, zone boot/shutdown, setting resource, zones devices and config, mounting loopback and conventional file system, plumb nics.

✓   <u>Zsched</u> :- Every active zone has this process. Track per zone how many kernel threads are running.

First zoneadmd started and then zsched is started.

2.6. Enable Networking in non-global Zone

Networking is a feature by which our system is able to communicate with other systems or nodes. The first thing that comes in our mind when we talk about networking is node's IP address.

IP address can be assigned to any non-global zone using below two ways:

1.   <u>Shared IP</u> :- Uses same global eth interface, and assigns virtual IP inside the non-global zone.

Drawbacks:-

- Low Bandwidth
- No network management inside non global zone, since the device can only be controlled in global zone.
- Only global zone admin can change the IP, availability dependent on global zone card. (ce0:1, ce0:2)

2. 	Exclusive IP :- From Solaris 9 onwards the concept of exclusive IP is introduced. When we dedicate a NIC to a particular zone, it is called exclusive IP.

Advantages:-

• 	Complete bandwidth

• 	Network management becomes easy. (ce1, ce2)

Disadvantage:

• 	Cost of additional hardware NIC card.

bash-3.2# zoneadm list -civ

ID NAME	STATUS	PATH	BRAND	IP
0 global	running	/	native	**shared**

In the above output, we can see IP type of global zone is shared.

### 2.7. 	Zone States

Solaris Zone or Container can have different states depending upon whether the zone is running, or powered off, etc. To understand them better, we need to see these different states.

1. 	Undefined (not yet defined/created)

2. 	Configured (zone is created but not configured, xml file exists for the zone)

3. 	Incomplete (not installed successfully)

4. 	Installed (when the zone gets installed successfully)

5. 	Ready (when we boot the installed zone it becomes ready, immediately it will go to running state)

6. 	Running (currently the zone is running)

7. 	Shutting down and down (when we shut down, the zone go into installed state)

/etc/zones/ is the directory which is updated with new xml file when any zone is created.

2.8. What is LOFS?

When we mount an already mounted partition directory or mount point on another directory in the same server then it is called as LOFS or LOopback FileSystem. You may be thinking what is the use of this LOFS mount point, and why we will mount same data mount point at two locations on the same server.

The main motive behind creating loopback filesystem is to fool the system that data is kept at one more alternate location or path and the advantage over this is that, we can even mount this as read-only protecting the original data, and allowing applications to use it as if its available right there.

You will see this concept in solaris local containers where the system files partition is mounted again inside the local zone as LOFS in read only format to save large amount of disk space and redundant data on the server.

Mounting a loopback filesystem (LOFS).

We will now see how we can mount the same directory again on another directory by mentioning its filesystem type as LOFS.

bash-3.2# mkdir /solaris10
bash-3.2# mount /dev/dsk/c0d0s0 /solaris10
mount: /dev/dsk/c0d0s0 is already mounted or /solaris10 is busy

Note:- Here we can see an already mounted partition can't be remounted in UNIX, however in LINUX we can mount it again.

Now we need to mount it as LOFS filesystem.

bash-3.2# mount -F lofs / /solaris10

bash-3.2# df -h

Filesystem   size   used avail capacity Mounted on
/dev/dsk/c0d0s0   14G   9.9G 3.5G   75%   /
/devices   0K   0K   0K   0%   /devices
ctfs   0K   0K   0K   0%   /system/contract
/   **14G   9.9G   3.5G   75%   /solaris10**

We can even mount any sub directory to other directory and so on. For example:- Make two directories under this lofs /solaris

bash-3.2# mkdir /dir1 /dir2

bash-3.2# pwd

/

bash-3.2# mount -F lofs /dir1 /dir2

bash-3.2# df -h | grep -i dir

/dir1   14G 9.9G 3.5G   75%   /dir2

Now dir1 is mounted on dir2, means dir2 simply refers data inside dir1.

2.9.   Zone Vs Container

We are calling Oracle Solaris Containers as zones and zones as containers. However there is a slight difference between them.

If resource management can be done in non-global zone then it is known as container. For example:- if we assign dedicated memory, cpu, etc to some zones then they will be called as containers.

A Zone may be a container or not.

2.10. Quick Tip 2: How to identify the local or global zone.

When you list the zones using zoneadm list command, the id is always 0 for global zone and more than 0 for non-global zone. The name is "global" for global zone.

#zoneadm list –civ

3. Zone Model Types

In Solaris, a zone can be created by using different options based on which we have two types of zone model available. We need to decide the zone model type while creating zone.

We can't convert between these zone types after creation.

1. Sparse root model (small zone)
✓ Only configuration files are copied, rest system files and packages are linked through loopback LOFS filesystem.
✓ Zone path on some slice → /export/zone_name/ with **permission 600.**
✓ /lib, /platform, /sbin, /usr are called as critical directories and mounted via LOFS, no data is copied, same directories will be mounted as read only.
✓ Apart from this we have seperate /etc, /var, /opt, /export/home directories.
✓ So it takes very less space for example:- 100MB only to create /etc/, /var, /adm, etc.
✓ Main drawback:- We can't install any OS related patch.

2. Whole root model (big zone)
✓ /lib, /usr, /sbin, and /platform are copied instead of sharing from global zone.

✓   Can install all patches except kernel patch. Kernel patch can only be installed on global zone.

✓   Take huge space as whole filesystem is copied.

3.1. <u>Quick Tip 3</u>: Identify whole root or sparse zone.

Go to any directory /lib, /sbin and try touching any file. If its read only and you are not able to write then it's a sparse root zone.

Also you can view the filesystem type from "mount –v" command, if it shows LOFS filesystem then it's a sparse root zone.

In case you are able to write in these directories /lib, /sbin then you are in whole root zone.

3.2. <u>Quick Tip 4</u>: Difference between vmware and solaris zones?

In VM, we have disk files which can't be accessed offline when the nodes are down but solaris zone data can be accessed from global zone when the zones are down.

In zones, we can install solaris, or linux(also called LX branded zones, only redhat/centos OS Zone can be created, no support for debian OS versions).

4.   Zone components

A zone consists of few things which are called as its components. These components altogether makes a zone functional and ready to serve as an independent operating system.

1.   Zone name → Name of the zone.
2.   Path to zone root → Path where new zone will be installed

3.   Zone network interfaces → Plumb interfaces and assign ip address to the zone.

4.   File systms mounted → Different filesystems mounted in the zone.

5.   Configured devices and resource management → The number of resources available for sparse or whole root zone from global zone and the devices shared with them.

We will look how to configure all these zone components in the next sections.

5.   Zone Commands

Before going with zone setup, we should know what all commands or utilities available for zone management. Oracle Solaris provides mainly two types of zone commands, one for configuration and other for administration which is used after the zone is configured.

1.   Zonecfg :- Used for creating zone, deleting zone, add/remove network card, etc configuration of the zone.

2.   Zoneadm :- For zone wide admin activities, installing, login, booting, shutting, migrating, etc. Once the zone is configured, we use this command for complete zone administration. One of the most frequently used command.

3.   Zonename :- Shows name of the zone.

bash-3.2# zonename

global

Oracle has made very clear and transparent mechanism to configure and administrator zones by giving only two commands, in which one is used for configuration, and other is for administration. So whenever you want to do any operation you should be clear, if you want to change some configuration, example adding a new NIC card, make changes in zone configuration xml file then you will use zonecfg command, and in case you want to perform admin activities on the zone like forcefully restart zone, etc then you will use zoneadm command.

6.   Zone Setup

Now we will see how to do zone setup i.e. how to create a new virtual operating system i.e. oracle solaris zone/container. First we will configure the zone(zonecfg), and thereafter we will install and boot the zone(zoneadm).

Zone Configuration

1.   Recommended is to create a separate slice of 2GB(minimum) from format. Any ufs or zfs.

2.   Mount the slice, say on /export/zone1 and now start creating new zone.

First check what all zones already available
bash-3.2# zoneadm list -cv

ID NAME	STATUS	PATH	BRAND	IP
0 global	running	/	native	shared

bash-3.2#

So no zones configured yet. Let's start creating a zone named saket-zone.
bash-3.2# zonecfg -z saket-zone
saket-zone: No such zone configured
Use 'create' to begin configuring a new zone.
zonecfg:saket-zone>

For sparse root zone:
zonecfg:saket-zone> create

For whole root zone, pass b argument with create command:
zonecfg:saket-zone> create –b

6.1.   Exclusive IP configuration

In this section, we will look how to dedicate a physical NIC to a zone and assign an IP address to it independent from the global zone.

Set ip_type=exclusive
Add net
Set physical=e100g2
end

Note:- If we do not give any ip address during configuration then it will be asked when we boot the zone after configuration.

We will see in next section where you can run above commands to configure exclusive ip address.

6.2.   Adding sound card to a zone

Similar to nic card addition, we can also add devices like sound card to our zone like below.

add device
set match=/dev/sound/*
end
We will see how to do this during zone creation step in the next sections.

6.3. Steps for Zone Creation

Here we will see how to configure the zone from beginning and learn what all configuration needs to be done and how to add NIC card, sound card whose commands we have seen in earlier sections.

To start creating the zone, first we need to configure zone, so we will use zonecfg command with new zone name followed by argument "-z"

bash-3.2# zonecfg -z saket-zone
saket-zone: No such zone configured
Use 'create' to begin configuring a new zone.
zonecfg:saket-zone>
zonecfg:saket-zone> create   ## start creating sparse zone
zonecfg:saket-zone> set zonepath=/export/zone1 ## dir where zone will be installed
zonecfg:saket-zone> set autoboot=true ## auto boot with global zone
zonecfg:saket-zone> add inherit-pkg-dir ### links /opt also as LOFS so that global zone apps available in sparse zone.
zonecfg:saket-zone:inherit-pkg-dir> set dir=/opt/sfw ### this is the directory where we can install the new softwares in this newly created non global zone.
zonecfg:saket-zone:inherit-pkg-dir> end
zonecfg:saket-zone> add net
zonecfg:saket-zone:net> set physical=e1000g0 ### no virtual interface id need to be given, it will be taken automatically.
zonecfg:saket-zone:net> set address=192.168.20.111
zonecfg:saket-zone:net> end
zonecfg:saket-zone> verify   ### verify if the settings defined are correct.
zonecfg:saket-zone> commit ### creates the xml file under /etc/zones
zonecfg:saket-zone> exit

bash-3.2#

The zone is now configured and the nic card is added with IP address.

We can also check the new zone status.

bash-3.2# zoneadm list -cv

ID	NAME	STATUS	PATH	BRAND	IP
0	global	running	/	native	shared
-	saket-zone	configured	/export/zone1	native	shared

6.4.   Viewing the created zone configuration

We can view a zone configuration and all the configured devices, options and based on that add/remove/change the configuration. Since we are talking about configuration lookup and modification, hence we will use zonecfg command.

bash-3.2# zonecfg -z saket-zone info

zonename: saket-zone

zonepath: /export/zone1

brand: native

autoboot: true

bootargs:

pool:

limitpriv:

scheduling-class:

ip-type: shared

hostid:

inherit-pkg-dir:

        dir: /lib

inherit-pkg-dir:

        dir: /platform

inherit-pkg-dir:

```
        dir: /sbin
inherit-pkg-dir:
        dir: /usr
inherit-pkg-dir:
dir: /opt/sfw        ##### make sure this directory exists, otherwise
create  ##### this directory using "mkdir /opt/sfw" command.
net:
        address: 192.168.20.111
        physical: e1000g0
        defrouter not specified
bash-3.2#
```

6.5.   Verify new Zone

After zone configuration, before we go ahead with zone installation, we should verify the zone to avoid any errors while installing. Zone verification will check whether all configured options are satisfied and if it is fine to go ahead with installation.

bash-3.2# **zoneadm -z saket-zone verify**

/export/zone1 must be owner executable.

/export/zone1 must not be group readable.

/export/zone1 must not be world readable.

could not verify zonepath /export/zone1 because of the above errors.

zoneadm: zone saket-zone failed to verify

As we can see above, our zone failed to verify with permission errors on /export/zone1. Lets correct these errors by setting correct permissions on the zone directory.

bash-3.2# chmod 700 /export/zone1

Now when we verify our zone, it will be successful.
bash-3.2# zoneadm -z saket-zone verify

Since now our zone is verified and had not thrown any error, so we can go ahead and install this zone.

6.6.   Install Zone

Now since our zone is verified, we will install this newly configured zone now. Now since we will install the zone, which is not related to zone configuration change, hence we will use zoneadm command with install option.

bash-3.2# **zoneadm -z saket-zone install**
Preparing to install zone <saket-zone>.
Creating list of files to copy from the global zone.
Copying <9130> files to the zone.
Initializing zone product registry.
Determining zone package initialization order.
Preparing to initialize <1225> packages on the zone.
Initialized <1225> packages on zone.
Zone <saket-zone> is initialized.
Installation of these packages generated errors: <SUNWusrdir
SUNWoptdir>
Installation of <2> packages was skipped.
Installation of these packages generated warnings: <SUNWsmmgr>
The file </export/zone1/root/var/sadm/system/logs/install_log>
contains a log of the zone installation.

After above installation when we look at the zone status, it will show the zone in installed state.

```
bash-3.2# zoneadm list -cv
  ID NAME          STATUS    PATH                   BRAND   IP
  0 global         running   /                      native  shared
  - saket-zone     installed /export/zone1                  native  shared
```

6.7.   Boot Zone

Now since the zone is installed, so its like an OS installed on a PC which is shut down. So the next step is to switch on the PC i.e. boot the new OS. Hence the next step is to boot this new zone.

```
bash-3.2# zoneadm -z saket-zone boot
zoneadm: zone 'saket-zone': WARNING: e1000g0:2: no matching subnet
found in netmasks(4) for 192.168.20.111; using default of 255.255.255.0.
bash-3.2#
```

```
h-3.2# zoneadm list -cv
  ID NAME          STATUS    PATH                   BRAND   IP
  0 global         running   /                      native  shared
  1 saket-zone     running   /export/zone1                  native  shared
```

6.8.   Login to the zone

The newly configured zone is not booted and the status shown is running. So we are not good to login on the new zone. Oracle Solaris provides two ways to login on the zone either on the terminal or on the console.

Zlogin –C <zonename> (-c → console)

Zlogin <zonename> (login to the terminal)

First time when we login to the zone, we need to login with "-C"or on console, since OS will setup date/time, etc. Lets have a look what happens when we first time login on the console after zone creation and bootup.

bash-3.2# **zlogin -C saket-zone**
[Connected to zone 'saket-zone' console]

Select a Language
  0. English
  1. es
  2. fr
Please make a choice (0 - 2), or press h or ? for help: 0

Select a Locale
  0. English (C - 7-bit ASCII)
  1. Canada (English) (UTF-8)
  2. Canada-English (ISO8859-1)
  3. U.S.A. (en_US.ISO8859-1)
  4. U.S.A. (en_US.ISO8859-15)
  5. Go Back to Previous Screen

Please make a choice (0 - 5), or press h or ? for help: 0

It will ask few other simple configuration options, complete those steps to finish new OS setup, and then it will drop you on the login shell.

Observe few things from local zone.

1.   Check the newly configured interface and you will observe the shared NIC interface virtual device is created with ":2" and the IP address is assigned.

bash-3.2# ifconfig -a
lo0:1:
flags=2001000849<UP,LOOPBACK,RUNNING,MULTICAST,IPv4,VIRTUAL> mtu 8232 index 1
        inet 127.0.0.1 netmask ff000000
e1000g0:2:
flags=1000843<UP,BROADCAST,RUNNING,MULTICAST,IPv4> mtu 1500 index 2
        inet 192.168.20.111 netmask ffffff00 broadcast 192.168.20.255
bash-3.2#

2.   Another thing to observe is that when we check available zones using zoneadm list command we can see only local zone with id =2, which is not equal to 0 which means this is not a global zone.

bash-3.2# zoneadm list -cv

ID	NAME	STATUS	PATH	BRAND	IP
2	saket-zone	running	/	native	shared

3.   Also when you check the mounted partitions, you can see that few partitions including /lib is mounted read-only with partition type LOFS.

bash-3.2# mount -v | grep -i lib

/lib on /lib type lofs **read-only**/setuid/nodevices/rstchown/nosub/dev=1980000 on Wed Apr 2 23:30:56 2014

6.9.   <u>Quick Tip 5</u>: Identify where the zones are installed ?

We can quickly view where the zone is installed by observing output of zoneadm list command.

```
bash-3.2# zoneadm list -cv
  ID NAME          STATUS    PATH              BRAND   IP
   0 global        running   /                 native  shared
   2 saket-zone    running   /export/zone1     native  shared

bash-3.2# cd /export/zone1/
bash-3.2# ls -ltr
total 20
drwx------  2 root   root     8192 Apr  2 23:04 lost+found
drwxr-xr-x 12 root   sys      1024 Apr  3 01:00 dev
drwxr-xr-x 18 root   root      512 Apr  3 01:01 root
```

The root filesystem is available inside root directory under the zone install directory.

```
bash-3.2# cd root/
bash-3.2# ls
bin    etc     home    lib    net    platform  sbin    tmp    var
dev    export  kernel  mnt    opt    proc      system  usr
```

Here you can create any file/dir which will reflect in local zone.

6.10. Halt the Zone.

Now since the zone is installed and running, we can access the node directly from outside with the IP address assigned to the node. Suppose you need to change some zone configuration and want to stop the node, so either you can shutdown the zone by logging into zone or you can directly halt the zone. We will see how to halt the zone using zoneadm command.

bash-3.2# zoneadm -z saket-zone halt

bash-3.2# zoneadm list -cv

ID NAME	STATUS	PATH	BRAND	IP
0 global	running	/	native	shared
- saket-zone	installed	/export/zone1	native	shared

So now the zone will come up in installed state since the zone is shut down.

Now lets boot the zone again.

zoneadm -z saket-zone boot

Note:- Now observe the id, it is incremented by 1.

bash-3.2# zoneadm list -cv

ID NAME	STATUS	PATH	BRAND	IP
0 global	running	/	native	shared
3 saket-zone	running	/export/zone1	native	shared

6.11. Quick Tip 6: Check files of local zone from non global zone without login.

We can also fire commands on local zone without logging into the zone using another new command called "zlogin". Zlogin is a simple command which is used to login into any non global zone from global zone.

```
-bash-3.2# zlogin saket-zone ls –l
total 560
lrwxrwxrwx  1 root    root        9 Apr  2 22:23 bin -> ./usr/bin
drwxr-xr-x 12 root    sys      1024 Apr  2 23:53 dev
drwxr-xr-x 78 root    sys      4096 Apr  2 23:53 etc
drwxr-xr-x  2 root    sys       512 Apr  2 21:46 export
```

6.12.   Quick Tip 7: Where are the files of zone configuration kept?

We know that everything in linux or Unix is a file, and when we make any changes it gets stored/modified in some file. When we configure any zone, the changes are stored in some files. Lets have a look where are these files kept and what changes are made.

```
bash-3.2# pwd
/etc/zones
bash-3.2# ls -ltr
total 10
-r--r--r--  1 root    bin       402 Jun 21  2007 SUNWlx.xml
-r--r--r--  1 root    bin       562 Aug  9  2007 SUNWdefault.xml
-r--r--r--  1 root    bin       392 Aug  9  2007 SUNWblank.xml
-r--r--r--  1 root    bin       777 Mar 12  2008 SUNWtsoldef.xml
-rw-r--r--  1 root    sys       285 Jun 28  2011 index
-rw-r--r--  1 root    sys       285 Jan 30  2015 saket-zone.xml

bash-3.2# cat index
global:installed:/
saket-zone:installed:/export/zone1:46c2f581-fed1-c876-c9d0-
c352d6e28811
bash-3.2#
```

```
bash-3.2# more saket-zone.xml
<?xml version="1.0" encoding="UTF-8"?>
<!DOCTYPE zone PUBLIC "-//Sun Microsystems Inc//DTD
Zones//EN" "file:///usr/share/lib/xml/dtd/zonecfg.dtd.1">
<!--
    DO NOT EDIT THIS FILE.  Use zonecfg(1M) instead.
-->
<zone name="saket-zone" zonepath="/export/zone1" autoboot="true">
  <inherited-pkg-dir directory="/lib"/>
  <inherited-pkg-dir directory="/platform"/>
  <inherited-pkg-dir directory="/sbin"/>
  <inherited-pkg-dir directory="/usr"/>
  <inherited-pkg-dir directory="/opt/sfw"/>
  <network address="192.168.20.111" physical="e1000g0"/>
</zone>
bash-3.2#
```

It is not recommended to edit these files, however in emergency situation we do take backup of these files and edit the parameters required.

6.13.   Remove the zone

Now we know how to configure, install, boot and halt the zone. Next step is to understand how to remove the zone completely from the system.

There are three steps to remove the zone.
First halt i.e. shut down the zone.
#zoneadm –z saket-zone halt (shuts down)

a.   Now uninstall the zone which removes the files from the partition.
zoneadm –z saket-zone uninstall (uninstall the files)

b.   Now delete the configuration files to remove zone from completely from the system.
zoneadm –z saket-zone delete (deletes the xml configuration file).

7.   Categories of non-global zone

The non global zone i.e. sparse or whole root zones can be categorized into three different types depending upon which operating system/version we are going to install. To understand these types let us have a look what are these different categorizations of non global zone.

7.1.   Native Zone

Also called default zone where global OS version and non-global OS version are same. Lets say you have installed Solaris 10 zone on a Solaris 10 OS or global zone then this zone will be called as Native zone.

bash-3.2# zoneadm list -cv
```
  ID NAME          STATUS    PATH                    BRAND   IP
   0 global        running   /                       native  shared
   8 saket-zone    running   /export/zone1           native  shared
```

7.2.   Branded zone

a.   When we bring Solaris 8 or Solaris 9 under non-global zone, it is called as Branded Zone. The branded zone is supported from solaris 10 u6 onwards. So make sure you have Solaris version 10_U6 or above.

b.   To install branded zone, we need to first install solaris 8 or solaris 9 packages. Once these are installed, configure required zone with template ("-t" option) file installed with the above packages.
Zonecfg –z sol8
➤   Create –t **SYSsolaris8**

c.   OS backup of solaris8, or solaris 8 OS image file and copy into solaris 10 global zone.
d.   Install the zone giving reference of the Soalris 8 backup(in .flar format usually) or Solaris 8 image file mount point.
zoneadm –z sol9 install –u attach <source file of solaris8 backup> ### in case of migration
zoneadm –z sol9 install –u attach <solaris image mount point> ## in case of new install

7.2.1. <u>Quick Tip 8</u>: How to mount an iso file in Solaris?
We have studied LOFS i.e loopback filesystem, similarly to mount iso images we need a loopback filesystem driver also called as LOFI which is responsible for mounting the files as block devices on the system itself. To make use if this LOFI or loopback filesystem driver, we will use the utility lofiadm.

Let's first add this file as loopback block device on the system using "-a" option.

bash-3.2# lofiadm -a /var/opt/upgrade/pkgs/1_190.iso
/dev/lofi/1
Now we have block device name available to use in the same manner we use other devices.
bash-3.2# mount -o ro -F hsfs /dev/lofi/1 /tmp/mnt28033

7.3.   Lx-Brand Zone

When we deploy linux OS in Solaris x86 as non-global zone, then this type of zone is called as LX branded zone. The installation is quite simple.

zoneadm -z lx-zone install -d archive_path

Where archive_path is the iso image, or backup tar archive of complete Linux OS.

8.   Actions on a Zone

We have seen how to configure the zone, how to boot it, and how to login into the zone i.e. complete zone setup. However there are few common actions that you should know as a system administrator like how to rename a zone, how to move zone data, etc. We will look how to take these different actions on a zone in this section.

8.1.   Renaming a Zone

We can rename the zone easily, however to take this into effect we need to reboot the zone. Hence it can't be done at runtime, and requires a reboot.

global#zonecfg –z saket-zone
zonecfg:work-zone#set zonename=play-zone
zonecfg:work-zone #Commit
zonecfg:work-zone #exit

After changing above configuration, reboot the zone.

8.2. Moving a Zone

To move a zone i.e. to move all files/dirs to some other directory, we need to halt the zone. The syntax of the command is as follows:
#zoneadm –z great-zone move /newpath

bash-3.2# zoneadm -z great-zone move /export/zone2
Moving across file-systems; copying zonepath /export/zone1...
Cleaning up zonepath /export/zone1...rm: Unable to remove directory /export/zone1: Device busy
zoneadm: zone 'great-zone': '/usr/bin/rm -rf' failed with exit code 2.

zoneadm: could not remove zonepath: Empty document

The zone is moved successfully but the zonepath i.e. /export/zone1 is not removed successfully that's why we get this error. So if you want you can remove it manually and reboot the zone from new path.

8.3. Clone a Zone

While cloning a zone, everything is copied exactly however we need to change three configuration options to create the zone successfully. Obviously if you clone a zone, you can't have same ip address or hostname, so that it will not clash with existing zone.

1.   Zone path (where zone will be mounted)
2.   Zone Name and Hostname
3.   IP address

Steps to clone a zone.
1.   Halt the zone
zonecfg –z great-zone halt

2.   Export the configuration file of the already created zone.
zonecfg –z great-zone export –f /export/zones/master   ####(file in which to export)
Lets see this on my system.
bash-3.2# **zonecfg -z great-zone export -f /mysolaris/zonemaster**
bash-3.2# **file /mysolaris/zonemaster**
/mysolaris/zonemaster: assembler program text

3.   Edit the file exported and correct zonepath, and ip address.
bash-3.2# **vi /mysolaris/zonemaster**
"/mysolaris/zonemaster" 23 lines, 329 characters
create -b
set **zonepath=/export/zone3**
set autoboot=true
set ip-type=shared
add inherit-pkg-dir
set **address=192.168.20.112**
set physical=e1000g0

4.   Now Configure new Zone
bash-3.2# **zonecfg -z vrygreat-zone -f /mysolaris/zonemaster**
bash-3.2#

5.   Check the newly configured zone
bash-3.2# **zoneadm list -cv**

ID NAME	STATUS	PATH	BRAND	IP
0 global	running	/	native	shared
10 great-zone	running	/export/zone2	native	shared
- **vrygreat-zone**	**configured**	/export/zone2	native	shared

6.   Clone the zone

bash-3.2# **zoneadm -z vrygreat-zone clone great-zone**

vrygreat-zone zonepath (/export/zone2) and great-zone zonepath (/export/zone2) overlap.

could not verify zonepath /export/zone2 because of the above errors.

zoneadm: zone vrygreat-zone failed to verify

The above command will clone the zone successfully if you don't receive above error. Suppose you get the above error, It means we have not changed ip address or zonepath. So again change the file and restore the configuration and clone.

Delete the configured zone.

bash-3.2# zonecfg -z vrygreat-zone delete

Are you sure you want to delete zone vrygreat-zone (y/[n])? y

bash-3.2#

Edit the file again and change zonepath and ip address and reconfigure clone

bash-3.2# zonecfg -z vrygreat-zone -f /mysolaris/zonemaster

Try to clone again

bash-3.2# **zoneadm -z vrygreat-zone clone great-zone**

/export/zone3 must not be group readable.

/export/zone3 must not be group executable.

/export/zone3 must not be world readable.

/export/zone3 must not be world executable.

could not verify zonepath /export/zone3 because of the above errors.

zoneadm: zone vrygreat-zone failed to verify

<u>Change permission of new mount point</u>
bash-3.2# **chmod 700 /export/zone3**
bash-3.2#
bash-3.2# **zoneadm -z vrygreat-zone clone great-zone**

This time it will be successful and the zone will be cloned.

8.4.   Migrate a Zone
We can also migrate a zone from one host to another host. For migration of zone, we need to halt the system, it can't be done on the fly.

1.   Halt the zone
zoneadm –z great-zone halt

2.   Detach the zone
zoneadm –z great-zone detach

3.   Migrate the data

On host1:
cd /export/zones
tar -cf abc.tar work-zone

On host2:
cd /export/zones
tar -xf abc.tar

4.   Create the zone config on host2.

Zonecfg –z saket-zone
create –a /export/zones/work-zone ## same file which is copied
commit
exit

5.   Now the zone is configured. Attach it to host2.
zoneadm –z work-zone attach

8.5.   Adding exclusive IP into an existing zone

Suppose you want to add a new dedicated NIC card to a non global zone and then assign IP address to this nic card. To achieve this task, we can follow few simple steps.

a.   Halt the zone
zoneadm –z saket-zone halt

b.   Enter into configuration
#zonecfg –z saket-zone
#remove net
#set ip-type=exclusive
#add net
Net>set physical=e1000g1
Net>end
#commit
#exit

c.   Boot the zone.

d.   Plumb the new IP and make it permanent.

a.   Check the current IPs.
Ifconfig –a

b.   Plumb new interface so that the system can identify the device.
ifconfig e1000g1 plumb
You can check the device will be available under /dev of local zone.

c.   Now set the ip address
vi /etc/hostname.e1000g1
zone1   ### enter the hostname of the zone.

#vi /etc/hosts
192.168.20.30 zone1 ### enter the main interface e1000g2 ip address.

Now check if ip is assigned correctly by restarting network service.
Ifconfig e1000g2 unplumb
svcadm –v restart network/physical
ifconfig –a

9.   **Quick Tip 9: Two ways to reach server before its OS gets installed.**
There are two ways we can reach the Solaris physical server in case its IP is not reachable directly.

1.   Via Serial Console, or SC card (fall on sc prompt.)
Sc> **break**
Sc>**console –f** (to goto console forcefully)

2.   When there is no console card available then we can login via serial port available on the server (now we directly fall into ok prompt)

Benefits of console

1.   Console card has a chip: OBP (NVRAM) which is 1mb chip that stores all required data for remote access.

2.   We can poweron the server remotely.

3.   Check server status/health remotely.

10.   Quick Tip 10: How to check whether we have console card/sc card. ?

We can check whether our system has sc card available or not by analyzing below command output.

bash-3.2# **prtconf -v | grep -i rsc**

In case we get any output then the driver of SC Card is loaded and hence the console is available otherwise there is no console available on the system.

11.   Quick Tip 11: Solaris Diagnostic Commands

The diagnostic commands are very useful in identifying problems on our solaris system. Here I have listed only few common diagnostic commands, however depending upon the requirement, we need to change the approach towards problem diagnostic.

a.   **#prtdiag –v**

➢   Checks the system hardware and runs the diagnostic. Less information on x86 systems.

➢   Shows OBP and POST version

- ➤ Memory and CPU details
- ➤ List of on board devices

b.   **#prtconf -vp | more** (show system information, but don't run diagnostics)
- ➤ Shows memory and CPU information
- ➤ Detailed information of all devices

c.   **# iostat –eE (shows disk errors)**

```
      ---- errors ---
device  s/w h/w trn tot
cmdk0  0  0  0  0
fd0    0  0  0  0
sd0    0  0  0  0
sd1    0  0  0  0
nfs1   0  0  0  0
cmdk0    Soft Errors: 0 Hard Errors: 0 Transport Errors: 0
Model: VMware Virtual  Revision:  Serial No: 110000000000000 Size: 17.18GB <17179706880 bytes>
Media Error: 0 Device Not Ready: 0 No Device: 0 Recoverable: 0
Illegal Request: 0
```

d. Dmesg and /var/adm/messages file

```
bash-3.2# dmesg | tail
Jan 30 17:42:00 SolarisLab1 sendmail[3616]: [ID 702911 mail.crit] My unqualified host name (vsserver1) unknown; sleeping for retry
Jan 30 17:42:00 SolarisLab1 sendmail[3606]: [ID 702911 mail.alert] unable to qualify my own domain name (vsserver1) -- using short name
```

bash-3.2# tail /var/adm/messages
Jan 30 17:42:00 SolarisLab1 sendmail[3616]: [ID 702911 mail.crit] My unqualified host name (vsserver1) unknown; sleeping for retry
Jan 30 17:42:00 SolarisLab1 sendmail[3606]: [ID 702911 mail.alert] unable to qualify my own domain name (vsserver1) -- using short name

12. Quick Tip 12: How to login to Solaris OS when no console available.

There are two serial ports ttya and ttyb usually available on oracle server. So we can connect any other server in network to one of the serial console and can access the node via that serial port, let say ttya.

```
# tip -9600 /dev/ttya
connected
{3} ok
```

13. OK Prompt

OK prompt is available on Oracle Solaris SPARC servers. OK prompt or open boot firmware is first introduced by Sun, and thereafter it is used by many different non x86 based servers like Apple, IBM, etc. Open Boot Prompt or OBP is a standard which defines different interfaces of the computer hardware or firmware.

To understand it easily, you can compare it with GRUB in linux. Similarly it is also loaded on system PROM from where it is loaded, and then detects different system hardware, and thereafter runs bootstrap program to detect and boot the Operating system.

The Oracle Solaris SPARC server provides us with OK prompt or open firmware for managing the bootstrap process of our OS, and this open boot or OK prompt provides many advanced features, one of the most important is to edit open boot prompt parameters at OS level. Let us have a look at few of the basic OK prompt commands.

13.1. Basic OK prompt commands

ok page	To clear the screen
#.	To exit from the ok prompt
ok banner	Shows the obp version and ram details.
Ok probe-scsi	Shows the hard disks
Ok siftingshow	Will show all commands starting from show keyword.
Ok show-nets	To see all network cards
Ok watch-net-all	Check which network card is up or cable connected.
Ok devalias	Tells all device aliases set at ok prompt.
Ok nvalias	To create a new alias
Ok nvunalias disk21	To remove the aliases
Ok reset-all	To save and exit
Ok printenv	Shows all paramters at OK prompt.
Ok setenv	To change. On OS, eeprom is available.
Ok boot disk	Boot from device whose alais is disk.In case first disk is failed. Mention another disk/mirror from which you want to boot OS.

There are many other commands available on the ok prompt. For complete list of commands, we need to refer to the guide given by oracle during server setup.

13.2.   How to reach to OK prompt from Solaris OS?
Since the ok prompt is responsible to load the bootstrap program, so to check ok prompt you need to halt the system first. One of the easy ways to reach at OK prompt is like below.

1.   First set auto-boot to false.
eeprom auto-boot?=false
Auto-boot is one of ok prompt variable which defines whether to auto-boot system from ok prompt or not. So this parameter must always be true so that whenever we reboot out system, it doesn't fall back at OK prompt.

2.   Now login to the console and run init 0 on server to reach at OK prompt.
init 0
You need to login at console to access the OK prompt, since server goes down.

13.3.   Editing OK boot prompt variables from Solaris OS.
Here we will see how to edit OK prompt variables directly from our Solaris OS terminal session or from shell. Solaris provides a very nice command called "eeprom" to edit the ok boot prompt paramters directly from the OS.

eprom   ### This will display all ok prompt
variables
eprom parameter?=value   ### ? is used in case of some parameters.

For example:-
eprom auto-boot?=true   ### Sets the auto-boot value to true. Now whenever the system reaches ok prompt, it will be automatically rebooted.

14.   Quick Tip 13: How to see where the system got hanged while booting?
Since solaris does a silent boot, so we cannot see the status where the system got stuck during boot in normal course.

To see where our system is hanged while boot, we can use below command from OK prompt.
Ok **boot -v**
-v for verbose and will display all details while booting OS.

15.   Quick Tip 14: How to know MAC address of NIC cards in x86/sparc box ?
One of the interesting question is how can we see MAC or hardware address of NIC cards in any x86 or SPARC server.

OS already installed
In case OS is already installed then we can simply run ifconfig and find the MAC address mentioned next to ether.

bash-3.2# ifconfig -a

lo0:
flags=2001000849<UP,LOOPBACK,RUNNING,MULTICAST,IPv4,VIRTUAL> mtu 8232 index 1
        inet 127.0.0.1 netmask ff000000
e1000g0:
flags=1000843<UP,BROADCAST,RUNNING,MULTICAST,IPv4> mtu 1500 index 2
        inet 192.168.2.2 netmask ffffff00 broadcast 192.168.2.255
        ether 0:c:29:f2:e:1

0 is usually omitted, so the real MAC address will be 00:c:29:f2:e:1.

OS not installed
In case the Solaris OS is not yet installed and we are planning to install OS via network or jumpstart, and need to know the MAC address, then we need to follow below trick.

Boot from network and see the MAC address as our system will broadcast the MAC address to get IP address.

16.   SVM
SVM or Solaris Volume Manager is one of the techniques to manage disks in unix. Like LVM or linux volume manager, it supports creating volume and adding/removing new slices/disks in the volume at runtime. SVM was earlier named as online disksuite which helps in managing disk partitions alongwith RAID-0, RAID-1, RAID 5, or RAID10 configuration.

16.1. Comparison with LVM to understand SVM

In linux, we used to create logical volumes on volume group, but here we create a logical volume say /dev/md/dsk/d0 and we can add/remove slices in this volume. Here how many disks added/configured depends which raid level we want to configure. Ideally people used to configure raid 1 and include two slices of same size in a volume, so it will create a replica on both slices and keep syncing it.

In LVM, the information about LVs/PVs/VGs are kept under the same disk by reserving few blocks of disk space. But in SVM we need to create a metadb, and for storing this metadb we need to create few slices(4mb space required to save 1 copy of metadb, so in case we need to save 5 copies then we need 20mb of disk space) and this makes it a little complex to understand for linux administrators. However after you know how SVM maintains metadb and how it works with SVM disks, you will find it very easy to deal with it.

16.2. To check if svm is configured or not on the server.

The first step to move forward with practical knowledge to understand SVM, we should know how to check if SVM is configured or not on a server. So if SVM is configured then it is sure that a metadevice database will be created which stores the SVM configuration. Hence we can check if metadevice database exists or not.

Metadb command shows the metadevice database.

bash-3.2# **metadb**

metadb: system11: there are no existing databases

metastat command shows the status of each metadevice.

bash-3.2# **metastat**

metastat: system11: there are no existing databases

Since there is no output, hence there is no SVM configured on the server at present.

16.3. Advantage of bringing disks under SVM
If we bring any device under svm, it will not delete data, just replicate the data across the disks.

Only in case of raid5, it will delete existing data so as to distribute the data across the disks under raid 5 configuration. For other raid levels, it just replicate the data and hence no loss of data.

In SVM, we need to create state database replicas. Replica is the database which stores what all volumes, and filesystems are created.
½ + 1 =2 replicas must be healthy for SVM to work, for this reason we recommend to save at least 2 replicas of metadb on 2 disks.

16.4. Check Health status of replicas
Metadb is very useful command to see the status of all slices on which out meta device state database is saved. The "-i" option checks all metadevices for meta database and shows the status of different database health.

```
# metadb –I
-bash-3.2# metadb -i
        flags        first blk    block count
    a m  pc luo        16          8192        /dev/dsk/c2t1d0s4
    a    pc luo       8208         8192        /dev/dsk/c2t1d0s4
    a    pc luo       16400        8192        /dev/dsk/c2t1d0s4
```

          a   pc luo   24592   8192   /dev/dsk/c2t1d0s4

o - replica active prior to last mddb configuration change
 u - replica is up to date
 l - locator for this replica was read successfully
 p - replica's location was patched in kernel
 m - replica is master, this is replica selected as input
 a - replica is active, commits are occurring to this replica

16.5.   Creation of State replica Database

Before creating any volume under SVM first we need to create state replica database(or a private region) to save the volume or filesystem details. For this we need to create small slices of around 20mb or as per our requirements.

Let's see an example where we create a slice to keep 4 replicas of our Meta Database.

1.   First create one slice from format command
Multiple replicas on one slice of 4mb (4 replicas then preferred to take ~20mb)
Or, we can have one slice for 1 replica to have better stability.

2.   Now create db replica. Create 4 replicas on one disk.
bash-3.2# **metadb -a -f -c 4 c2t1d0s4**

-c states the number of replicas on the slice c2t1d0s4.

Now we can check health status of our replicas. If anything in upper case, then there is some error/issue, otherwise its fine.

bash-3.2# **metadb -i**

flags			first blk	block count	
a	u	16	8192	/dev/dsk/c2t1d0s4
a	u	8208	8192	/dev/dsk/c2t1d0s4
a	u	16400	8192	/dev/dsk/c2t1d0s4
a	u	24592	8192	/dev/dsk/c2t1d0s4

We have created the State replicas. So now we have the space to store the solaris volume information on the disk. Hence we can create the new volumes over the slices which we want to include under the SVM.

16.6.   Concat Volume

Now we have created the metadevice state replica database. So we can create new volumes or filesystems under SVM or solaris volume manager. In this section we will see how to create a solaris volume, say d0 with two partitions in concatenation.

We can create d0 to d255 volumes in one solaris system.

The command syntax will be as follows:
metainit –f d0(name of new volume) 2(2 individual slices volumes) 1(identifies one of the slice)

For example:- 2 disks c0t0d0s7 and c1t0d0s5 are added and a volume d0 is created.
metainit -f d0 2 1 c0t0d0s7 1 c1t0d0s5

16.7.   Stripe Volume

Similar to concat volume, here we will learn how to create stripe volume under SVM.

A volume d0 is created in stripe by using below command, stripe-width by default is 16k, however we will define 32k or 64 for a little fast transactions.

metainit d0(name of new volume) 1(1 stripe) 2(using 2 slices) c0t0d0s7 c1t0d0s5 –i <stripe-width 32k>

#metainit d0 1 2 c0t0d0s7 c1t0d0s5 –i 32k

Vfstab File changes

Now change the path in vfstab file to mount the specific partition with new metadevice name.

From:

/dev/dsk/c0t0d0s7 /dev/rdsk/c0t0d0s7 /mypartition ufs 2 yes -

To:

/dev/md/dsk/d0 /dev/md/rdsk/d0 /mypartition ufs 2 yes -

Remount the filesystem

Umount and mount the filesystem.

umount /mypartition

mount /mypartition

16.8.   Grow FS in case of concat volume

In SVM, any new disk can be added into concat volume at runtime without any downtime and it helps to grow the filesystem size on the fly. The command we will use to grow the concat volume is growfs. Growfs command is used to expand any UFS filesystem without impacting the data, -M options displays the mount point of the partition.

#growfs –M /mypartition /dev/md/rdsk/d0

16.9.   Root filesystem mirroring (raid 1)

Here we will see how to create RAID 1 or mirror volume. The command and syntax will be same, however first we will create two concat/stripe volumes and then we will add them to create RAID-1 Volume. Obviously if we are talking about RAID-1 then the slice size should be exactly same.

Note:- Raid-1 must be created with raid0. Because in case you want to increase space then you can easily add space to raid-0 concat volumes and increase raid-1 space, otherwise you will face major issues later.

SVM doesn't support disk to disk mirroring. (we have to do slice to slice mirroring)
After creating partition on first hard disk, copy prtvtoc table from this hard disk to the other hard disk to create raid0 volumes of same size and then add them in raid1 volume.

1.   Create separate slice on both hard disks for replicas (2 replicas on each disk)
Initialize the metainit on both disks.
metainit –f d11 1 1 c0t0d0s1
metainit –f d12 1 1 c1t0d0s1
(metainit –f(force) d11(meta device/volume name to create) 1(in concat with 1 disk) (disk number 1) c0t0d0s1(slice number))

2.   Now create a volume d10 with mirror d11.
metainit d10 –m d11

3.   Now we need to fire below command to make this mirror as root device.

metaroot d10

/etc/vfstab and /etc/system is updated with new metadevice root entry.

4.   Reboot the machine

Init 6

5.   Now attach the other mirror d12 to d10 volume.

metattach d10 d12

6.   Check progress(how much sync is completed) with command **metastat**.

#metastat | grep –I sync

7.   In last, we need to go at OK promot, and then update secondary boot device with this hard disk.

Ok **nvalais backup_root <device_path>**

Ok **setenv boot-device disk backup_root net**

The above command defines two aliases for booting. First system will try to boot system with "disk", thereafter from "backup_root", and in the last "net".

Questions

1. What do you mean by virtualization?
2. How to check available zones on your system?
3. Mount your root(/) filesystem again on /mnt2 ?
4. What is SVM?
5. What do you mean by mirroring and striping?
6. What command you will use to check all Meta devices created on your system?
7. How to check available metadatabase?
8. How can you delete old metadb and create new metadb?
9. How to boot system in single user mode from OK prompt?
10. How to change auto-boot?= false from your solaris OS.

Chapter -7
Solaris Installation/Upgrade and Troubleshooting
Day 6

1.   Solaris OS installation

In this chapter we will learn how to install Solaris OS on a sample hardware with CD/DVD, and how to automate installation using jumpstart. Solaris OS provides us various options to go ahead with install using CD or DVD, like we can install in GUI, or using CLI(text mode).

However if you have gone through complete book till now then you can easily install Solaris OS without anyone's help using GUI or text mode. *The steps are really simple.*

a.   Insert the installation disk in your system CD DVD ROM.

b.   Now set the first boot disk priority as CD DVD from BIOS and then reboot the system, it will boot up from CD/DVD.

c.   Or in case we have SPARC hardware with OK prompt then we can use below commands:

a.   For GUI installation.

ok boot cdrom

The above command will contact the device of alias cdrom which is by default points to the CD/DVD drive.

b.   For text/CLI install

ok boot cdrom - text

c.   Installing from CLI console session.

ok boot cdrom – nowin

d. Once the system is booted from CD/DVD, just follow on screen instructions to install the OS on the hardware.

1.1 Requirements

The minimum requirement of Solaris 10 varies depending upon the update which we are going to install and for which architecture sparc or x86 servers. Hence here we will look at the recommended requirement for smooth operation of our solaris 10 server. Solaris 10 Operating system is free, except the source code, a license is required for support whereas in linux we can even download source code.

For Sparc Architecture
➢   1 GB RAM or physical memory since zfs root filesystem is supported from update 9.
➢   Disk Space of 5GB for installation
➢   Access to bootable CDROM or DVD or installation server(jumpstart server).

For x86/x64:
➢   120MHz or faster processor
➢   1 GB RAM since ZFS root filesystem is supported from update 9.
➢   Disk Space of 5GB for installation
➢   Access to bootable CDROM/DVD or installation server

Note: We can check compatibility at sun.com/bigadmin/hcl.

1.2 Two ways to install OS

Here we will check different ways to install Oracle Solaris 10 on our system. Majorly we can divide Installation ways in two types.

a.   Standard Solaris Installer
a.   GUI

b.   CLI
c.   Jumpstart
d.   Upgrade

b.   Flash Archive installation
a.   Solaris flash archive
b.   WAN Boot

As we can see above, the two ways of Solaris installation includes one way of standard installation, and other way is flash archive installation. The standard installation includes installation from CD/DVD, or from jumpstart server. Another way is to use Solaris flash archive (.flar files) to install OS, or by booting it from WAN.

1.2.1   Standard Installation

We have already seen how to do the standard installation using cd/dvd in the first section, however let's have a look at it again.

1.2.1.1 Installation on SPARC machine

On SPARC machine, we are provided with OK prompt or Openboot firmware, hence we can use "boot cdrom" command to call cdrom alais which points to CD/DVD device.

Ok boot cdrom   #### Starts the installation in GUI.
Ok boot cdrom – nowin ### It will assume you are using Console, and hence drops you to command line mode from GUI.
Ok boot cdrom – text ### to do installation in text or CLI mode.

1.2.1.2 Installation on x86 Machine

On X86 machine, you can install Solaris 10 simply by following the on-screen steps. You need to select first boot device in BIOS and then reboot your system.

1.2.2 Flash archive installation

The flash archive is a backup copy of some existing solaris installation, which can be backed up and installed on other nodes as well. Such type of installation is used in many product based companies where they incorporate product based packages, customization in the OS, and then create a flash archive and advise the customers to do upgrade/installation from this falsh archive without any hassle.

➢ For cloning or restoration purpose.
➢ Complete OS backup can be taken.
➢ Also flash archive can be used in case of Operating System corruption. In the case of corruption, boot the server from flash archive location like below:
Ok boot tape #### in case the flash archive is on tape.
➢ Used for disaster recovery

Flar flash archive utility was used till solaris 10. From solaris 11, we have distribution creator instead of flar utlity, to create cd/dvd.

2   Upgrade Solaris

We can also upgrade solaris from old versions to solaris 10. The Oracle Solaris can be upgraded from Solaris 8 to 10, or from solaris 8 to solaris 9, or from Solaris version 9 to 10.
But the upgrade from solaris 10 to solaris 11 is not possible.

2.1   Standard upgrade

The standard upgrade process involves the usage of CD/DVD to perform the upgrade.
➢ If you are currently logged on the server, then first check and detach the mirror before upgrading.
bash-3.2# metastat -p
d31 -m d11 d21 2
d11 1 1 /dev/dsk/c5t5000CCA016DA11DDd0s1 -h hsp002

d21 1 1 /dev/dsk/c4t5000CCA016DDB1A5d0s1 -h hsp002
d30 -m d10 d20 1
d10 1 1 /dev/dsk/c5t5000CCA016DA11DDd0s0 -h hsp001
d20 1 1 /dev/dsk/c4t5000CCA016DDB1A5d0s0 -h hsp001

Now detach required mirrors.
bash-3.2# metadetach d31 d11
d31: submirror d11 is detached
bash-3.2# metadetach d30 d10
d30: submirror d10 is detached

Now we will perform the upgrade. Mirrors are detached so that in case upgrade fails then we can go ahead and boot the system from other disk which has current OS backup.

➢   Insert solaris 10 CD/DVD.
➢   Set autoboot = false so that system will not boot automatically after reboot.
eeprom auto-boot?=true
eeprom | grep –I auto   ### check the parameter value
➢   Now reboot the server and then boot from CD.
Ok boot cdrom
➢   It will ask you to install or upgrade OS. Select Upgrade OS and press return.

If anything gets wrong, boot from other disk and attach the first disk and sync data.

2.2   Live upgrade.

One of the interesting features of solaris is live upgrade. Live upgrade allows us to upgrade our operating system without any downtime and the system is upgraded on the fly except kernel patch which obviously needs a reboot. Hence a server can be upgraded with just 10 minutes of downtime and rest of the patches can be installed on the running system. Suppose we are upgrading from Solaris 9 to Solaris 10, then there are two requirements that must be met in order to do live upgrade.

a.   Needs a separate disk
b.   Need to install LU package on Solaris 9 first disk.

Concept of Live Upgrade

Mostly we use SVM to setup RAID filesystem to maintain fault tolerance against a disk failure. Suppose you have a RAID-1 setup with two disks in sync. So first we will detach one disk and then perform live upgrade on the disk from which system is booted and if the overall upgrade fails at any point then we will boot our server from second detached disk and attach the first disk back to sync old data. Then the system will be back to old state.

In case the upgrade gets fine, then we will attach the detached disk and the new OS will be synced on both disks. Usually when the upgrade is fine, we let the customer test the upgraded system for few days/weeks and then attach the disk, so it keeps an option open where we can restore the OS back to old state.

3   Configuring JumpStart Installation using Solaris 10 OS

To speed up the process of OS installation and setup, we can configure a jumpstart server from where the new server can pick the OS install setup and its initial network configuration.

For solaris, we can setup only one jumpstart system which can act as jumpstart server for any Solaris version. It implies the same server can be a jumpstart for solaris 8 or 9 or 10.

Suppose your administrator has already setup the jumpstart in your network and ask you to install the server. Then you need to perform below actions.

For Sparc Systems, goto ok prompt and run below commands.
Ok **boot net – install**
Above command will contact jumpstart and start the installation.

For jumpstart server to identify the client machine, we need to know the MAC address of client machine and make an entry on jumpstart server.

Knowing Mac address
On sparc,
Ok> banner   ##### shows the mac address

On x86,
Press f12 to boot from network, and shows the MAC address of NIC. Note mac address and break the system install and then add this MAC address on jumpstart server.

3.1   Services provided by jumpstart server.
Solaris jumpstart server provides cross platform support to provide installer service for different solaris versions. Now since it provides a complete installation service, so it can also be used to recover a corrupt OS. Also we can setup DHCP, or few other services on the same jumpstart server to utilize all server resources as per the requirements.

Jumpstart server provides many useful services, some of which are as listed below.
1.   Provides installation service.
2.   Boot service (can be used to boot into single user mode.)
3.   Identification service or configuration service

3.2   Jump Start Server Config
Linux or Unix maintains a MAC to IP address table which is looked up by Jumpstart server to assign hostname corresponding to the mentioned

MAC address. This table or database referred is stored in ethers file, and hence sometimes called as ether. We can also setup our system as jumpstart server and automate the Solaris installation and troubleshooting by following few steps as mentioned below.

1.   Make an entry in the below ethers file mentioning the MAC address and corresponding hostname.
vi /etc/ethers
<mac>   <hostname>
3:00:50:33:88:12 SolarisLab99

When this mac sends a request to our jumpstart server, it is assigned the mentioned hostname.

2.   As we know ethers file maintains table w.r.t MAC address or ip address. So the entry made in first step with hostname must be validated by translating the mentioned hostname to ip address.
So now we need to define hostname entry in /etc/hosts file so that our system can determine IP address with this hostname.
vi /etc/hosts
<ip address> <hostname>

3.   Insert and mount the installation media on this new jumpstart server.
Vold → volume management daemon(vold) is responsible for mouting external media on the server automatically. Check if its running then your media will be automatically mounted.

-bash-3.2# ps -ef | grep -i vold
    root   577   1   0 10:10:54 ?   0:00 /usr/sbin/vold -f /etc/vold.conf
    root 2685 1893   0 11:41:27 pts/1   0:00 grep -i vold

-bash-3.2# rmformat
Looking for devices...

1. Volmgt Node: /vol/dev/aliases/cdrom0
   Logical Node: /dev/rdsk/c1t0d0s2
   Physical Node: /pci@0,0/pci-ide@7,1/ide@1/sd@0,0
   Connected Device: NECVMWar VMware IDE CDR10 1.00
   Device Type: DVD Reader/Writer

-bash-3.2# /etc/init.d/volmgt stop

sh-3.2# /etc/init.d/volmgt start
volume management starting.

Otherwise mount it manually by checking cfgadm –al and then
mounting the respective media.

4.   After inserting media.
Go inside to the dvd mountpoint and copy installation media contents to
the directory /export/install by using the script "setup_install_server".
cd /cdrom/cdrom0/s0/Solaris10/Tools
./setup_install_server /export/install ###to dump the solaris dvd
image in this path.

5.   Goto /cdrom/cdrom0/s0/Solaris_10/Misc/Jumpstart_sample
and copy the sample cofiguration files under /export/config.
cd /cdrom/cdrom0/s0/Solaris_10/Misc/Jumpstart_sample
mkdir /export/config
cp –r * /export/config/

6.   Make changes in config files under /export/config
And then validate jumpstart files.
./check

7.   Share the jumpstart directory.
vi /etc/dfs/dfstab
share –o ro /export/config

shareall

8.   Add Clients to Jumpstart based on which OS version they want to install.
cd Solaris_10/Tools
./add_install_client –s sun8:/export/install –p sun8:/export/config/ -c sun8:/export/config sun122 sun4u
    -s -→ source of media
-p → profile location
 –c → config file location
Sun122 → hostname of client taken from /etc/ethers
Sun4u → architecture

For different versions of solaris, we can create separate filesystems and dump medias accordingly. Decide the installation path in the command fired at jumpstart server.
In case of any mistake, run script ./remove_client to remove the client and add the client back.

4   Quick Tip 1: To see the MAC address of machines contacted our machine.

-bash-3.2# arp -a
Net to Media Table: IPv4

Device	IP Address	Mask	Flags	Phys Addr
e1000g1	172.16.159.255	255.255.255.255		
e1000g0	224.0.0.2	255.255.255.255		01:00:5e:00:00:02
e1000g1	224.0.0.2	255.255.255.255		01:00:5e:00:00:02
e1000g1	224.0.0.22	255.255.255.255		01:00:5e:00:00:16
e1000g0	224.0.0.22	255.255.255.255		01:00:5e:00:00:16
e1000g1	172.16.159.1	255.255.255.255	o	00:50:56:c0:00:08
e1000g0	192.168.1.111	255.255.255.255	SPLA	00:0c:29:2c:ad:dc
e1000g1	172.16.159.11	255.255.255.255	SPLA	00:0c:29:2c:ad:e6
e1000g0	system11	255.255.255.255	SPLA	00:0c:29:2c:ad:dc

e1000g1 224.0.0.0	240.0.0.0	SM	01:00:5e:00:00:00
e1000g0 224.0.0.0	240.0.0.0	SM	01:00:5e:00:00:00

The above table is saved in cache and will be removed on a reboot. Arp is used to send the IP and MAC.

5 Quick Tip 2: How to check how many usb drives are connected?

-bash-3.2# **cfgadm -al | more**

cfgadm: Configuration administration not supported: Error: hotplug service is probably not running, please use 'svcadm enable hotplug' to enable the service. See cfgadm_shp(1M) for more details.

Ap_Id	Type	Receptacle	Occupant	Condition
c2	scsi-bus	connected	configured	unknown
c2::dsk/c2t0d0	disk	connected	configured	unknown
c2::dsk/c2t1d0	disk	connected	configured	unknown
c2::dsk/c2t2d0	disk	connected	configured	unknown
c2::dsk/c2t3d0	disk	connected	configured	unknown
c2::dsk/c2t4d0	disk	connected	configured	unknown

6 Quick Tip 3: What is meant by sun4u and sun4v in sparc ?

When we run uname –a on SPARC solaris system, we see either sun4u or sun4v in the output alongwith server name and number.

root@bhminsat1 # **uname -a**
SunOS bhminsat1 5.10 Generic_147440-26 **sun4u** sparc SUNW,Netra-T12

sun4u and sun4v represents the hardware architecture type whether it supports virtual cpu threads or not, in simple language, it is an easy way to determine whether a server has single core cpu or multi core cpu.

Sun4u
For those sparc systems which has single or multiple physical processors but do not have any cores. It means single core technology where the cpu doesn't support virtualization.
For example:- sun fire, sun ultra, sun blade.

You can check cpu cores using below command.

-bash-3.2# **psrinfo -v**
Status of virtual processor 0 as of: 04/04/2014 12:02:39
  on-line since 04/04/2014 10:10:45.
  The i386 processor operates at 2600 MHz,
      and has an i387 compatible floating point processor.

Sun4v
Sun4v is mentioned for those sparc systems which have single or multiple physical processors with a single core or multicore technology. The processors which shows sun4v supports virtualization.

For example:- sun T series (T1000, T2000, etc)
Sun M Serries (M1000, M2000) → latest high end server in solaris. These are the servers which can even support another level of virtualization, means we have a vm machine inside a VM on these servers. We can create and manage LDOM's(logical partitioning of hardware also called Logical DOmain) or OVM(oracle virtual machine) on these servers.

7   Quick Tip 4: How to disable cpu(s) on a sparc system?
1.   Check the processor id with psrinfo –v
Different processors will be shown with different ids.
bash-3.2# psrinfo -pv
The physical processor has 1 virtual processor (0)
  x86 (chipid 0x0 GenuineIntel family 6 model 58 step 9 clock 2592 MHz)
      Intel(r) Core(tm) i5-3320M CPU @ 2.60GHz
bash-3.2#

2.   Now suppose we want to take a processor offline whose id is 3. So run below command.

psradm –f 3

Now in case you want to bring it back online, then you can execute below command.

prsadm –n 3

8   LU (live upgrade)

Live upgrade as described earlier is a way to upgrade our system with minimum downtime and allows us to keep a backup of old system, so in case of any issue we can recover to old system state.

Why we perform live Upgrade in Solaris?

Suppose you want to upgrade your production server, however you can't simply go ahead without prior testing and for testing you need to have an exact replica test server, which is not possible for each and every server. So Solaris had introduced a concept of Live upgrade and introduced this tool in year 2001 with Solaris release 8u10 onwards wherein a single server with two disks in raid can be upgraded safely. Hence the main reasons for introducing the live upgrade can be summarized as.

➢   Due to lack of test server, we have live upgrade.

➢   Do patching in duplicate boot environment. If its fine, replicate it in live Boot environment, otherwise restore old boot environment.

To check the boot environments configured, we can use lustatus command.

-bash-3.2# lustatus
ERROR: No boot environments are configured on this system

ERROR: cannot determine list of all boot environment names

As we know solaris standard upgrade takes a lot of time and sometimes its very hard to get so long downtime in case of production/live servers. So to make this task fast forward, Oracle introduced a new way of upgrading the solaris system called live upgrade in which almost all the patches/packages are installed in the running system and thereafter the system is rebooted so as to apply these patches. So the overall downtime is now reduced to the time taken for a reboot of the system. However in case we need to install kernel patch then we may need extra time as such patches can't be installed on live system.

With the help of LU, we create BE.

8.1 BE (Boot environment)/Cloning

BE is a clone of boot disk. It is used to do live upgrade of sol8, sol9, or sol10 and easy fallback to old non−upgraded system in case of issues.

Live upgrade is very useful when we want to test some new patch, or new software. Metadetach and meattach sync takes more time as compared to BE creation. So usually LU is performed to create a backup copy/clone and test the patch.

No need to change any parameters at ok prompt when activating new BE on sparc systems.

To perform LU, first we need to clone our root disk and create a new BE on which we will test the upgrade.

8.2 Steps to clone a disk
➢ First copy the partition table of our root hard disk to a file.
-bash-3.2# prtvtoc /dev/rdsk/c0d0s2 > /mysolaris/prtvtoc_main

➢ Now format the new *same size hard disk* with this exported partition file.
-bash-3.2# fmthard -s /mysolaris/prtvtoc_main /dev/rdsk/c2t2d0s2
fmthard: New volume table of contents now in place.

➢ Now clone the root hard disk contents i.e. create a new BE for LU.
lucreate -c "before_upgrade" -m /:/dev/dsk/c2t2d0s0 :ufs -n "after_upgrade"
-c → Takes current BE name
-m → keeps the same swap space
/ is the partition
-n → new boot environment BE to be created
New disk name to format in ufs.

Lucreate assigns current environment name as "before_upgrade" and then copies data of root directory / to the new disk /dev/dsk/c2t2d0s0 in ufs format and name this new boot environment as "after_upgrade".

OR,

We can also use lucreate command interactively, but that seems a little complex for beginners to interact with this command options.

Let's see how to run this command and how it is executed.
-bash-3.2# **lucreate -c "before_upgrade" -m /:/dev/dsk/c2t2d0s0:ufs -n "after_upgrade"**
Determining types of file systems supported
Validating file system requests
Preparing logical storage devices
Preparing physical storage devices
Configuring physical storage devices
Configuring logical storage devices
Checking GRUB menu...
Analyzing system configuration.

No name for current boot environment.

Current boot environment is named <before_upgrade>.

Creating initial configuration for primary boot environment <before_upgrade>.

INFORMATION: No BEs are configured on this system.

The device </dev/dsk/c0d0s0> is not a root device for any boot environment; cannot get BE ID.

PBE configuration successful: PBE name <before_upgrade> PBE Boot Device </dev/dsk/c0d0s0>.

Updating boot environment description database on all BEs.

Updating system configuration files.

The device </dev/dsk/c2t2d0s0> is not a root device for any boot environment; cannot get BE ID.

Creating configuration for boot environment <after_upgrade>.

Source boot environment is <before_upgrade>.

Creating file systems on boot environment <after_upgrade>.

Creating <ufs> file system for </> in zone <global> on </dev/dsk/c2t2d0s0>.

Mounting file systems for boot environment <after_upgrade>.

Calculating required sizes of file systems for boot environment <after_upgrade>.

Populating file systems on boot environment <after_upgrade>.

Analyzing zones.

Mounting ABE <after_upgrade>.

Generating file list.

Unmounting ABE <after_upgrade>.

Fixing properties on ZFS datasets in ABE.

Reverting state of zones in PBE <before_upgrade>.

Making boot environment <after_upgrade> bootable.

Updating bootenv.rc on ABE <after_upgrade>.

File </boot/grub/menu.lst> propagation successful

Copied GRUB menu from PBE to ABE

No entry for BE <after_upgrade> in GRUB menu

Population of boot environment <after_upgrade> successful.

Creation of boot environment <after_upgrade> successful.

4. Check the new BE created.
-bash-3.2# **lustatus**

Boot Environment Name	Is Complete	Active Now	Active On Reboot	Can Delete	Copy Status
before_upgrade	yes	yes	yes	no	-
after_upgrade	yes	no	no	yes	-

If we want to boot from other environment, then we need to activate this BE.

First check lu if all the partitions are correctly shown in this output.
-bash-3.2# **lufslist after_upgrade**
        boot environment name: after_upgrade

Filesystem	fstype	device size	Mounted on	Mount Options
/dev/dsk/c0d0s1	swap	2155023360	-	-
/dev/dsk/c2t2d0s0	ufs	14756152320	/	-
/dev/dsk/c2t0d0s3	ufs	838978560	/oradb	-
/dev/dsk/c2t4d0s0	ufs	2136997888	/export/zone1	-

➢   Now activate LU.
-bash-3.2# **luactivate after_upgrade**
System has findroot enabled GRUB
Generating boot-sign, partition and slice information for PBE <before_upgrade>
Generating boot-sign for ABE <after_upgrade>
Generating partition and slice information for ABE <after_upgrade>
Boot menu exists.
Generating multiboot menu entries for PBE.

Generating multiboot menu entries for ABE.

➢ Now you can test if the new boot environment is setup by rebooting the server.
init 6

The server will be booted from new environment and if it is booted fine then you can try to do upgrade, test patches on this new environment, keeping the old environment safe in case of any issue while upgrade.

8.3 Quick Tip 5: How to select alternative BE in case the system doesn't come up after reboot from new BE?
On Sparc, we can see installed BEs from "boot -L" command.

Ok boot –L   New command introduced which will show all BEs.
In case above command doesn't list the BEs, then we need to check the devalias to see the hard disks available and try to boot from other hard disks by mentioning the hard disk drive in front of boot command.

On x86, we can select the BE to boot from the grub menu.

If you want to remove BE, rename lutab file and /etc/lu directory and keep them safe to some other directory. In case you need to restore BE, you can place these files back.
In case you want to delete LU permanently, use ludelete command. And you may use the hard disk for any other use.

8.4 How to test a patch on a BE by mounting it temporarily.
First we will mount the BE temporarily.
-bash-3.2# lumount -n after_upgrade -m /mylu
/mylu

Now we can install and test the patches on this mounted BE by changing the –R i.e. root path for this patch.
pkgadd -R /mylu/ -d . SUNWoptdir

Now umount BE.
-bash-3.2# luumount /mylu/
We can also use non global zone for testing patches.

9   Quick Tip 6: How to refresh/mount only NFS entries in vfstab?

We can also refresh only the remote file systems on our solaris box (the command also works on newer versions of linux). Mountall command when passed with an option "-r" will mount only the remote/nfs file systems.
mountall –r

10   Troubleshooting topics

Here we will look few common issues faced in our Solaris operating system and how to resolve such issues.

10.1   Breaking root password (On SPARC and on x86)

Sometimes we forget the root password and as we know without root privilege we can't do any admin activities on our system. So to get the root password, we can use failsafe mode in Solaris. Lets have a look at the steps you need to perform to reset the root password.

On Sparc:
1.   Init 0   ## to goto ok prompt.
2.   Ok boot –F failsafe   ### boot the system in failsafe

On x86,
From grub menu select second option solaris failsafe.

<u>Quick Note:</u> If cursor is rotating in clockwise direction then everything is fine.
If it rotates in anti clockwise direction, then there may be some issue.

1.   Now when the system boots up in failsafe, It will ask if you wish to mount root filesystem read-write on /a (/a also called memory directory).

In case of you want to do fsck, type "no" and you will be dropped to # prompt.
In case of breaking root password, press yes to mount filesystem on /a and set the password in shadow file.

2.   Now for editing /a/etc/shadow file, we need to set the terminal and editor.
export TERM=vt100
export editor=vi
Remove the password, and save the file.
Reboot the system and change the password.

In case, the system is booted from CD.
1.   Run format and go inside each disk and check for root partition.
2.   Mount the partition and change the password.

10.2   How to troubleshoot ufs booting problem?
In case of ufs filesystem boot issue and we are dropped to # prompt saying it can't start the OS. In such cases, we need to remount / partition in rw mode and then correct vfstab/system file. Or investigate if further problems exist.
1.   Check what all partitions are mounted.
#df –h
Usually we can see the root partition will be mounted with physical path as seen below.

/devices/pci@0,0/pci-ide@7,1/ide@0/cmdk@0,0:a 14G 9.9G 3.5G 75% /

And when we check "mount –v" command, you may also realize that / is mounted read only.

2.   Now we need to identify the logical path of the disk and mount it as rw using below command.

mount –o remount,rw /dev/dsk/c0t0d0s0 /

You can identify the root disk by going into each disk under format command, or an easy way is to identify from the physical path directly like "0,0:a" represents the disk at 0 controller and 0th target with first slice is root partition of the hard disk. However it depends upon hard disk format and how it is used.

3.   Now check /etc/vfstab and /etc/system file for errors and correct the issue.

You can yourself induce such error by editing /etc/vfstab file and change / or root filesystem entry, lets say you remove "/" and reboot your system. Your system will fall in maintenance mode with root filesystem mounted read only and now you need to correct vftsab file entry to successfully boot the system back.

10.3   How to correct ZFS pools in case not coming up on boot?

There are few scenarios when the zpool is not mounting successfully when the system boots, and there is some problem with zpool on our system. The first troubleshooting in such case is to check if the zpool cache has some issue. First we will check ZFS pool health by command zpool status and in case we feel something wrong, then we will reload new cache from backup stored on the disk. Simply remove the cache and import the pools back from the backup saved on our hard disk.

1.   Remove the zpools cache.

rm /etc/zfs/zpool.cache

2.   Reboot the system.
Init 6
Now pools will be disabled when the system will reboot next time.

3.   Now import the required pools back.
zpool import
zpool import –f oracle
zpool import –f <sap>

10.4   How to recover root filesystem problem in case of ZFS.

In case our root filesystem in on ZFS, then we can't mount the filesystem easily like in UFS by saying mount command. For this we need to boot our OS with CDROM, and then we can import the rpool(root filesystem pool) under any arbitrary mount point say /a and then we can investigate issues with the filesystem.

1.   Boot OS in single user mode using CD drive.
Ok boot cdrom –s
Or use grub to boot into single user mode in case of x86.

2.   Mount the root filesystem to /a
#zpool import /a rpool

Now you can do troubleshooting to check and correct system files to recover root filesystem.

10.5   Mounting zfs using /etc/vfstab

We can also mount the ZFS filesystems by using vfstab file, i.e. by using default feature of our operating system.

We have /oracle pool created on our system where we have below two filesystems created and mounted by ZFS automatically.

```
ZFS Filesystem        → Mountpoint
Oracle/linux                → /oracle/linux
Oracle/hpux                 → /oracle/hpux
```

a.   Now we will mount oracle/hpux via vfstab file on reboot instead of zfs. For this we need to change the mount option of this filesystem to legacy under zfs and then manually define under vfstab.

Set the mount point to legacy.
#zfs set mountpoint=legacy mypool/data
Immediately it will be umounted automatically.

b.   Create a new directory where to mount the file.
mkdir /mydata

c.   Add the entry in vfstab file.
mypool/data-   /mydata   zfs   -   yes   -

d.   Now run mountall command.
mountall
And check if this new filesystem is mounted automatically or not.

10.6   Editing boot options in x86 to boot in single user mode.

When Solaris is installed on x86 architecture then since it uses GRUB to boot OS. So we can pass few options with the kernel in the grub to boot our OS in single user or in any of the modes available.

The most common options that can be passed to the kernel while booting are as follows.
-s   single user mode
-v   verbose mode
-x   boot without in cluster
-a   interactive mode

For example:- to boot Solaris in single user mode, I have edited kernel line and appended "-s".

```
   GNU GRUB  version 0.97  (638K lower / 522176K upper memory)

 ┌─────────────────────────────────────────────────────────────────┐
 │ findroot (rootfs0,0,a)                                           │
 │ kernel /platform/i86pc/multiboot -s                             │
 │ module /platform/i86pc/boot_archive                             │
 │                                                                  │
 │                                                                  │
 │                                                                  │
 │                                                                  │
 │                                                                  │
 │                                                                  │
 │                                                                  │
 └─────────────────────────────────────────────────────────────────┘
    Use the ↑ and ↓ keys to select which entry is highlighted.
    Press 'b' to boot, 'e' to edit the selected command in the
    boot sequence, 'c' for a command-line, 'o' to open a new line
    after ('O' for before) the selected line, 'd' to remove the
    selected line, or escape to go back to the main menu.
```

In case you need to run fsck on root filesystem then boot the OS in failsafe mode which is mentioned as second option in the grub boot menu. In failsafe, the root is mounted under /a, not on / and hence we can do fsck on root filesystem.

10.7   Understanding findroot to fast identify root disk.

The findroot command is similar to the root command used by GRUB previously (still used in few linux distros), has enhanced capabilities for discovering the mentioned targeted disk, regardless of the boot device. The advancement of findroot command is that it _also supports booting from an Oracle Solaris ZFS root file system._

If you look entry in grub under solaris, we find entries like below:

bash-3.2# cat /boot/grub/menu.lst| grep -v '^#'

default 0
splashimage /boot/grub/splash.xpm.gz
timeout 10
title before_upgrade
findroot (BE_before_upgrade,0,a)
kernel /platform/i86pc/multiboot
module /platform/i86pc/boot_archive

In above three lines, kernel and module are loaded from /platform/i86pc in case of 32-bit x86 systems and findroot refers the first sectors of the mentioned boot environment i.e. "before_upgrade", "BE_" denotes this is boot environment created via Live upgrade. "0" refers to the target and "a" specifies that it is the first slice.

10.8   Repairing Primary superblock in Solaris

One of the strange problems that we used to face as a Unix admin is when we are not able to repair the disk partition even with normal fsck command. In most of such cases, the superblock of the hard disk gets corrupted and we need to run fsck with new backup superblock number.

-bash-3.2# **fsck /dev/dsk/c2t0d0s0**
** /dev/rdsk/c2t0d0s0
BAD SUPERBLOCK AT BLOCK 16: NUMBER OF DIRECTORIES OUT OF RANGE
LOOK FOR ALTERNATE SUPERBLOCKS WITH MKFS? ^C

a.   Check the available backup superblock number(s).

-bash-3.2# **newfs -N /dev/dsk/c2t0d0s0**
/dev/rdsk/c2t0d0s0:   1028160 sectors in 68 cylinders of 240 tracks, 63 sectors
     502.0MB in 14 cyl groups (5 c/g, 36.91MB/g, 17536 i/g)
super-block backups (for fsck -F ufs -o b=#) at:

32, **75696**, 151360, 227024, 302688, 378352, 454016, 529680, 605344, 681008,
 756672, 832336, 908000, 983664

From second block onwards, we can see there are many backup superblock numbers present. Any of these superblock number can be used to recover the partition but the recommended one is second since the chance of restoration is maximum with this superblock number. In case the fsck fails with this superblock number, then we can try other superblock numbers also but the chance of recovery is very less.

b.   Now try to do fsck with this alternate superblock number.
-bash-3.2# **fsck -y -o b=75696 /dev/dsk/c2t0d0s0**

Now the fsck will run with new superblock present at this block and try to recover the partition. In case it fails, then there are chances that your data is corrupt and you may need to restore it from some backup or DR site.

10.9   How to reconfigure all network settings?

Suppose you cloned your server using LU, or dd command, or any other technique and now you want to reconfigure all network settings like hostname, ip address, etc.
For this task, Oracle Solaris provides a very nice command to remove all network settings and then automatically asks you to reconfigure them back on reboot.

sys-unconfig

All network settings will be removed and everything will be asked when the system rebooted. On sparc:- system will halt at ok prompt and you may need to run command "boot", on x86 the system will be rebooted.

bash-3.2# **sys-unconfig**

WARNING
This program will unconfigure your system. It will cause it
to revert to a "blank" system - it will not have a name or know
about other systems or networks.
This program will also halt the system.
Do you want to continue (y/n) ? y
updating /platform/i86pc/boot_archive

10.10   First point of troubleshooting in case SPARC server is in cyclic reboot.

Suppose your solaris server is in cyclic reboot and you are not aware
why it is taking cyclic reboot, so first step is to identify where it is halting
and taking a reboot.

For this we need to boot our system into interactive mode two or may be
more times to identify and skip the service which is generating error at
boot time.

Sc> **break**   sends the break signal to OS that we need to goto ok
prompt
Sc> **console –f**
Ok **boot –a**   reboots the system and will now boot the server in
interactive mode.

10.11   How to continue with OS installation in case of any issue in connectivity and installation halted?

Suppose you are installing the Solaris OS via network and there is some
connectivity issue occurs and the installation failed and you are dropped
to shell.
 In such cases, usually the installation is halted and we are dropped to
root shell saying "it can't continue". To resume the installation from the
point it gets halted, we need to run below command.

install-solaris

Now the installation will resume from the exact last point where it gets interrupted.

10.12   Why Solaris 11 installation failing again and again with enough RAM?

Solaris 11 is purely 64 bit and our system must be VT(virtual technology) enabled(in bios) to install Solaris 11. In case your system is not VT enabled, the installation will fail.

10.13   Troubleshooting GUI in Solaris

Solaris provides a wonderful tool called kdmconfig to troubleshoot few GUI issues arises because of its limited support on x86 platform initially. With kdmconfig we can change gui devices like video card, mouse pointer, etc.

kdmconfig

10.14   Quick Tip 7: Not able to store files larger than 2 GB.

Sometimes you may encounter an error where a user is not able to store large files of size, say more than 2GB on the server. In this case we need to investigate step by step.

a.   First check if any quota set for you.
bash-3.2$ repquota -va
quotactl: no quotas file on any mounted file system
If quota is set than ask system administrator to increase the quota using edquota command.

b.   The next thing we can check if there is any limit set on current shell.

```
bash-3.2$ ulimit -a
core file size        (blocks, -c) unlimited
data seg size          (kbytes, -d) unlimited
file size            (blocks, -f) unlimited
open files                 (-n) 256
pipe size          (512 bytes, -p) 10
stack size            (kbytes, -s) 10240
cpu time             (seconds, -t) unlimited
max user processes          (-u) 6261
virtual memory        (kbytes, -v) unlimited
bash-3.2$
```

In case you find the file size parameter is fixed to 2Gb then you can increase this by using below command.

```
bash-3.2$ ulimit unlimited
```
If you want to make the ulimit value permanent then make an entry in any of the startup file /etc/profile, or /etc/default/login for the new ulimit value.
ULIMIT=0

c.   If ulimit is also fine, then we can check how the filesystem is mounted, is it restricting large files.
```
bash-3.2$ mount | grep -i large
/ on /dev/dsk/c0d1s0
read/write/setuid/devices/rstchown/intr/nolargefiles/logging/xattr/
onerror=panic/dev=1980000 on Sun Feb  1 04:37:33 2015
bash-3.2$
```

So our filesystem is mounted with nolargefiles option and hence it is not allowing to store large files above 2GB. Edit vfstab file and enter an option largefiles to enable saving large files on the filesystem.

Here we have seen a simple troubleshooting for the particular scenario. Similarly you need to identify what all things can cause the specific problem and based on that we can proceed further.

10.15   Metadb of 2 disks are corrupted. We need atleast 50% metadb up. What should we do?

If you got a chance to work as unix administrator then you will surely face this type of issue where more than 50% of metadb got corrupt and the system goes into read only mode. For example:- I have also faced below scenario.

```
root@ry1vs01a>metadb -i
      flags first blk block count
  a m p lu 16 8192 /dev/dsk/c5t5000CCA016DA11DDd0s7
  a p l 8208 8192 /dev/dsk/c5t5000CCA016DA11DDd0s7
   M u 16 unknown /dev/dsk/c4t5000CCA016DDB1A5d0s7
   M u 8208 unknown /dev/dsk/c4t5000CCA016DDB1A5d0s7
   M u 16 unknown /dev/dsk/c3t5000CCA022607A01d0s7   → corrupt
metadb
   M u 8208 unknown /dev/dsk/c3t5000CCA022607A01d0s7
```

Here we can see out of 6 metadevice database, 4 got corrupted and this is the reason our system is going into maintenance mode.
Now to recover the system, we will follow below steps:

a.   You will be dropped to maintenance mode after entering root password. And the system will most probably in read only mode mounted directly with physical hard drive path.

So the first step is to make the system mounted in read-write since we can't make changes to metadb unless it can be changed on disk.

root@ry1vs01a>df -h /
Filesystem size used avail capacity Mounted on
/pci@0,0/pci8086,3c0a@3,2/pci1000,3050@0/iport@8/disk@w5000cca01 6da11dd,0:a
            259G 159G 98G 62% /

Determine the root disk physical path.
echo | format | grep –i w5000cca016da11dd
bash-3.2# echo | format | grep -in w5000cca016da11dd
16:
/pci@0,0/pci8086,3c0a@3,2/pci1000,3050@0/iport@8/disk@w5000cca01 6da11dd,0:a
bash-3.2#
Now run format, and check disk logical path.

b.   Now mount the root partition read-write from disk logical path.
mount –o remount,rw /dev/dsk/c1t0d0s0 /

Note: Always make sure you don't mount directly or from metadevice and, since its already corrupted. In this case session may hang and display below error.
root@ry1vs01a>mount -o remount,rw /
WARNING: Error writing ufs log statWARNING: init(1M) exited on

fatal signae

lWARNING: ufs lo 1 for / changed tate to Error

0:W ARNING: Pleaserumount(1M) / and run fsck(1M)

estarting automatically

WARNING: exec(/sbin/init) failed with errno 5.

WARNING: failed to restart init(1M) (err=5): system reboot required

Once the partition is mounted read-write, we can go ahead to correct metadb error.

c.   Now check the metadevice database.

```
root@ry1vs01a>metadb -i
    flags first blk block count
  a m p lu 16 8192 /dev/dsk/c5t5000CCA016DA11DDd0s7
  a p l 8208 8192 /dev/dsk/c5t5000CCA016DA11DDd0s7
  M u 16 unknown /dev/dsk/c4t5000CCA016DDB1A5d0s7
  M u 8208 unknown /dev/dsk/c4t5000CCA016DDB1A5d0s7
   M u 16 unknown /dev/dsk/c3t5000CCA022607A01d0s7   ---▢
corrupt metadb
   M u 8208 unknown /dev/dsk/c3t5000CCA022607A01d0s7
```

To make the system bootable we should have more than 50% metadb in fine state. Two metadb are fine, however 4 are in corrupt state, so we need to delete 3 metadb.

```
# metadb –d c4t5000CCA016DDB1A5d0s7
# metadb –d c3t5000CCA022607A01d0s7
```

Now check metadb status. Only two correct metadb will be shown. Now we have only two correct metadevice database remaining, hence we can reboot the system now and it will come up. The system got panic because it could not detect the database replica on main disk and hence failed to start.

10.16 OK boot prompt options for SPARC systems.

Here we will see different options that can be used on ok prompt for booting the system. We should know these options so that in emergency situation we know what can be achieved through this.

Ok boot   Boots from first hard disk

Ok boot –s   Boots the server in single user mode(ask for the root password)

Ok boot cdrom   Boot from cd/dvd and start installation

Ok boot cdrom –s   Never ask for root password, and boots in single user mode with cd. Never asks for the root password.

Ok boot –F failsafe   Booting from hard disk without any need of root password. Boot from hard disk, useful in breaking root password without any cd drive.This is supported only from u9.

Ok boot net – install To pull installation from jumpstart server.

Ok boot net –s   Booting in single user mode from jumpstart server.

Ok boot –v   Verbose boot

Ok boot –a   Interactive boot (ask for everything while booting. Suppose anything is wrong in /etc/system file we can use this option)

Ok boot –x   Don't join cluster, boot without joining into cluster.

Ok boot –r   Reconfigure reboot→ if new device added. Suppose new external hard disk attached, and its not detected(showing message no hardware found).

10.17 Updating BE using luupgrade

In live upgrade, we have seen the concept of BE, but we haven't checked one of the main command luupgrade which automatically upgrades the alternate BE and helps us to update the boot environment on running node. Lets see an example to clear how this command works.

luupgrade -f -n newBE -s /tmp/mnt4423 -a /tmp/mnt4423/1_19089-CXP9024789_1.3122.flar

Luupgrade command installs or upgrades packages or operating system from the mentioned location, disk image or flar archive. In the above command, following options are used.

-n newBE → Name of the BE which will receive an OS installation/upgrade.
-s /tmp/mnt4423 → For adding packages, /tmp/mnt4423 is the path of a directory containing packages to add.
-a /tmp/mnt4423/1_19089-CXP9024789_1.3122.flar → This is the path of the flash archive which we want to install.
-f → luupgrade command uses -f to install the operating system from a Solaris Flash archive. Installing an archive overwrites all files on the target BE.

Similarly you can use this command to do upgrade from cd/dvd image or from other backup locations.

Questions
1. What do you mean by live upgrade?
2. What is BE?
3. What do you mean by ZFS Pool?
4. What do you mean by jumpstart installation and where we should use it?

APPENDIX

1.   UNIX System V

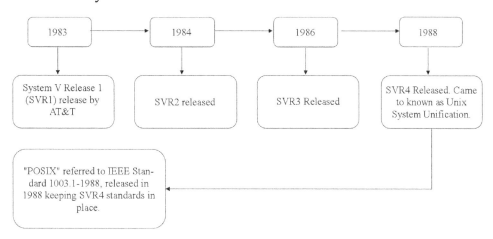

Fig. 1 AT&T's Unix System V(SysV) Release Cycle & POSIX

Unix operating system was at peak of its development in 1970s and 1980s by AT&T. Finally in year 1983, the first commercial UNIX system was released by AT&T which is named as System V (or SysV). Unix System V also known as SVR1(System V Release 1). After its release there are further enhancements and we have following versions of UNIX released.

➢   SVR2 :- System V Release 2 released in April, 1984 introduced copy on write, demand paging, and also added many shell functions.

➢   SVR3 :- System V Release 3 released in 1986 introduced Remote File System(RFS) which allowed remote accessibility of devices like cdrom, and also introduced a new way of inter process communication with STREAMS.

➢   SVR4 :- System V Release 4 launched on October 1988. SVR4 was the most stable commercial release, and hence it is also called as Unix System Unification.

➢   SVR4.2:- Launched in 1992, also called UnixWare, included Veritas File system(VxFS) first time.

➢   SVR5 or UnixWare 7:- Released for large scale servers in year 1997.

➢   SVR6:- Supposed to release in 2004 year end, however the plan got canceled, it was supposed to support 64 bit OS.

With the release of SVR4, in year 1988, IEEE(Institute of Electrical and Electronics Engineers) has introduced some standards how processes are created and controlled in a UNIX OS, how different OS signals sent and received, segmentations or memory violations, different BUS errors, etc. These standards are called as POSIX(Portable Operating System Interface). Based on these a Unix or Unix-Like system or application is called as fully POSIX complaint or partial POSIX complaint.

POSIX defines the common standards like what shells ran on an OS, how the process communication happens, etc, which can be used to identify if the OS and the application are compatible with each other. Solaris is certified fully POSIX complaint. Most of the linux distributions are also mostly POSIX complaint; however these are not POSIX certified. RHEL(Redhat Enterprise Linux) Server also provides full POSIX compliance.

2.   Unix License

The unix operating system may or may not need license for its operation, whereas a Linux operating system doesn't require any license for its operation even for commercial usage, its always free and licensed under GNU GPL i.e. GNU General Public license where GNU is a recursive acronym and stands for GNU's not unix which means this is not a Unix OS which will require a license for its usage.

Various Other Unix Operating Systems majorly used

Unix OS Variant	Short Description
IBM AIX	Proprietary Unix OS sold by IBM. AIX was first OS which introduced journaling filesystem. AIX Version 1

	was introduced in 1986 (in IBM 6150 RT workstation) which was based on UNIX System V Release 1 and 2. The Latest Release if AIX Version 71. TL(Technology level) 3 which was launched in November, 2013.
HP-UX	HP-UX or Hewlett-Packard UniX is HP proprietary Unix Operating System which was released in year 1984 and this OS is also based on Unix System V specification. The current latest version of this OS available is HP-UX 11i v3 with update 13.
BSD Variants	BSD or Berkeley Software Distribution is also a UNIX variant which was released in 1977 under University of California, Barkeley, and its development halted in 1995 with its last release of 4.4. Lite-2 as its development team was dissolved during that time. After the dissolution of its development team, this closed source unix OS was available as free software from 1991. After that, there are many versions of BSD maintained like FreeBSD, NetBSD, OpenBSD, and DragonFlyBSD.
OpenSolaris	OpenSolaris is an open source Solaris like OS released by Sun to give a tough competition to Redhat Linux, however this is no longer officially supported now after oracle took over Sun.
MAC OS X	Mac OS X, the well-known Apple Inc Unix based operating system. It is usually shipped with Apple notebooks also known as Macbook(s). The series of MAC OS was first introduced in year 1984, and the latest release of this OS available is 10.10.3 (released on Feb 5, 2015) which is currently available for developers only and will be soon officially anounced.

3.   Solaris 10 is now no more free to use

Solaris 10 is one of the most stable releases of the Oracle Solaris version, which was earlier provided to user free to use and they can take license in case of support required from Oracle. However now Oracle has limited the free usage till 90 days, after which the users must attain a license for commercial use of the operating system.

Don't get disappointed with this, I personally feel we should know what are the differences between unix and linux, and should be able to work on both the operating systems freely, since the difference is only in their kernels. We also have OpenSolaris available with free open source code, which can be used to setup on our server for free.

OpenSolaris is an open source variant of Solaris which was created by Sun and is only unix version based on System V which is available as open source. OpenSolaris is licensed under Sun's open source Common Development and Distribution License (CDDL) and hence it will remain free to use for lifetime. However all features of Solaris are not available in opensolaris, since after Oracle overtook Sun in year 2010, it discontinued the open development of OpenSolaris.

4.   Linux License

Linux OS came into picture in 1991 when Linus Torvalds designed his own kernel and assembled all free or open source software to create a complete free and open source Operating system. The operating system is completely free to use, we can even modify its source code, and distribute it further with the same license. Since this is completely free, this software falls under GNU General Public license. There are many Linux distributions now available in the market which are very well designed and makes linux dominate the market over other unix or windows versions. We can't say a Linux distribution is good over other until we know insiders of both Operating systems, however based upon user ratings and experience we can rate various Linux distributions.

a.   Best Enterprise Linux

RHEL(Redhat Enterprise Linux) is considered best when we talk about enterprise use and reliability is our first concern. SUSE Linux can also be used with almost equal reliability in place of Redhat for enterprise purpose. However we can use any Linux version, but these two distributions considered well for enterprise use.

b.   Best Desktop Version

Ubuntu is one of the best desktop version available for a user to install with various easy to use options like install new games/softwares just a click away.

c.   Best Linux security Distribution

BackTrack Linux is considered one of the best distribution when we talk about network security and troubleshooting. Its very well designed OS to troubleshoot network issues and also helps hackers to accomplish their task fast.

d.   Oracle Linux

To give Redhat a touch competition, Oracle has introduced its own linux distribution based on redhat linux, with Oracle logos and art added to it. The main focus of Oracle is to earn revenue by providing support to this oracle Linux, and that too cheaper than Redhat. To build trust among users, oracle even calls its Oracle lnux as unbreakable linux.

5.   Meaning of different directories inside /devices

We have already seen that /devices directory contains a list of all device drivers (including buses) and /dev contains links to these drivers. /devices directory is specific to Solaris Operating system and the paths under /dev is a general UNIX standard. To understand what all drivers are there in this directory, we will check each directory and understand what is meant by this driver.

```
bash-3.2# ls  /devices/
agpgart        iscsi:devctl    pci@0,0:intr    scsi_vhci:devctl
agpgart:agpgart  objmgr        pci@0,0:reg     xsvc
cpus           options         pseudo          xsvc:xsvc
isa            pci@0,0         pseudo:devctl
iscsi          pci@0,0:devctl  scsi_vhci
bash-3.2#
```

Here we can see different directories like agpgart, obimgr, etc and few character files(with colon) like scsi:devctl, pci@0,0:intr, etc. Now we will look each directory and file separately to have an idea what all is there in this directory.

a.   AGPGART

AGP GART stands for accelerated graphics port -graphics address remapping table. As its name defines, this is the graphics driver introduced in Solaris operating system which allows us to run our games which require graphics card usage. This driver allows data transfer between system main memory and graphics memory.

Device File

```
crw-r--r--  1 root    sys      55,  0 Feb 21 18:04 /devices/agpgart:agpgart
```

This device directory is empty.
```
/devices/agpgart:
total 0
```

b.   iscsi Driver

ISCSI(Internet Small Computer System Interface) is an internet protocol which allows linking data storage from different remote storage locations on our local system and vice versa. It means we can mount a remote ISCSI storage location(usually as a disk) on our system, and can also share some storage space from our server to any remote location.

For sharing storage from our local system towards the network, we need to have this driver /devices/iscsi:devctl. The remote server accesses this driver and allows remote devices to gain access of the shared storage. In case your system doesn't show this device then it means you can't share your system storage via ISCSI.

You can verify whether a module is loaded or not by using prtconf or modinfo.
bash-3.2# prtconf -P | grep -i iscsi
   iscsi, instance #0

bash-3.2# modinfo | grep -i iscsi
106 fffffffff7c9a000 37428 73 1 iscsi (Sun iSCSI Initiator v20110524-0)
108 fffffffff7c20000 f518 - 1 idm (iSCSI Data Mover)
bash-3.2#

Since the module is loaded, we should have the device file.
bash-3.2# ls -ltr /devices/iscsi*
crw------- 1 root   sys   73, 0 Feb 21 17:12 iscsi:devctl
iscsi:
total 0

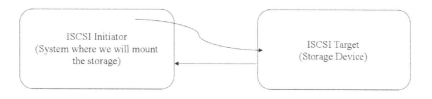

Fig.2. ISCSI Storage Device on UNIX

ISCSI initiator is the system where we will access and mount the ISCSI Target, i.e. storage disk shared by any remote/target system.

c.   PCI Devices

We usually see most of the devices are named with PCI in their path name. You must be curious to know what this PCI is when we talk about devices in our UNIX system. For example:- When we list /devices directory then we can see below output.

```
bash-3.2# ls /devices
agpgart        iscsi:devctl      pci@0,0:intr      scsi_vhci:devctl
agpgart:agpgart  objmgr         pci@0,0:reg       xsvc
cpus           options         pseudo          xsvc:xsvc
isa            pci@0,0         pseudo:devctl
iscsi          pci@0,0:devctl   scsi_vhci
bash-3.2#
```

PCI or Peripheral Computer Interconnect represents a bus that connects different hardware devices to our system. This is the reason we can see many devices with PCI in their physical name representing system bus through which the device is connected. When I list all PCI devices under /devices, I can see below devices on my system.

```
bash-3.2# ls -l /devices/ | grep -i pci
drwxr-xr-x 39 root   sys        1536 May  2 2013 pci@0,0
crw------- 1 root    sys     183, 255 Feb 21 18:57 pci@0,0:devctl
crw------- 1 root    sys     183, 252 Feb 21 18:57 pci@0,0:intr
crw------- 1 root    sys     183, 253 Feb 21 18:57 pci@0,0:reg
bash-3.2#
```

Here we have one directory with name "pci@0,0" and three character/device files. Oracle Solaris operating system is very interesting when we talk about device management here. It creates separate directories for each BUS which contains all devices' address connected to that bus. Here since we have only one directory, it means my system has only one BUS available for all devices and the BUS ids are started from 0, so I can say "pci0,0 is the first BUS with id 0 available on my system". Similarly next BUS ids will be 1,2, and so on.

My BUS name is ""pci@0,0", here PCI denotes we are talking about a device connected to a bus(or bus itself), and "0,0" shows the device number of this BUS is 0, and function number is also 0. Hence the details I have now from "pci@0,0" is "Bus Number:0 with Device Number:0, and Function Number:0" is available on my system.

d.   What is 183,255 shown in long list output?

When we do long list to any character or block device, instead of size we will see two numbers separated by a comma. This pair "183,255" is called as the device number, where 183 is the device major number and 255 is the device minor number. Our solaris system uses these major and minor numbers to uniquely identify a complete device and sub devices attached to this major device. The major number will represent whole device and the minor number helps OS to identify different sub devices attached to this major device. The device number is used by our kernel for performing different operations on the block device such as IO operations.

Each major number is linked to an instance name, which is used by many programs to identify the major number device, or nexus device where to send the request. We can see this instance name from /etc/name_to_major file.

bash-3.2# cat /etc/name_to_major | grep -i 183
npe 183

Here npe is host to major PCIe nexus driver linked to device major number 183. You can view the driver name through modinfo.

```
bash-3.2# modinfo | grep -i npe
 36 ffffffffff7830718  6d30 183   1  npe (Host to PCIe nexus driver 1.11)
```

Now you might be thinking its bit confusing, running so many commands, but it is not. It is just a start of this too wide UNIX Operating system where we have a lot to learn more.

e.   :devctl :intr and :reg Minor Devices

We have seen three character devices with names pci@0,0:devctl, pci@0,0:intr, and pci@0,0:reg. If you have observed, "pci@0,0" is the name of the bus, so how come these three devices with its name ? These three devices "pci@0,0:devctl", "pci@0,0:intr", and "pci@0,0:reg" are called as minor devices of the major device "pci@0,0". A minor device is automatically created by major device and whenever this device is referenced the same driver of major device is used. The major device is also called as nexus device which means it's a parent of multiple small devices attached to this device, usually a nexus device is represented by a directory under /devices. Hence we can conclude that the filename is <representative name>:<minor node name> where < representative name > corresponds to <node name>@<bus address> where node name is pci, bus address is 0,0 and the minor node names are devctl, intr, and reg.

➤   pci@0,0:intr :- This minor device will handle all interrupts happened during input output calls towards the major device.

➤   pci@0,0:reg :- Helps to modify the major device registers, very powerful and dangerous device, may crash the system immediately, however its equally helpful also.

➤   pci@0,0:devctl :- devctl is the main minor device which takes requests from different programs and manage their execution on the device i.e. provides resource management. This is the reason we usually see devctl type of minor node for almost every major device available on our system.

We can view all such devices in prtconf output with "-P" option to display details of all pseudo devices as well.

bash-3.2# prtconf -Pv | grep -in intr
330:              dev_path=/pci@0,0:intr
bash-3.2#

bash-3.2# prtconf -Pv | grep -in devctl
111:              dev_path=/scsi_vhci:devctl
324:              dev_path=/pci@0,0:devctl
403:               **dev_path=/pci@0,0/pci8086,7191@1**:devctl
1204:   dev_path=/pci@0,0/pci15ad,1976@10:devctl
1437:   dev_path=/pci@0,0/pci15ad,790@11:devctl
1625:   dev_path=/pci@0,0/pci15ad,7a0@15:devctl
1687:   dev_path=/pci@0,0/pci15ad,7a0@15,1:devctl
1749:   dev_path=/pci@0,0/pci15ad,7a0@15,2:devctl
3485:   dev_path=/pci@0,0/pci15ad,7a0@18,6:devctl
3547:   dev_path=/pci@0,0/pci15ad,7a0@18,7:devctl
3596:   dev_path=/iscsi:devctl
3606:   dev_path=/pseudo:devctl
3616:   dev_path=/pseudo/zconsnex@1:devctl

We can observe above output, there is only one minor node of intr type but devctl minor node exists for each major/minor device.

f.   Understanding dev_path=/pci@0,0/pci8086,7191@1

The sub device with name "pci8086,7191@1" available inside major device "pci@0,0". PCI8086 represents an Intel Device with device ID 7191 at address 1. This address is meaningful only to the parent device.

g. Other Drivers in my /devices directory

➢ X Services kernel Driver (xsvc) :- XSCV is the kernel module or driver provided by Xi Graphics, Inc. which enables graphics on our Solaris server.

➢ ISA Bus Driver:- Solaris also support ISA bus, and the respective drivers are loaded with the directory named isa under /devices.

➢ SCSI VHCI:- SCSI Virtual Host Controller Interconnect driver is used for SCSI-3 devices when used in multipathing.

➢ CPUS :- CPUS contains different cpu instances, instance #0,1,2, etc.

➢ Objmgr:- Object Manager involves management of portable and independent objects(which does not depend on system architecture) on our Solaris operating system like LDAP user management.

h. Pseudo Devices

When I look into my /devices directory, I can see one directory called pseudo which contains a lot of files or drivers. Does my system contain so many hardware devices?

About 330 driver files are there.
bash-3.2# ls -l /devices/pseudo | wc -l
   330

bash-3.2# ls /devices/pseudo | head
aggr@0
aggr@0:ctl
arp@0
arp@0:arp
biosdrv@0
biosdrv@0:biosdrv
bl@0
bl@0:bl
clone@0
clone@0:ptm

bash-3.2#

As the name implies, "pseudo" directory contains all fake devices of our system which are installed by different essential OS software but they don't have any corresponding separate hardware. For example:- for every virtual terminal on which we work, solaris creates a pseudo devices and make it available so that we can work on it.

For example:- check your terminal type and number.
bash-3.2# tty
/dev/pts/4

Do a long list, you will see a pseudo or fake device which makes it possible for us to access the system terminal.

bash-3.2# ls -l /dev/pts/4
lrwxrwxrwx 1 root   root   28 May 2 2013 /dev/pts/4 -> ../../devices/pseudo/pts@0:4
bash-3.2#

In other words we can say this directory /devices/pseudo contains all software devices installed on our system.

i.   Example of Device Naming

One of the most important thing when we work in solaris is to know how devices physical and logical path names are linked and what we understand when we see the physical path of a device. In my /devices directory, when I search for sd(SCSI/IDE disk), I can below results.
bash-3.2# find /devices/ -print | grep -i sd | more
/devices/pci@0,0/pci-ide@7,1/ide@1/sd@0,0
/devices/pci@0,0/pci-ide@7,1/ide@1/sd@0,0:a
/devices/pci@0,0/pci-ide@7,1/ide@1/sd@0,0:a,raw
/devices/pci@0,0/pci-ide@7,1/ide@1/sd@0,0:b
/devices/pci@0,0/pci-ide@7,1/ide@1/sd@0,0:b,raw
←---output truncated -→

What /devices/pci@0,0/pci-ide@7,1/ide@1/sd@0,0 represents?

pci@0,0 → PCI Bus at address 0,0.
pci-ide@7,1 → PCI IDE Controller(c0) located at address 7,1.
ide@1 → IDE hard drive located at address 1(i.e. target 1-sparc or disk1-x86). This address is meaningful to the parent device.
sd@0,0 → SCSI disk at address 0,0 on the IDE controller at address 1.So the disk name is either c0t1d0(sparc) or c0d1(x86). The sd name and driver also apply to SCSI, and CD-ROM devices.

Note:- On x86 platform, IDE and SATA hard disk drives do not use target controllers. The device names of these disks are represented by the controller (c3), disk (d#), and slice (s#).

Hence the name of the disk is c0d1 in my case, since I am working on x86 platform.

What is sd@0,0:a and sd@0,0:a,raw?

"a" represents the first slice i.e. s0, hence sd@0,0:a represents first slice on first disk attached to parent SCSI/IDE target i.e. /dev/dsk/c0d1s0.

",raw" represents the raw device path of this disk. Hence this physical path corresponds to /dev/rdsk/c0d1s0 logical drive.

LAB

In this lab, we will see some topics to practice few things we have learned from this book. To practice this lab, just open the solaris operating system in your PC/Lab, and perform the examples from beginning.

1.   Create a user lily with default shell "bash" and home directory /var/export/lily and map the home directory to /home/lily by autofs.

a.   First add user lily with given details and assign password to the user.
bash-3.2# useradd -d /home/lily -s /bin/bash lily

bash-3.2# passwd lily
New Password:
Re-enter new Password:
passwd: password successfully changed for lily
bash-3.2#

b.   Now make the home directory of this user and change permission.

mkdir -p /var/export/lily
chown lily /var/export/lily
chmod 755 /var/export/lily/

c.   Map the autofs home directory.
First check the entry in /etc/auto_master file.
bash-3.2# cat /etc/auto_master | grep -i home
/home   auto_home   -nobrowse

So the map is auto_home. Lets open this file and add the lily home directory.

bash-3.2# vi /etc/auto_home
"/etc/auto_home" 10 lines, 216 characters
+auto_home
lily   localhost:/var/export/lily

d.   Now try to switch to lily user and it should be successful.
bash-3.2# su - lily
Oracle Corporation SunOS 5.10   Generic Patch   January 2005
-bash-3.2$

2.   Display a greeting message "HELLO" to each user on login.

In Linux or Unix, we have a file /etc/motd known as "Message Of The Day(MOTD)" where we can insert any message to display to each user after login.
My system current file content is:
bash-3.2# cat /etc/motd
Oracle Corporation   SunOS 5.10   Generic Patch   January 2005

Now we can insert any new message in this file which we want to display to user.

For example:- Lets add HELLO to this file and when lily logs in, she will see this new message as well.
bash-3.2# cat /etc/motd
Oracle Corporation   SunOS 5.10   Generic Patch   January 2005
HELLO

bash-3.2# su - lily
Oracle Corporation   SunOS 5.10   Generic Patch   January 2005

HELLO
-bash-3.2$

3. Show a message "Welcome <username>" when a user logs in.

The task is quite simple, and we can achieve this task by simply entering the message into .profile file of the user. For example:- I have written below line to one of the user's profile file to print "welcome username" message on the screen.

-bash-3.2$ cat .profile
echo "*******Welcome $LOGNAME*******"

bash-3.2# su - lily
Oracle Corporation SunOS 5.10   Generic Patch   January 2005
*******Welcome lily*******
-bash-3.2$

4. Create a customized function in place of default rm command which asks users before deleting the data.

To achieve this, we can simply define an alias in our .profile file like "alias rm=rm -i"", however I would recommend you to create your own function specific to each command which helps you to achieve whatever you want by executing these commands.

Here I will create a function say ""newrm" and then execute this function whenever lily calls rm command.

Enter few lines of code in your .profile file like below I have done with lily's profile file:

```
-bash-3.2$ cat .profile
echo "*******Welcome $LOGNAME*******"

### function must be defined before calling it.
newrm()
{

#### $@ gets the argument given with rm command.
        echo "Beware you are removing the data $@";
        echo "Press y to confirm and n to cancel ?"

#### reads the data provided by user.
        read answer

                if [ "$answer" == "y" ]; then
                {
#### remove the file
                rm -i "$@"
                echo "File removed"
                }
                fi
                if [ "$answer" != 'y' ]; then
                {
                echo "File not removed."
                }
                fi
}

alias rm=newrm;
#### defines the alias rm which will call function newrm.
Now logout and login again to observe the changes with rm command.

-bash-3.2$ logout
```

```
bash-3.2# su - lily
Oracle Corporation SunOS 5.10    Generic Patch        January 2005
*******Welcome lily*******
-bash-3.2$ rm abc
Beware you are removing the data abc
Press y to confirm and n to cancel ?
y
rm: remove abc (yes/no)? yes
File removed
-bash-3.2$
```

In a similar fashion, you can create your customized commands, or modify any system commands to achieve different tasks on your system.

5.   Grant sudo access to lily with all commands.

SUDO (Substitute user do/Superuser do) is a UNIX utility which allows the system administrator to grant different command(s) access to specific user(s). We can grant a user access to ALL available system commands to give them temporary root equivalent rights. The sudo command is very useful to log user commands and to secure our system from outside attacks that can happen if root access is provided directly.

SUDO utility is distributed under a ISC-style license i.e. a permissive free software license which means its current release is free, however its under company rights whether its future releases will be provided free or not. To install this useful utility we can follow below steps.
SUDO Install Instructions

a.   Download stable and free sudo .tar.gz source package from its official site. http://www.sudo.ws/
b.   Once its download untar the file.
gunzip sudo-1.8.12.tar.gz

tar –xvf sudo-1.8.12.tar
cd sudo-1.8.12

c.   Now run the configure command to create the makefile of sudo.
bash-3.2# ./configure
configure: Configuring Sudo version 1.8.12
checking for gcc... gcc
checking whether the C compiler works... yes

In case the installer encounter any error like below:
checking for library containing strerror... none required
checking how to run the C preprocessor... gcc -E
checking for ar... no
checking for ranlib... no
configure: error: the "ar" utility is required to build sudo

        You need to export the path of the specific utility.
export PATH=$PATH:/usr/ccs/bin/
Now run the configure command again.

d.   Now we need to run make command to compile sudo.
make
for d in lib/util plugins/group_file plugins/sudoers
plugins/system_group src include doc examples; do \
------output truncated------

e.   Now we have the sudo install package files created. So we will
now install the sudo package.
bash-3.2# make install
for d in lib/util plugins/group_file plugins/sudoers
plugins/system_group src include doc examples; do \
   (cd $d && exec make pre-install) && continue; \
   exit $?; \
done

Installing sudo message catalogs: camkdir /usr/local
mkdir /usr/local/share
mkdir /usr/local/share/locale
---------output truncated -------------------

Granting lily sudo access

a.   First Edit sudo file with visudo command.
/usr/local/sbin/visudo

b.   Now enter below line and save & quit the file.
lily ALL=(ALL) ALL

c.   That's it ! Now lily has access to all available commands.

bash-3.2# su - lily
Oracle Corporation SunOS 5.10   Generic Patch   January 2005
*******Welcome lily*******

-bash-3.2$ /usr/local/bin/sudo -l
We trust you have received the usual lecture from the local System
Administrator. It usually boils down to these three things:
    #1) Respect the privacy of others.
    #2) Think before you type.
    #3) With great power comes great responsibility.
Password:

User lily may run the following commands on SolarisLab1:
    (ALL) ALL
-bash-3.2$

6. Log all Lily's sudo commands.

Here we will see another interesting topic which we generally use to setup on our Linux and Unix servers i.e. to do auditing with sudo command logs. SUDO makes it simplier for an administrator to do the RCA(root cause analysis) in case of some issue occurred due to wrong command fired and it also allows us to identify which user has executed the command and caused the issue on the server. The command also helps us to know how to recover the fault caused.

To know what all commands fired by a user using sudo, we can enable sudo logging by using below steps.

a.   Open sudoers file and add one line under Defaults.
 #visudo
Add below line.
Defaults@local7 log_host, log_year, logfile=/var/log/sudo.log

b.   Now create this new log file.
touch /var/log/sudo.log

c.   In the end, we will restart the syslog service.
svcadm restart svc:/system/system-log:default

d.   Now login with lily user and execute few commands.
# su – lily
$ sudo –l
$ sudo cat /etc/shadow

e.   In the end we can view our new logs inside /var/log/sudo.log file.
bash-3.2# cat /var/log/sudo.log

Mar 10 21:36:14 SolarisLab1 sudo: [ID 702911 auth.notice]   lily :
TTY=pts/4 ; PWD=/home/lily ; USER=root ;
COMMAND=/usr/bin/cat /etc/shadow
Mar 10 21:38:29 SolarisLab1 sudo: [ID 702911 auth.notice]   lily :
TTY=pts/4 ; PWD=/home/lily ; USER=root ; COMMAND=list
bash-3.2#

7.   Hack: Make fool of sudo logging

We can also bypass sudo logging and hide our commands from sudo
logs by becoming super user or root using sudo. Some ways to become
root user using sudo are as follows:

a.   <u>By Switch user :-</u> We can switch to root user account by using
sudo.

-bash-3.2$ sudo su -
Oracle Corporation SunOS 5.10   Generic Patch   January 2005
You have new mail.
welcome to solaris lab
#
Now whatever we will type will be stored in root history file, and there
will be no sudo logs created.

b.   <u>Another way</u> to become root is to use system inbuilt shell access.
This trick is also used by many of us as a hack to gain root access and to
avoid sudo logs on our name.
-bash-3.2$ sudo bash
bash-3.2#   ← You became root

Now no commands will be logged under sudo logging.

You can restrict su command accesss, however bash shell access can't be restricted, hence many of our colleagues use this method to gain root access.

8. Hack BASH shell so that it doesn't save commands in the history.

Suppose you want to execute few commands and doesn't want the administrator to know that you have executed these commands. So either we can remove complete history, however it is not a good choice as it will remove all exisitng commands as well. So to achieve this we can hack the environment variable to bypass current session commands to be saved in history file.

bash-3.2# su - lily
Oracle Corporation   SunOS 5.10   Generic Patch   January 2005
*******Welcome lily*******
-bash-3.2$ sudo bash
Password:
bash-3.2# export HISTFILE=/dev/null ← saves all commands to null on exit.
bash-3.2# cat /etc/passwd
Now whatever command you run, when you exit, the system will write the commands to /dev/null which will be removed as soon as you exit the current session.

9. SSH Troubleshooting
Suppose a user is not able to do ssh towards a host. To troubleshoot such issue we should have access to the system console and thereafter only we can check the issue on server. However initial troubleshooting we can carry out by checking few things below.

a.   Try to ping the server and check if the host is up.
ping 172.16.159.33

b.   If the host is reachable, second thing is to check whether ssh service is running on host or not. You can check this by logging into the server through console

bash-3.2# svcs ssh
STATE   STIME   FMRI
online   19:01:42 svc:/network/ssh:default
bash-3.2#

c.   If the ssh service is also running, try to run ssh command in verbose mode to see where its rejecting the connection to the server.

root@L9AHG13:~# ssh -vvv 172.16.159.33
OpenSSH_5.9p1 Debian-5ubuntu1.4, OpenSSL 1.0.1 14 Mar 2012
debug1: Reading configuration data /etc/ssh/ssh_config
debug1: /etc/ssh/ssh_config line 19: Applying options for *
debug2: ssh_connect: needpriv 0
debug1: Connecting to 172.16.159.33 [172.16.159.33] port 22.
debug1: Connection established.
debug1: permanently_set_uid: 0/0
debug1: identity file /root/.ssh/id_rsa type -1

d.   Once you get where its rejecting the connection, you can proceed the troubleshooting. One of the important thing to check is whether gateway is reachable from the server or not.

bash-3.2# netstat -r
Routing Table: IPv4

Destination	Gateway	Flags	Ref	Use	Interface
172.16.159.0	172.16.159.33	U	1	2	e1000g0:1
192.168.2.0	vsserver1	U	1	0	e1000g0
224.0.0.0	vsserver1	U	1	0	e1000g0
localhost	localhost	UH	1	113	lo0

bash-3.2#

Here we have all gateways reachable. If gateway is not reachable, you may not be able to access the server from outside.

e. Few Other Things to Checks
o   Check /etc/hosts.allow and /etc/hosts.deny files to identify which hosts/networks are denied.
o   Check ssh configuration, root login is denied from this file generally /etc/ssh/sshd_config. Also sometimes we change the port of ssh and user thinks ssh is not working.
o   Check if there is any rule in IPfilter.
bash-3.2# ipfstat -io
empty list for ipfilter(out)
empty list for ipfilter(in)

bash-3.2# svcs ipfilter
STATE   STIME   FMRI
disabled   19:00:23 svc:/network/ipfilter:default

Similarly there could be another issue like user is locked, network latency, etc, you need to check the output of these commands as well as log files to conclude where the issue exists.

10.   Chat with other Users in Unix

You must be thinking is there any way of sending a message to a particular user or to all users on the system. Unix also provides few utilities to achieve this, however we will discuss the most common utilities which are usually found installed with the OS.

a.   Broadcasting message to all logged in Users using wall command.

-bash-3.2$ echo "Please save and logoff, we are going to reboot the system" | wall

All users will see below message on their screen:

Broadcast Message from lily (pts/4) on SolarisLab1 Fri Mar 13 20:44:00...
Please save and logoff, we are going to reboot the system

b.   Sending message to Specific logged in Users.

First check what all users are logged in and on which terminal.
-bash-3.2$ w
 8:45pm up 1:45, 4 users, load average: 0.01, 0.01, 0.01
User   tty   login@ idle JCPU PCPU what
root   console   7:04pm 1:45   /usr/dt/bin/sdt_shell -c ?   u
root   pts/3   7:10pm 1:35   sh
lily   pts/4   7:44pm   w
root   pts/5   7:41pm   2   write lily
-bash-3.2$

Suppose you want to send message to root user who is logged at pts/5 terminal. So we can use below command.

-bash-3.2$ write root pts/5
Hello

Root User will receive:
Message from lily on SolarisLab1 (pts/4) [Fri Mar 13 19:46:44] ...
hello

bash-3.2# write lily
hello

Now the above message will be sent to lily's screen.

c.   A root user can also directly send the message by mentioning the terminal pseudo device path.
bash-3.2# echo "hello lily" > /dev/pts/4

The message will be printed on lily's screen.
-bash-3.2$ <EOT>
hello lily

Few other utilities available to achieve this task are talk, or mail depending on our need.

FEW ISSUES

I have faced many issues as a Unix or Linux administrator, however few issues require deep analysis and thorough research to conclude the issue. So I thought to share such issues through this book. These are some issues which helps us to enhance our understanding and knowledge towards the operating system. Let us discuss few such issues here.

1.   Importance of Kernel Messages "swapper: page allocation failure."

a.   Customer is getting below error messages in log files on the server. First we will check dmesg and /var/adm/messages file and check these kernel messages and note down different messages.

ryivrap3 kernel: [<ffffffff8100de85>] ? do_softirq+0x65/0xa0 Jan 14 04:38:35 ryivrap3 kernel: [<ffffffff81073ca5>] ?
 irq_exit+0x85/0x90 Jan 14 04:38:35 ryivrap3 kernel: [<ffffffff81505c25>] ? do_IRQ+0x75/0xf0 Jan 14 04:38:35 ryivrap3 kernel:

[<ffffffff8100ba53>] ? ret_from_intr+0x0/0x11 Jan 14 04:38:35 ryivrap3 kernel: <EOI> [<ffffffff812cd9fe>] ? intel_idle+0xde/0x170
 Jan 14 04:38:35 ryivrap3 kernel: [<ffffffff812cd9e1>] ? intel_idle+0xc1/0x170 Jan 14 04:38:35 ryivrap3 kernel: [<ffffffff81407757>]
 ? cpuidle_idle_call+0xa7/0x140 Jan 14 04:38:35 ryivrap3 kernel: [<ffffffff81009e06>] ? cpu_idle+0xb6/0x110 Jan 14 04:38:35 ryivrap3
 kernel: [<ffffffff814f6e0f>] ? start_secondary+0x22a/0x26d Jan 14 04:38:40 ryivrap3 kernel: swapper: page allocation failure.
 order:4, mode:0x20 Jan 14 04:38:40 ryivrap3 kernel: Pid: 0, comm: swapper Not tainted 2.6.32-279.2.1.el6.x86_64 #1 Jan 14 04:38:40
 ryivrap3 kernel: Call Trace:
 Jan 14 04:38:40 ryivrap3 kernel: <IRQ> [<ffffffff811276cf>] ? __alloc_pages_nodemask+0x77f/0x940
Jan 21 04:36:47 ryivrap3 kernel: swapper: page allocation failure. order:3, mode
:0x20
Jan 21 04:37:17 ryivrap3 kernel: swapper: page allocation failure. order:3, mode
:0x20

What this error signifies ?
The error message tells us that the system main process (with PID 0) which has initiated the init runlevel and process for memory thread management itself generated an error when:
a.   Order:4 i.e. *16 pages from swap memory* with mode 0x20(kernel grants access to emergency pages as well) were *failed to load in memory*.

Why it failed to load pages in memory ?
The most common reason why a page is failed to load into memory is due to memory outage or less memory available during that moment. Hence to resolve this issue, we may need to increase swap or physical memory on our server.

2.   Interface links flapping over.

Here I will show you a very interesting issue where the two NIC cards on a Unix(Solaris) server which are in multipathing failover continuously on each other without any issue on NICs.

The server is configured using *probe based IPMP(IP multipathing) with active-active configuration.*

In probe based configuration, the server used to send the 10 ICMP echo/ping requests from the dummy/deprecated interfaces (as shown below), and in case it doesn't receive reply it used to failover to another NIC.

e1000g0:1:
flags=9040843<UP,BROADCAST,RUNNING,MULTICAST,DEPRECATED,IPv4,NOFAILOVER> mtu 1500 index 3
    inet 172.20.110.225 netmask ffffff00 broadcast 172.20.110.255
e1000g0:2:
flags=1040843<UP,BROADCAST,RUNNING,MULTICAST,DEPRECATED,IPv4> mtu 1500 index 3
    inet 172.20.110.234 netmask ffffff00 broadcast 172.20.110.255

a.   First we will check what errors are appearing; we are getting NIC failure messages as seen below in /var/adm/messages file.
Feb 19 14:41:10 stcvs4a in.mpathd[372]: [ID 832587 daemon.error] Successfully failed over from NIC e1000g2 to NIC e1000g0
Feb 19 14:41:16 stcvs4a in.mpathd[372]: [ID 299542 daemon.error] NIC repair detected on e1000g2 of group pub
Feb 19 14:41:16 stcvs4a in.mpathd[372]: [ID 620804 daemon.error] Successfully failed back to NIC e1000g2
Feb 19 15:41:05 stcvs4a in.mpathd[372]: [ID 594170 daemon.error] NIC failure detected on e1000g0 of group pub
Feb 19 15:41:05 stcvs4a in.mpathd[372]: [ID 832587 daemon.error] Successfully failed over from NIC e1000g0 to NIC e1000g2

Feb 19 15:41:12 stcvs4a in.mpathd[372]: [ID 299542 daemon.error] NIC repair detected on e1000g0 of group pub
Feb 19 15:41:12 stcvs4a in.mpathd[372]: [ID 620804 daemon.error] Successfully failed back to NIC e1000g0

The error message denotes that our router is not responding to server requests timely.

b.   The second step is to check the multipath daemon configuration file i.e. /etc/default/mpathd. In mpath(multi-path) configuration, we can see that failure detection time is very less i.e. 3000ms or 3sec

```
bash-3.2# cat /etc/default/mpathd
#
#pragma ident   "@(#)mpathd.dfl 1.2    00/07/17 SMI"
#
# Time taken by mpathd to detect a NIC failure in ms. The minimum time
# that can be specified is 100 ms.
#
FAILURE_DETECTION_TIME=3000
```

However it is recommended to set its value to 10seconds to detect the actual NIC failure and thereafter reload the IPMP configuration files.

```
# first set it to 10sec, and then restart like below
# pkill -HUP in.mpathd

### will reload files for the process: root   372    1  0  Apr 29 ?
709:52 /usr/lib/inet/in.mpathd -a
```

c.   Another thing we should check here is whether auto-negotiation is on or off. It is always recommended to have auto-negotiation ON so the NIC cards can work flawlessly.

```
bash-3.2# ndd -get /dev/e1000g0 adv_autoneg_cap
```

0

bash-3.2# ndd -get /dev/e1000g2 adv_autoneg_cap

0

We need to turn it on to make it in sync with router.

ndd -set/dev/e1000g0 adv_autoneg_cap 1

ndd -set/dev/e1000g0 adv_autoneg_cap 1

d.   Now observe for some time if we still see the messages. If no, then make above setting permanent by adding these ndd commands in any server startup script like /etc/profile.

If yes, then it means the router is still not responding to probes sent from the server. We can check this by collecting explorer on the server.

/opt/SUNWexplo/bin/explorer

While explorer is running you may see below messages in the /var/adm/messages log file depicting problem with the router in this case.

Feb 19 20:43:16 stcvs4a in.mpathd[372]: [ID 214330 daemon.error]

Feb 19 20:43:16 stcvs4a Probe stats on (inet e1000g0)

Feb 19 20:43:16 stcvs4a Number of probes sent 59915018

Feb 19 20:43:16 stcvs4a Number of probe acks received 59856326

Feb 19 20:43:16 stcvs4a Number of probes/acks lost 58536   -----□

Packets are currently lost, _no ACK from router._

Feb 19 20:43:16 stcvs4a Number of valid unacknowled probes 0

Feb 19 20:43:16 stcvs4a Number of ambiguous probe acks received 0

You may see similar issues in your Unix box also. This error usually occurs when there is some intermittent problem with router.

3.   SMI Label issue on x86 servers.

Many of the times when we try to upgrade our Unix Operating system, or try to re-install it, we encounter an error message saying SMI label is not set.

Line 1636: ERROR: Disk c3t5000CCA022784709d0 is not SMI labeled, and metadb slice c3t5000CCA022784709d0s7 is invalid
    Line 1812: ERROR: Disk c4t5000CCA016DDB1A5d0 is not SMI labeled, and metadb slice c4t5000CCA016DDB1A5d0s7 is invalid

It means above disks are not SMI labeled and you need to change it to SMI label before proceeding with upgrade.
However when we check in format(format→ select disk→fdisk→print), then we will see the label is already SMI i.e. Solaris2. However still we see this message that disks are not SMI labeled.

The SMI/EFI disks fdisk partition should not start with 0th cylinder.

		Cylinders				
Partition	Status	Type	Start	End	Length	%
=========	======	============	=====	===	======	===
1		Solaris2	0	36471	36471	100

The start cylinder should be 1 instead of 0. So here we need to re-create fdisk partition with 0th cylinder by manually deleting the partition under format→fdisk and then re-creating it.

4.   Invalid Fdisk partition issue on Solaris x86 servers.

We have seen smi label error in last topic; however we may also encounter one more common error while doing Solaris Unix Upgrade or re-installation which says "Invalid fdisk partition".

ERROR: fdisk partition table invalid (c5t5000CCA016DA11DDd0)

What this error signifies ? :- When the disk is *installed/replaced on the server* and integrated into SVM(solaris volume manager), it's *not* formatted with fdisk on x86 server which is mandatory.

In most of the cases, it is caused after disk replacement activity when we forget to create fdisk partition. In rare cases, when there is no disk replacement activity performed, this problem exists from the starting when the node is first implemented or installed.

The fdisk partition creation is *required* in *x86* servers, *not on sparc* Servers.

The error indicated that for each disk on both systems the fdisk partition didn't exist, not that it was corrupt or was unavailable.

The 'fmthard' utility does not check the presence of an fdisk partition when writing a VTOC(Volume Table of Contents) label to a disk. Therefore if a new disk is introduced into the system which does not have the fdisk partition of type 'Solaris' (0xbf) and

Fmthard is used to label the disk without first running 'fdisk </dev/rdsk/cXtXdXp0>';
the disk will not contain a valid partition and will not be usable.

It's quite common in disk replacement action plans for SVM mirrored root disks to see a step where the customer is instructed to copy the VTOC from the remaining good disk in the mirror to the newly replaced disk using:

prtvtoc /dev/rdsk/<good_disk>s2 | fmthard -s - /dev/rdsk/<new_disk>s2

On an x86 host, the prtvtoc/fmthard completes successfully but does not create an fdisk partition and appears to write the VTOC earlier on the disk than if it were constrained by and fdisk partition table (i.e. disk _content_ must be _trashed_ in order to correct the partitioning.

5.   Check Disk Health (Server taking auto-reboot).

The most common issue when we deal with Solaris SVM disks is a problem with disk drive, i.e. the drive has introduced some hardware issue and we may face issues/error messages on the server like below.

> Server automatically taking auto-reboot
> Server hangs frequently.
> The file systems going into read-only mode impacting server operations.
> Server is operating fine, but we may see error messages in the log file like below

Feb 1 22:20:49 northminsat1 metacheck[9193]: [ID 702911 local1.error] d0: d10 S
tate: Okay d20 State: Needs maintenance
Feb 1 22:24:57 northminsat1 metacheck[10221]: [ID 702911 local1.error] d0: d10
State: Okay d20 State: Needs maintenance

To check the server health, login on the server and check output of below commands.

a.   First we will check server health (i.e. if any hardware error).

bash-3.2# fmadm faulty
bash-3.2#

b.   Now we will check if there is any issue with hard disks configured in SVM.

metastat | grep –I state
State: Okay
State: Okay
State: Needs Maintenance
State: Okay
State: Okay

In case you see any disk with "Needs maintenance", then it shows a problem with the hard disk. You need to chase local hardware support to check if there is any amber light blinking on the server and if yes, then replace this disk with new one.

c.   Another most useful command to check system hardware is prtdiag which is used to display the system diagnostic information . So we can use this command in verbose mode to display all available information and can see states of different devices to confirm if everything is fine.

/usr/platform/`uname -m`/sbin/prtdiag –v

Similar to hard disk issue, you can use above commands to check the complete system hardware, however you may need to run few more utilities(dladm/ifconfig for NIC or network status) to check other things as per the issue.

6.   Hack some UNIX/Linux command ?

In Unix/Linux, we have some environment variables that control how our shell will function and what all resources it will use and from where. To hack some command we will use the environment variable "PATH".

The PATH environment variable contains different paths where our system checks for the commands/executables and executes them.

bash-3.2# echo $PATH
/opt/EABpython/bin:/usr/sbin:/usr/bin:/usr/sbin:/usr/dt/bin:/usr/sfw/bin:/usr/openwin/bin:/opt/EABfds/bin:/opt/EABcsutls/bin:/opt/EABcsConfig/bin:/opt/sfw/bin:/opt/EABfdslic/bin

Now suppose we want to hack command "uname".

a.   First check actual path of uname command.
bash-3.2# which uname
/usr/bin/uname

b.   The "/usr/bin" is the third directory as mentioned in PATH environment variable. It means there is no uname command found in first two directories and hence the system searches in third directory and executes the command.

c.   So we will now create another uname command in a directory path which exists before /usr/bin in PATH command output.

➢   Create the new file with contents you want to display.
bash-3.2# echo 'echo "uname command is hacked"' >>
/opt/EABpython/bin/uname
bash-3.2#
bash-3.2# cat /opt/EABpython/bin/uname
echo "uname command is hacked"

➢   Make the script executable
bash-3.2# chmod +x /opt/EABpython/bin/uname
bash-3.2#

➢   Now try to run the command and see the output.

bash-3.2# uname -a
uname command is hacked

You can even create your script and handle the different arguments of this command. When you have created your script you can move original command and then fool your users with customized commands.

In case the command is from first directory in PATH environment variable then you can add your own directory path in this variable and export it.
export PATH=/opt/bin:$PATH where /opt/bin is our customized directory and then you can add this in end of the profile file to make the change permanent.

As an unix administrator I have also seen few issues where multiple copies of a command exists and users say the command is not working. So this is also a good point to check when troubleshooting issues with commands.

7.   Repairing GRUB in Unix.

GRUB or Grand Unified Boot loader exists on sector 0 of boot disk or mirror which loads our Unix Operating System(in case of x86 systems). Sometimes due to disk activities on server, the GRUB gets corrupted or may be not installed. For example:- Suppose a faulty root mirror disk is replaced on server, and the administrator simply copies the prtvtoc and contents but forget to install grub, in this case the system will not boot from this new replaced hard disk.

Our system will not be able to boot and does not show the boot menu. To resolve this issue, we need to re-install the grub on sector 0 of boot disk.

a.   First boot the server from CD.
b.   Now check #format and # prtvtoc diskname to check the root disk and mount its root partition on some directory say, /mnt2.

c.   Now run below command to reintstall grub. Enter the correct root disk name.

bash-3.2# /sbin/installgrub /mnt2/boot/grub/stage1 /mnt2/boot/grub/stage2 /dev/rdsk/c0t5000CCA0254BBE15d0s0
stage1 written to partition 0 sector 0 (abs 16065)
stage2 written to partition 0, 273 sectors starting at 50 (abs 16115)
bash-3.2#

d.   That's it! Now you can reboot the system to see its booting now.

The GRUB install is also required in case we have installed Windows after Unix/Linux installation, as this will also remove the GRUB. Or in general whenever our hard disk sector0 faces some problem we need to reinstall grub.

8.   Understanding Password less authentication. Why its important and how it can save us from unobvious situations?

Password Less authentication (PLA) allows us to authenticate different users and grant them access of our LINUX/UNIX node without asking for password while authentication i.e. why it is called as Password less authentication.

Suppose you want to give access of your system to a user, say Mahesh then you will create his account and give him login credentials. Now suppose you don't want to ask for password whenever Mahesh logs in. It means whenever Mahesh do ssh <to your machine> he should login without entering the password.

To achieve this, Mahesh will generate a private and public key pair and share the public key with the world. You will take this public key and add on your machine under his account. Now whenever Mahesh do ssh from the machine where his private key is kept then he will be able to login without entering the password. The system will match private and public key pair and authenticates the user.

As an admin you can add this key to any account, and can grant Mahesh access to any account, even root. However Mahesh can only add this public key to the accessible account and setup password less authentication.

Why its important and how it can save us from unobvious situations?
You can find usual answers that it saves time by skipping the password and hence it is helpful. However we have faced few practical situations where PLA is the only way which helped us to troubleshoot the issue.

Suppose our system root disk becomes faulty and not able to write anything, or just say our partitions (/ /var and /tmp) is full and now our system will not able to authenticate any user via password since it will not able to create any temporary file. So in case PLA is setup, the user can still login and troubleshoot the issue whether it is with hard disk or anything else.

We have faced a similar case where we were not able to login on the system since the hard disk has some issue and our OS is not able to write anything (not able to create any temporary file) and hence the authentication failed. In the end we found a user private key file who had earlier setup PLA and managed to login on the server.

Also PLA is considered more secure way of authentication as compared to password.

Public and Private Keys Algorithms
A user generates a pair of private and public keys and gives away public key to the world. When this user which has private key left behind, logs on to any server where public key is kept he/she is authenticated

without entering the password. The system authenticates this unique public-private key pair and accordingly allows/denies the user access.

These private and public key pair can be generated using different key generation Algorithms. These generated keys can further be encrypted for enhanced security in case required. Disgital Signature algorithm(DSA) and RSA(Ron Rivest, Adi Shamir and Leonard Adleman Algorithm) , are the two most widely used key generation algorithm available on almost every Linux/Unix distribution.

We will use RSA to generate public-private key pair and would recommend the same to you since it provides fast verification as compared to DSA. So a RSA key pair will be validated fast as compared to DSA key pair. And also DSA can only be used for signing or verification, whereas RSA can be used for encryption and decryption as well.

To enhance security it is recommended to create a 2048 bit key pair instead of 1024/512 bit. So whether you create DSA or RSA key, it is always recommended to generate a 2048 bit pair. RSA keys allows us to encrypt messages using its public key and then decrypt the messages with its private key and hence we will recommend to use RSA key pair so that it can be further used to encrypt/decrypt messages if required.

Now we will setup PLA setup to lily's account, followed by a diagram to understand the steps required.

Fig. 2 Password less Authentication

a.   First the root user on Host A will generate the key pair if already not available.

 # ssh-keygen -t rsa -b 2048
Generating public/private rsa key pair.
Enter file in which to save the key (/root/.ssh/id_rsa):
Enter passphrase (empty for no passphrase):
Enter same passphrase again:
Your identification has been saved in /root/.ssh/id_rsa.
Your public key has been saved in /root/.ssh/id_rsa.pub.
The key fingerprint is:
1f:ef:c6:65:00:8f:91:16:c6:44:ed:f4:16:92:fb:83
root@L9AHG13.egi.ericsson.com
The key's randomart image is:
+--[RSA 2048]----+
| +=+ . |
| .* = . |
| . B + . |
| . = o |
| S . = |
| . oE = |
| ...o . |

```
|        .o   |
|          ..  |
+-----------------+
#
```

b.   Now we will transfer the public key /root/.ssh/id_rsa.pub to the host B under the account where we want to login without entering password.

\# scp /root/.ssh/id_rsa.pub lily@172.16.159.33:~lily/
Password:
id_rsa.pub   100% 411   0.4KB/s 00:00
\#

c.   Now we will login to Host B with lily's account and copy this key in authorized file.

Check our key file is available.

-bash-3.2$ ls –ltr id*
-rw-r--r-- 1 lily   other   411 Mar 15 21:11 id_rsa.pub

-bash-3.2$ cd .ssh
-bash: cd: .ssh: No such file or directory

.ssh directory is not available. So we will create this directory and authorized_keys file under it.

-bash-3.2$ mkdir .ssh
-bash-3.2$ cat id_rsa.pub >> .ssh/authorized_keys

d.   Now that's it ! You can go back to root user account on Host A and try to login to lily account and see the magic.

\# ssh lily@172.16.159.33
Last login: Sun Mar 15 21:14:00 2015 from 172.16.159.1
Oracle Corporation   SunOS 5.10   Generic Patch January 2005
*******Welcome lily*******
-bash-3.2$

We can see the root user can login to lily's account without entering any password. Similarly you can setup PLA between any user(s) and in between any server(s).

9. Changing a process timezone in UNIX.

When we execute any process/thread, our system assigns the current timezone to the process. The timezone defines where the server is located, for example if the server is located in India, its timezone will be IST(Indian Standard Time, GMT+5:30) and is the same server is in NY(New York), USA then the timezone will be EDT(Eastern Daylight Time, GMT-4:00). And the beauty of our Unix Server is that it will adjust the time automatically according to the timezone.

Importance of Timezone ?
The timezone plays very important part in case of few java processes which communicate regularly with other servers in the network. Suppose one system is under one timezone and the other server is in another timezone, then in this case our system can become unstable during communication due to mismatch in timestamp and you may not able to track where the issue exists.

We have faced many issues due to different timezones of the communicating processes and it had also caused a large outage since they are not able to sync and hence throws errors.

To assign a new timezone to a process we will use an environment variable "TZ" (TimeZone) which is picked by different processes during startup.

a.   Check Timezone assigned to a process
bash-3.2# pargs -e 1595 | grep -i TZ
envp[17]: TZ=Asia/Calcutta

where TZ is the environment variable and 1595 is the process id. It may be possible that no TZ variable exists, in this case, current system timezone/location will be assigned.

b.   Current timezone of our server and value of TZ variable
bash-3.2# date
Monday, March 16, 2015 05:08:40 PM IST

bash-3.2# export TZ="America/New_York"

bash-3.2# date
Monday, March 16, 2015 07:43:10 AM EDT

c.   Now lets start a new process, and check which timezone is assigned to it.

bash-3.2# tcsh   ### starts tcsh shell, a new process.
root@SolarisLab1>echo $$ ### gets process id of current shell.
5977
root@SolarisLab1>pargs -e 5977 | grep -i TZ   ### gets timezone of pid 5977.
envp[18]: TZ=America/New_York
root@SolarisLab1>

        Note:- Now the timezone of the new process is EDTof New York/America). We can't modify the timezone of already running process, we need to stop it and then run it again with new TZ variable value.

Similar to TZ variable, UNIX assigns many more environment variable to each process and we can even modify them to satisfy the requirements of different programs. A sample list of available variables on my system can be seen below.

```
bash-3.2# pargs -e 1595 | more
1595:  bash
envp[0]:
MANPATH=/usr/share/man:/usr/openwin/man:/usr/dt/man:/opt/
EABfds/man:/op
t/EABcsutls/man
envp[1]: LC_MONETARY=en_US.ISO8859-1
envp[2]: TERM=xterm
envp[3]: SHELL=/sbin/sh
envp[4]: SSH_CLIENT=172.16.159.1 52453 22
envp[5]: LC_NUMERIC=en_US.ISO8859-1
envp[6]: OLDPWD=/
envp[7]: SSH_TTY=/dev/pts/5
envp[8]: USER=root
.............
<output truncated>
.............
envp[25]: ORACLE_HOME=/opt/oracle
envp[26]: LC_TIME=en_US.ISO8859-1
envp[27]: _=/usr/bin/man
```

So there are 27 environment variables defined for this process named "bash". Similar to UNIX, in LINUX also we can get the environment variable list by looking at the file /proc/<pid>/environ.

```
#  xargs -n 1 -0 /proc/PID/environ  | grep TZ        ### For Linux,
replace PID with the process id.
```

Xargs improves the readability of the file output.

10.   Mirror too small error in metattach even when size of the partition is same.

Many of the times we face issue with metadevice when trying to attach the mirrors saying "submirror too small to attach". The error could be like below:

Failure when running "metattach d30 d2".
ERROR: metattach: vs02b: d2: submirror too small to attach
ERROR:

a.   <u>Checking and Correcting Submirror Size</u>

In such cases, we need to check the size of d30 and d2 submirrors. d2 submirror should be equal or greater than d30 submirror. We can check it by following ways:
a.   Going inside format→select disk→print→print, or
b.   By looking at output of metastat command.

In case the size is small, we can modify the size from the format→print→print and then delete and recreate partition with new size.

c.   <u>Checking Cylinder Range</u>

Now suppose the size is same in the above output, and still we are facing this issue then we need to check the number of cylinders and disk type.

bash-3.2# echo | format | grep -i c0t5000CCA0254F8B45d0
     2. c0t5000CCA0254F8B45d0 <**DEFAULT** cyl 36469 alt 2 hd 255 sec 63>

bash-3.2# echo | format | grep -i c0t5000CCA0254F8B45d0c0t5000CCA0254C9E51d0
     1. c0t5000CCA0254C9E51d0 <**HITACHI**-H106030SDSUN300G-A2B0 cyl 46871 alt 2 hd 20 sec 625>

We can see in the above output that one disk is of default solaris type with 36469 cylinders, and the other disk is of Hitachi type with 46871 cylinders. Now the issue is clear that d2 submirror has less cylinders than d30 because of which it is not able to attach with the large number of cylinder metadevice.

To resolve this issue first we need to correct the disk geometry with the same type and then we need to check if the cylinders are fine, otherwise we need to correct the cylinders as well.

d.   <u>Correcting Disk Geometry</u>
To correct the disk geometry we can follow below steps.

bash-3.2# **format**
Searching for disks...done

AVAILABLE DISK SELECTIONS:
     0. c0t5000CCA0254BBE15d0 <DEFAULT cyl 36469 alt 2 hd 255 sec 63>

/pci@0,0/pci8086,340a@3/pci1000,3050@0/iport@ff/disk@w5000cca0254bbe15,0
     1. c0t5000CCA0254C9E51d0 <HITACHI-H106030SDSUN300G-A2B0 cyl 46871 alt 2 hd 20 sec 625>

/pci@0,0/pci8086,340a@3/pci1000,3050@0/iport@ff/disk@w5000cca0254c9e51,0
     2. c0t5000CCA0254F8B45d0 <DEFAULT cyl 36469 alt 2 hd 255 sec 63>

/pci@0,0/pci8086,340a@3/pci1000,3050@0/iport@ff/disk@w5000cca0254f8b45,0

        3. c0t5000CCA0255036E5d0 <HITACHI-H106030SDSUN300G-A2B0
cyl 46871 alt 2 hd 20 sec 625>
- hit space for more or s to select -
Specify disk (enter its number): **0**
selecting c0t5000CCA0254BBE15d0
[disk formatted]

format> **type**
AVAILABLE DRIVE TYPES:
        0. Auto configure
        7. HITACHI-H106030SDSUN300G-A2B0
        8. DEFAULT
        9. other
Specify disk type (enter its number)[7]: **8**
selecting c0t1d0
[disk formatted]

format> **label**
Ready to label disk, continue? **y**

Now we can check the new partition table of our disk. In my case, the
cylinders came to be of same size and the partition also. You need to
make sure the first partition should start from 1 instead of 0 to avoid any
future issues with the disk and to make sure it remains available to hold
grub/boot data in case required.

Beyond This Book

I have tried to include most of the Unix Solaris Topics, however there is much more to learn when we talk about this operating system. Unix Is just like a universe and we have only seen few initial planets and now we are ready to explore other planets, and stars of this universe.

The roadmap to learn this operating system is a bit complex, after you have done with this book, you should go ahead with installing latest fedora and explore its features like the new kernel features, and new server(s) introduced, etc. Once you are familiar with both Linux and Solaris working environments, we can start with Linux development.

To start exploring bits and bytes of how linux is created, I would recommend you to go ahead by reading Linux from scratch (LFS), and Beyond Linux from Scratch (BLFS) books available on internet for free of cost licensed under a Creative Commons License.. After completing LFS, we should go ahead with Linux system programming to know how kernel and C library talks to each other. There are few books available for this in market; one of the nice books I have gone through is by Robert Love.

Once you have completed Linux System programming, the last step is to do hit and trial on the Linux kernel and understand its working, maybe you are able to modify and enhance its features. There are also few books available for Linux kernel Development which you can refer to make a pathway towards your Linux or Unix Learning.

If you feel down anytime during your learning, sit back, relax and start again

www.ingramcontent.com/pod-product-compliance
Lightning Source LLC
LaVergne TN
LVHW062302060326
832902LV00013B/2010